BY BING WEST

One Million Steps: A Marine Platoon at War

The Wrong War: Grit, Strategy, and the Way Out of Afghanistan

The Strongest Tribe: War, Politics, and the Endgame in Iraq

No True Glory: A Frontline Account of the Battle for Fallujah

The Village

Naval Forces and Western Security: Sea Plan 2000 (editor)

Small Unit Action in Vietnam

The Pepperdogs

WITH SGT. DAKOTA MEYER, USMC (RET.)
*Into the Fire: A Firsthand Account
of the Most Extraordinary Battle in the Afghan War*

WITH MAJ. GEN. RAY L. SMITH, USMC (RET.)
The March Up: Taking Baghdad with the U.S. Marines

ONE MILLION STEPS

ONE MILLION STEPS

A Marine Platoon at War

BING WEST

Random House New York

Copyright © 2014 by Francis J. West, Jr.
Maps copyright © 2014 by David Lindroth Inc.

All rights reserved.

Published in the United States by Random House, an imprint
and division of Random House LLC, a Penguin
Random House Company, New York.

RANDOM HOUSE and the HOUSE colophon are registered
trademarks of Random House LLC.

Library of Congress Cataloging-in-Publication Data
West, Francis J.
One million steps : a marine platoon at war / Bing West.
pages   cm
Includes index.
ISBN 978-1-4000-6874-6
eBook ISBN 978-1-58836-933-8
1. West, Francis J.   2. Afghan War, 2001– —Personal narratives,
American.   3. Afghan War, 2001– —Campaigns—Afghanistan—Sangin
(Helmand).   4. United States. Marine Corps—History—Afghan War,
2001–   5. Marines—United States—Biography.   I. Title.
DS371.413.W46 2014
958.104'745—dc23
[B]
2014016063

Printed in the United States of America on acid-free paper

www.atrandom.com

2   4   6   8   9   7   5   3   1

First Edition

Title-spread photo: Cpl. Jordan Laird

Battalion 3/5 suffered the highest number of casualties in the war in Afghanistan. This is the story of one platoon in that distinguished battalion.

Preface

Suppose you're offered $15,000 to walk two and a half miles each day for six months. In total, you will take one million steps and be well paid for losing a few pounds. Interested?

There are a few provisos. First, you must live in a cave. Second, your exercise consists of walking across minefields. Third, each day men will try to kill you. The odds are 50-50 that you will die or lose a leg before you complete the one million steps. Still interested?

This is the story of fifty men who said yes. Third Platoon fought the hardest sustained battle of the Afghanistan war. When we think of courage, we imagine a man acting bravely in a terrifying situation that lasts for a minute or an hour. These men battled fiercely for 200 days. Because U.S. forces were leaving Afghanistan, they knew their effort was a footprint in the sand. Yet every day they went forth to find and kill the enemy. Half of them didn't make it intact to the end of their tour.

What kept them going?

When I embedded with 3rd Platoon, I felt at home with them because I'm a Marine infantryman, a grunt. That was how I was raised. After Pearl Harbor, my uncle and his baseball team joined the Marines. In 1942, I was two years old when they came home after seizing the island of Guadalcanal. The team spent their leave hanging out in their clubhouse in our attic. Assuming they were the resident babysitters, my mother placed me in their care.

Thus began my four-year education. After each campaign—Guadalcanal, Tarawa, Iwo Jima, Okinawa—the survivors returned to their clubhouse. They gave me a toy rifle and tiny uniform, played endless games, and smuggled me down the back stairs wrapped in a blanket when they went out. No boy ever had more protective or peculiar guardians.

A few months after my college graduation, I said good-bye to my parents and left for law school. Across from the train station, the Marine Corps had a recruiting station. When I returned home a few hours later, my mother simply said, "You joined the Marines, didn't you?"

Like thousands of my fellow grunts, I wore out several pairs of boots in the jungles of Vietnam. I wrote two books about that war, a manual of small unit tactics and the story of a squad that lived in a Vietnamese village for a year. Forty years later, I went back to war. Between 2003 and 2013, I embedded with dozens of Army and Marine units in repeated trips to Iraq and Afghanistan.

From one war to the next, I joined our grunt platoons and grew close to many who died in battle. In Afghanistan, the realities confronting the platoons mocked the proclamations of our generals. Our officials insisted that our troops act as nation builders, a Sisyphean task that confused both the Afghan tribes and our troops. Our generals promised victory, while insisting that killing the enemy could not win the war. Instead, our grunts were ordered to persuade medieval Islamic tribes to support a mendacious government in Kabul. This strategy was contrary to military and political logic.

We invaded Afghanistan to destroy the Al Qaeda terrorist organization. We stayed to build a nation. This required fighting the Taliban insurgents who were woven into the fabric of the society, while the Afghan government failed to foster a spirit of nationalism. Our grunts departed Afghanistan deeply skeptical of the wisdom of their senior commanders.

This is my sixth and final book about the wars in Iraq and Afghanistan. As I look back, it is clear that America and the West tried to do too much. When Saigon fell in 1975, the secretary of defense, James Schlesinger, assured our soldiers that "your cause was just and noble." That is equally true of Iraq and Afghanistan. A flawed war policy can coexist with a soldier's determination to fight for his country.

Afghanistan was America's longest war, persisting for thirteen years. The fiercest fighting took place in a farming community called Sangin in southern Afghanistan. In response to the Marine offensive in the fall of 2010, the Taliban mounted a stout resistance. Week after week, the casualty toll mounted. Appalled, the secretary of defense offered to pull the Marines back. The Marines refused.

Third Platoon was one of three platoons in Kilo Company; Kilo was one of three rifle companies in 3/5—the 3rd Battalion of the 5th Marine Regiment. When I arrived in January of 2011, 3rd Platoon was locked in mortal combat. Their lieutenant was in a hospital with an amputated leg. Their inspirational sergeant, who led in every fight, was dead. One of their squad leaders was gone, and his replacement was limping around with a bullet wound, fearing he would be sent to the rear if he sought treatment.

They lived in caves outside friendly lines, without computer connections. Twice a month, they called home to lie about how safe they were. Each day, they patrolled in search of a ghostlike enemy who planted mines to maim them. When a Marine was struck down, the others bound his wounds, stood guard while he was evacuated, and resumed the patrol. Each night, they returned to their caves, scratched stick figures of their kills on a wall next to the skins of coyotes, and roasted goats over their campfires, rituals little changed from that of war parties centuries ago.

Based on the platoon's hand-printed log, two embeds, and months of interviews, I try to describe what 3rd Platoon did. In six months, 3rd Platoon conducted about 400 foot patrols and engaged in 171 firefights. Imagine being on one patrol, and then another and another, always expecting to be blown to bits. Had these Marines been policemen anywhere in the States, the intensity of their battles would have made front-page news every week. To 3rd Platoon, each week only meant a few more stories shared around the campfire.

In Vietnam, our casualties were more numerous, because many more of us were fighting. But we didn't have it harder. Today's grunts are more muscular than we were back then, but not as good-looking. Aside from that, the differences aren't great. In a platoon then and now, you lived, laughed, fought, killed, and died in about the same numbers.

Seven decades ago, my uncle, Sgt. Walter West, gave me a picture of the 1943 assault against the island of Tarawa. Sgt. Alex Deykeroff, who appears in this book, has that same picture on his Facebook page. Time does not separate Sergeant Deykeroff in Afghanistan from Sergeant West in the Pacific islands or from me in Vietnam or from my son who fought in Iraq. Marines have gone to war before us, with us, and after us. The dead, the living, and the unborn are links in an unbroken Marine tradition of service in war.

The infantry—specifically Marine grunts—comprise the heart of this book. The theme is cohesion, how one platoon—fifty young men—fused into a resolute fighting machine. Third Platoon knew we were pulling out of Afghanistan. Yet they didn't slack off. When their leaders fell, they raised up new ones and continued to attack. Six months of daily patrolling. One million steps, with steady losses from start to finish.

Who are these men? What spirit sustained them?

Contents

CONTENTS

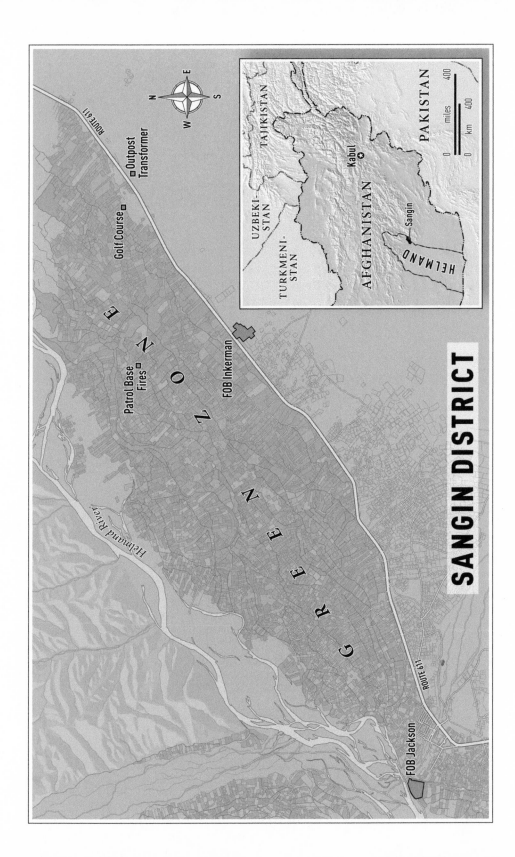

SANGIN DISTRICT

Introduction

The Setting

Sangin was the most violent district in Afghanistan, a remote farmland in southern Helmand Province at the bottom of the country.
Beginning in 2006, British forces defended the government compound next to the district market, while the Taliban controlled the
outlying fields where poppy was grown in abundance. To profit from
the opium export, the Taliban planted thousands of land mines
around the British outposts and attacked every patrol that sallied
forth. Afghan officials never ventured beyond the market. Helicopters provided resupply only at night. Daylight flying was too dangerous. By 2010, Sangin was isolated and under siege.

Then the U.S. Marines were sent in.

"What does Sangin mean?" four-star Marine general John Kelly said when it was over. "They sent us there to fight—so we fought."

The British Effort

In 2001, America and its allies invaded Afghanistan in response to the destruction of the Twin Towers. However, the invasion was botched, allowing the Al Qaeda terrorists to escape into Pakistan, along with the Taliban Islamists who had harbored them. America then stayed to build a democratic nation. As President George W. Bush explained, nation building was America's "moral obligation."

The U.S. commander, Gen. Tommy Franks, claimed that the Taliban had been "squeezed into extinction." By 2005, however, the Taliban had surged back. Helmand Province in the south was in danger of being completely overrun. Sharing an open border with Pakistan, Helmand accounted for 70 percent of the world's opium and heroin supply. *The New York Times* reported $155 million in drug money went into Taliban coffers.

Helmand had to be brought under government control. The tribes in the province were Pashtuns, as were the Taliban. The few Afghan soldiers were northern Tajiks who spoke a different language and hovered inside a few bases. So in 2006, the British sent in a 5,000-man brigade. But the province, 300 miles in length and home to a million farmers, was half the size of England, far beyond the control of 5,000 soldiers. One British general likened the effort to "mowing the lawn," with the Taliban returning as soon as the British left an area.

At the top of the province lay Sangin, a 200-square-mile rectangle of farmlands, bordered on the west by the Helmand River and on the east by a rutted road called Route 611. Beyond those boundaries lay miles of uninhabitable desert. Near and around the district market about 15,000 Pashtuns lived in a maze of one-story cinder-block-and-mud houses and slypes bare of shade trees. To the north, several thousand farmers lived in compounds in the middle of vast fields of corn and poppy.

Next to the market, the British established a Forward Operating Base (FOB) called Jackson that was under constant siege. The Brits decided that trying to control the outlying farming areas was not worth the cost in casualties. By staying inside their forts, however, they were routinely attacked.

The British opened schools and built up the market. Dozens of stores with gaily colored goods lined the "Avenue of Hope," a half-mile-long strip of Route 611 next to Jackson. Despite the constant attacks, a British general explained, "The central theme of the counterinsurgency, winning the hearts and minds, was still core to our plans."

But no Afghan official wanted to serve in the district and the few police refused to venture beyond the market. Riding in motorbikes and pickup trucks, the Taliban drove around the outlying farmlands in teams of five to twenty, paid and supplied by patronage networks called mahaz. Operations were directed by military commissioners, or nizami, who reported to the main headquarters in Quetta, Pakistan, eighty miles to the east. The Taliban in Pakistan provided hardened Punjabi fighters, some not even speaking Pashto, to train the locals in tactics and bomb making.

In Sangin, the Taliban drew most of its local fighters from the Ishaqzai tribe. The Taliban went from farm to farm, saying, "You are not Muslim unless you support jihad. Send at least one of your sons to fight with us." Left unsaid was that when the Taliban seized power, the cooperative tribes would be rewarded with a larger share of the poppy trade.

At the end of his tour, one British platoon leader wrote, "Sangin was no safer than when we found it. In fact, it was more dangerous and getting even more so." A soldier described his outpost as "ringed in." The British troops called the district "Sangingrad," a reference to the World War II siege of Stalingrad. Finally, the Afghan provincial governor asked the British to "stop referring to Sangin as a district, when all you occupy is a base."

Marine-istan

With the situation out of control in Sangin and across Helmand Province, in mid-2009 President Barack Obama authorized the U.S. Marines to move in. The Marines were the vanguard in a surge of 30,000 American troops that the president said would last only for eighteen months. From the first day of their deployment, the Marines knew they would be leaving based on a calendar rather than victory.

One sweltering night in July of 2009, I was sitting with a few newly arrived Marines in an outpost in Helmand when a helicopter landed. A wiry Marine with close-cropped gray hair hopped out and called us together.

"Here's the deal," Brig. Gen. Larry Nicholson rasped, the red battle scar on his neck glistening in the candlelight. "We're here to take their home turf from the Taliban. I want you to patrol until your asses fall off. Run every fucker who shoots at you out of the district."

I had first met Nicholson in 2006, when he was a colonel fighting in Fallujah. Back then, when Nicholson met with the city council, he promised fair treatment.

"I have pulled Marines who do not act properly out of the city," he said. "They had betrayed my trust; I lost confidence in them."

At the same time, he threw up a dirt berm around the city, erected concrete walls sealing off each neighborhood, and placed Marines on every street corner. Once the insurgents were killed in one neighborhood, he moved on to the next. He ground down the enemy.

Marines fight the way the Chicago Bears play football; they line up and run over the opposition. Nicholson's commander, Maj. Gen. James Mattis, had set the tone in Iraq, telling defiant sheiks, "I'm pleading with you, with tears in my eyes: If you fuck with me, I'll kill you all."

Now in Afghanistan, Nicholson issued the same clear order every corporal could understand. The mission: drive the enemy out of Helmand by walking every foot of farmland. Nicholson spread his forces out along the Helmand River where the people lived, with orders to clear their way south. Sangin, in the remote north, would wait until last.

At the higher levels, though, a more sophisticated, or squishy, philosophy prevailed. A few weeks before the Marines arrived, Adm. Mike Mullen, the chairman of the Joint Chiefs of Staff, had announced that America, after eight years of fighting, finally had "the right strategy" for Afghanistan. Mullen explained that the U.S. troops were building a nation. As a model, he praised the book *Three Cups of Tea*, which espoused village-level projects, and spent a day visiting a girls school in Afghanistan. America's top military leader had replaced war with social evangelism. The Muslim tribes would be converted by the secular gods of liberalism—schools, electricity, and other benefits bestowed from America via Kabul. "We can't," Mullen asserted, "kill our way to victory." Empathy was to be the path forward.

Confusion about the Marines' role deepened a few months after they arrived in Helmand. The White House changed the mission from "defeat" to "diminish" the Taliban. Asked to explain the meaning of "diminish," the chairman of the Joint Chiefs was stumped.

"I urge our troops," he said, "to think carefully about how they will accomplish the mission they have been assigned."

Was the mission of the Marine Corps to act as a Peace Corps? Down in Helmand, 500 miles physically and psychologically removed from Kabul, Nicholson walked a fine line. The Marine command did not know they were going to war under such a cloud of bureaucratic confusion. Their focus was upon defeating the enemy.

The Marines are a small, tight outfit. Think of a golf ball—inside a hard shell are hundreds of tightly coiled elastics. An order relayed down the chain of command is like dropping that ball down a flight of stairs. From top to bottom, the golf ball bounces the same way with the same energy.

Tensions between the Marines and the top command grew. In February of 2010, the Marines pushed the Taliban out of one of their strongholds called Marjah. Gen. Stanley McChrystal, the top commander in Kabul, then announced, "We've got a government in a box, ready to roll in."

Two months and two governments in boxes later, the Marines were still struggling, without any competent Afghan officials, to flush out the secret Taliban cells controlling the villagers.

McChrystal responded by flying down to Marjah to berate the Marine battalion commander for being too slow. In reaction, the Marines silently assessed the top command in Kabul as disconnected from the realities of tribal loyalties and Afghan government incompetence.

When Nicholson finished his tour in mid-2010, the Marines had gained control of the southern portion of Helmand. Insisting that high-level staffs were giving them orders without understanding the battlefield, the Marine command successfully lobbied to take charge of most of Helmand, replacing the overstretched British. Free to design their own approach, the Marines cut down their task to one essential: fighting the enemy.

"We [Marines] can't fix the economy," Marine four-star Gen. James Conway said. "We can't fix the government. What we can do is affect the security."

In Marine parlance, security meant seeking out and destroying the enemy. But Secretary of Defense Robert Gates did not trust the war-fighting judgment of Marines. In his memoir, he wrote that his "biggest mistake" was not swiftly resolving high-level command issues.

"He [Conway] insisted all Marines deploy to a single area of responsibility," Gates wrote, "with Marine air cover and logistics. Only Helmand fitted Conway's conditions. . . . The Marine higher leadership put their own parochial service concerns above the requirements of the overall Afghan mission."

Karl Eikenberry, the American ambassador in Kabul, agreed, testily observing that, in addition to dealing with thirty-two nations, he now had to cope with "Marine-istan," yet another tribe operating by its own rules. To many observers, Marines had the subtlety of a steamroller, rolling forward at its own inexorable pace and going wherever it chose to go.

The Road to Sangin

The Marines chose to go to Sangin. After eighteen months of clearing southern Helmand, the Marines turned north. The British, having lost a hundred soldiers there and having made scant headway in four years, readily agreed to hand over the effort.

Gaining control of Sangin did have a wisp of strategic rationale. Route 611 wound sixty kilometers north from the center of Helmand to Sangin. From there, the road ran another twenty kilometers before ending at the Kajacki Dam. There, two hydroelectric turbines provided a trickle of power to a million Pashtuns. Since 2001, the Western coalition had tried to open 611 in order to transport a third turbine up to the dam. That increase in power generation would symbolize development in southern Afghanistan, but Taliban control of Sangin prevented any such demonstrations of progress.

Security in northern Helmand, to include Sangin, was the responsibility of the 2d Marine Regiment. By dint of personality, the commander, Col. Paul Kennedy, shaped the command climate—the rituals, task priorities, and combat behavior of 6,000 Marines. He talked in a fast Boston accent, assuming his listeners had processed what he had just said while his mind hurried on to the next thought.

Kennedy sopped up tactics. With a grunt's eye for terrain, he viewed vistas and landscapes as angles and planes for bullets. No setting was pastoral, and no scenery was soothing. When he looked at a map, he saw geometries of fire; when he walked across a field, he thought in terms of grazing fire; when he visited farms, he wondered where arms caches were hidden.

In 2004, Kennedy had led an 800-man battalion into the Iraqi city of Ramadi. He wanted to be friendly. The plan had been to wear no armor, walk the neighborhoods, fund projects, train the police, and leave. The insurgents mocked the Marines as shotak, a soft, sugary cake, and launched a full-scale assault to seize the city. The battle raged for a week. When the hospital and morgue overflowed, the Marines piled the bodies of rebels and former Iraqi soldiers on street corners, leaving burial to the residents.

After the battle, Kennedy wrote to the families in the States, "Previous to yesterday the terrorists thought that we were soft enough to challenge. . . . It will be a cold day in Hell before we are taken for granted again."

In September of 2010, Kennedy visited Sangin for a briefing by the departing British battalion. Thanks to the British, the Sangin market was secure. Why not leave the farms and hinterlands alone? Let the Taliban eat corn, tax the locals, smuggle opium, and rant in the rural mosques. Sangin was good—or bad—enough just as it was. Kennedy listened as the briefer pointed on the map to the positions of twenty-two forts, referring to them as the "Forward Line of Troops."

"If there's a forward line," Kennedy said, "then we've lost. The enemy's strategy is to hang in and bleed us until we decide it's not worth it. We don't play defense. My strategy is to smash them until they don't want to fight us anymore. We're going to own every ditch, path, field, and farm in this district."

Kennedy ordered half of the British forts closed. Many British officers disagreed.

"It's a hard pill to swallow," one officer said, "that the Rifles [a British battalion] put so much sweat and blood into establishing these patrol bases, only to have them be dismantled by the Americans. They are trying a new approach, but it was tried by us in the past and gave the Taliban the chance to plant IEDs [Improvised Explosive Devices] wherever they wanted."

Kennedy knew that gaining control of Sangin would be bloody. His battalion in Iraq had suffered thirty-five killed, the highest number for a battalion in that war. Although his tough game face never flickered in public, I had known him for ten years and had seen him alone in his office, writing the painful letters to the families.

But he was wary of funeral ceremonies while battle was still raging. A feeling of futility or loss can quickly crumble morale. The goal then becomes surviving for the rest of the tour. Patrols are cut short, the safer routes are repeated, and the enemy learns where he will be left alone.

"I won't foster a culture of victimhood," Kennedy said. "We're here to kill the enemy, not to mope when some of us die. If we get hit, we hit back harder."

When Kennedy was fighting in Ramadi in 2004, one of his companies ran into a hornet's nest. The Marines, riding in flimsy vehicles, were riddled. Nine died along a five-mile road bordered by unfordable irrigation ditches, allowing the enemy to hit and run at will. The company was furious about their tin-can vehicles and discouraged by the terrain. The battalion held a ceremony with stone faces and no tears. The next day, the company was out clearing the road again.

"A Marine is there to kill the other guy," Kennedy said. "That's how he has to think. Don't dwell on your losses. Make the other guy lose."

The generals let Kennedy run his own show. He talked to his boss three times a week. He didn't have to sit in on video teleconferences or submit PowerPoint briefs. He focused on developing Afghan leaders, deploying his battalions and insuring them air and logistics support. He encouraged Afghan officers, drank tea with the elders, sat cross-legged in meetings with mullahs, and gave farmers some seed and electric generators.

But after his experience in Ramadi, he took a dim view of man's kindness. To Kennedy, counterinsurgency, or COIN, was a branch of warfare, not an exercise in civics. He called his approach "Big Stick COIN," meaning: attack the enemy. He was the poster child for the Marine slogan: "Be polite, and have a plan for killing everyone you meet."

In late summer of 2010, Kennedy moved the 3rd Battalion of the 7th Marine Regiment, or 3/7, up to Sangin. Due to return shortly to the States, 3/7's task was to take over positions from the British and reconnoiter the district in preparation for the next Marine battalion.

Max, a Pashtun interpreter who had served with coalition forces since 2005, summarized what 3/7 found.

"IEDs were everywhere," Max told me. "The Marines had to fire rockets just to blow a safe path out of the market. The farmers turned their backs on us. I couldn't figure out who was a Taliban, and I'm pretty good at doing that. Man, Sangin's a crazy place."

Crazy was an apt word. For four years, the Taliban had exported opium and imported explosives. The farmers profited and in turn supported the Taliban, who planted thousands of IEDs around the British outposts. When the Marines began clearing operations farther to the south, more Taliban fled north to Sangin. Eventually the British were isolated inside their forts, while on the other side of the minefields the Taliban were safe inside farming compounds.

In early October of 2010, both the British troops and the Marine battalion 3/7 left. The 3rd Battalion of the 5th Marine Regiment, or 3/5, moved in. Kennedy ordered 3/5 to seize control of the farmlands. There would be no "Forward Line of Troops." For the next six months, the Marines would patrol constantly. On average, a Marine would walk two and a half miles each day. Six thousand steps a day. One million steps.

Table of Organization

Regimental Combat Team 2
  6,000 Marines
    Col. Kennedy

3/5 (3rd Battalion, 5th Marine Regiment) at
    Forward Operating Base (FOB) Jackson
  800 Marines
    Lt. Col. Morris

Company (Kilo) at FOB Inkerman
  140 Marines
    Capt. Johnson

1st Platoon at FOB Inkerman
  44 Marines
    Lt. Schueman

2d Platoon at Patrol Base Transformer
  40 Marines
    Lt. Donnelly
    Lt. Broun

3rd Platoon at Patrol Base Fires

    50 Marines

        Lt. West

        Lt. Garcia

        Platoon Sgt.—Staff Sgt. Cartier

3rd Platoon Squads

    1st Squad—Sgt. Esquibel

    2d Squad—Sgt. Deykeroff

    3rd Squad—Sgt. Thoman

        Sgt. McCulloch

    Sniper Section—Sgt. Abbate

        Sgt. Browning

    Mortar Section—Cpl. Moreno

ONE MILLION STEPS

SECTION TWO

Chapter 1

SHOCK

Day 1. The First 6,000 Steps

When 3/5 rolled into Sangin, its reputation had preceded it. In 2004, they had fought in Fallujah, a fierce battle sparked after four American contractors were lynched on a bridge. After the city was destroyed, a Marine scrawled on the bridge, "This is for the Americans of Blackwater that were murdered here in 2004. Semper Fidelis 3/5. P.S. Fuck you." In Sangin, the farmers were asking Max, 3/5's interpreter, "Why have these Marines come? They're not welcome."

The battalion commander, Lt. Col. Jason Morris, was capable, earnest, and formal. His father had served as a Marine in Vietnam, and Morris had won an award for outstanding leadership. Before deploying, he wrote to the families that the goal was "to increase security and bring economic development and stability to the Afghan people." That sounded more civic-minded than dangerous.

The 800 Marines in 3/5 had trained together for a year. Morris and the senior officers and NCOs were on their second and third combat tours. For the 700 excited junior Marines, Sangin was their first combat tour. Prior to flying out from California, Morris had called for one final gear inspection, amid grumblings about last-minute harassment.

"Colonel Morris looked right at me," Cpl. Kevin Smith, a sniper, said. "He asked if I was ready. He was sizing me up, not my gear. That's when it hit me. Holy shit, we're going to war!"

On October 13, 2010, an armored vehicle dropped Smith off at FOB (Forward Operating Base) Jackson, the battalion's headquarters next to the Sangin market. When Smith hopped on top of the turret to look around, a bullet pinged off its side. As he tumbled down, a British soldier called out, "Best to sit rather than stand out here."

Even before reaching FOB Jackson, 3/5 had lost Lance Cpl. John Sparks, twenty-three. He was shot and killed on a rooftop. He had grown up in a Chicago public housing complex and had hoped to join the Chicago police after his tour.

Now, an hour after arriving at Jackson, Smith had been shot at. In response, three Marines from the sniper section slipped into the nearby cornfields to conduct a quick security patrol. Moving quietly, they glanced down a row of corn and saw a man crouching with an AK, looking in the opposite direction. Two snipers dropped him with a "frame shot," each putting a bullet in the man's torso. Seconds later, a second man popped out of the corn and tried to drag the body away. They shot him too.

While Smith was out on that patrol with Cpl. Jordan Laird and Cpl. Jacob Ruiz, a massive mine shattered a 35,000-pound vehicle called an MRAP (Mine Resistant Ambush Protected), killing four Marines. All were on their first combat deployment.

By the end of the first day, Battalion 3/5 had taken five fatalities.

———

Marine units are organized on a simple three-part system. Forged over hundreds of battles, the system is focused downward and decentralized. The regiment, commanded by Kennedy, had three battalions. The 3/5 battalion, commanded by Morris, had three rifle companies. Each company had three rifle platoons. Each forty-four-man platoon had three squads. Each thirteen-man squad was divided into three four-man fire teams. In the field, a platoon usually had several attachments like engineers and snipers.

Sangin was shaped like a rectangle fifteen kilometers long and four kilometers wide. (See Map 1.) A copious flow of water fed thousands of irrigation ditches stretching from the Helmand River to Route 611. The vast expanse of well-watered fields stretching from the river to the road was called the Green Zone.

Morris sent his third company—Kilo—two kilometers north up 611 to an outpost called Inkerman, named for a fallen British soldier. Kilo's job was to control the Green Zone, where the Taliban were familiar with every field, ditch, compound, and back trail. They knew where they had planted IEDs and where they left open lanes.

Capt. Nick Johnson, the commander of Kilo Company, was a big, no-nonsense man with a keen interest in warfighting. The instructors back in the States had stressed reaching out to village elders and funding projects at the hamlet level. But with five killed on Day 1, he immediately shifted his focus to small-unit jungle tactics. His task was to clear from Inkerman on 611 to the Helmand River, a three-kilometer by three-kilometer rectangle.

Johnson initially kept two platoons at Inkerman and one at Outpost/Patrol Base Fires, an isolated fort one kilometer inside the Green Zone. Intent upon sending out several patrols daily, Johnson provided the platoons with maps that broke up the Green Zone into sec-

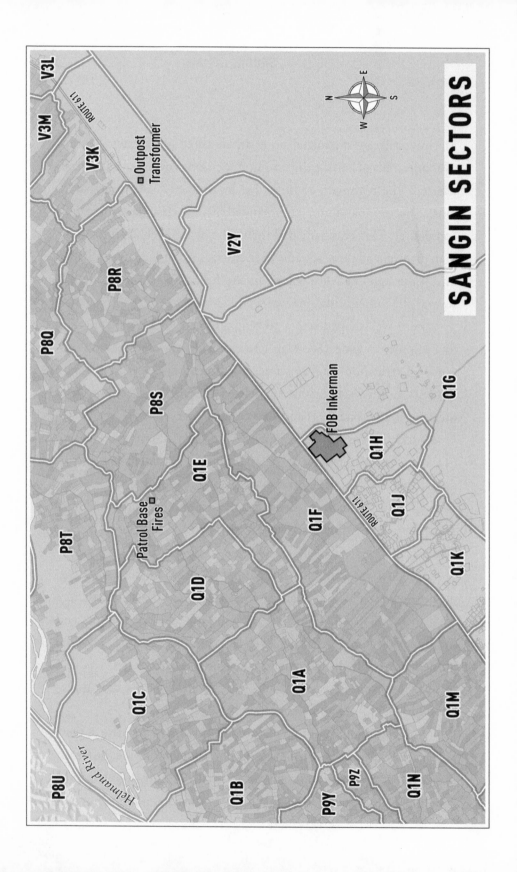

SANGIN SECTORS

tors designated by different sets of letters. This made it easier to direct reinforcements or indirect fire.

Day 2. 12,000 Steps

The next morning, a squad of thirteen Marines set off from Inkerman to scout to the northwest. When the squad was pinned down by two enemy machine guns, a second squad moved forward to help and was engaged from the flanks. Once linked together, the two squads threw out enough fire to prevent the Taliban from closing on them. Steady fire coming from different angles forced the squads to duck into an irrigation ditch. Unable to pull back, they radioed for help. In response, Sgt. Sean Johnson left Patrol Base Fires to flank the enemy with his squad.

"Hey, Sean," Sgt. Matt Abbate, the leader of a ten-man sniper section, called out, "we'll tag along to provide covering fire."

Drenched in sweat, Abbate had just returned from patrol. But the offer was typical of him. Of the seventy-odd sergeants in the battalion, Abbate, twenty-six, was the best liked. One Marine joked that Abbate was "the battalion mascot." An honor graduate from the reconnaissance swimmer's course, he had turned down an offer to transfer to the Navy SEALs. He was the battalion's top shot, held the endurance record, and grinned often. On battalion hikes in the High Sierras, he would fall back to carry the packs of those struggling to keep up.

His family in northern California were dedicated bikers and he told hilarious tales about his motorcycle escapades. His son, Carson, was two, and Matt was already planning their bike trips. He was everyone's outgoing big brother, smart, tough, carefree. On battalion movie nights, he would shout at the screen, making up wacky expressions and imitating movie actors. But once it came time for a mission, intensity replaced the smile.

"Outside the wire," Matt said, "you walk by faith, because no one knows where the next IED is. But we can't hesitate. We're here to shoot."

Covered by Abbate and four of his snipers, the squad departed from Fires. They could hear shooting a thousand meters to their east. The Taliban were using two Russian-made PKM machine guns with a slow, distinct cyclic rate that sounded like someone hammering on a steel pipe. Johnson cut to the north, hoping to come up on the rear of the enemy. Abbate and his snipers occasionally scrambled onto the roofs of farmhouses, trying to find targets in their scopes.

"I see guys in tree lines," Abbate called to Johnson. "The fuckers move around without weapons showing. I can't smoke them."

The rules of engagement required PID, or Positive Identification, which meant seeing that the man had a weapon or was talking on a radio in the middle of a firefight. In fact, Abbate was having a hard time seeing anyone. The summer corn hadn't yet been harvested and the fields were thick with heavy green stalks taller than a man. Once they plunged into a field, the Marines couldn't see ten feet. Each corn patch was about the size of a football field. The corn sucked the oxygen out of the air and the muddy ground oozed humidity. But to use the trails was to invite ambush.

The Marines walked in single file, the point man sweeping a metal detector called a Vallon back and forth. You can buy a Vallon on eBay, put earphones on your kids, and let them scamper along the beach, listening for the *ping!* of coins in the sand. In Sangin, the point man hoped the dials would quiver if a flashlight battery was detected.

The squad bounded by four-man fire teams across the openings between the fields, each four-man fire team covering the other. They waded across one canal in chest-deep muddy water, and then another. The enemy, knowing the Marines were trying to flank them, were chattering over their handheld radios and shifting positions. After crossing a dozen fields in the one-hundred-degree temperature, the Marines were exhausted, having sweated out more liquid than they were drinking from their CamelBaks.

In the cornfields, two separate groups of Marines and scattered enemy groups were maneuvering out of sight of one another. Bullets were zipping by from different angles. It was hard to tell who was firing at whom. But there hadn't been any friendly casualties and the enemy fire had slackened by the time Johnson's squad reached the other Marines. Running low on ammo, they decided to head west back to Patrol Base Fires by wading across a waist-deep canal.

Johnson's squad took up the rear. When Johnson's men reached the road paralleling the canal, the enemy unleashed a fusillade of machine gun fire. The Marines flopped down and LCpl. Alec Catherwood landed on a pressure plate. The blast hurled him into the canal, smashing apart his rifle and driving the red-hot barrel deep into Johnson's left thigh.

Improvised Explosive Devices—IEDs—were fiendishly simple. Despite entreaties from Washington to use other readily available chemicals, Pakistan persisted in manufacturing ammonium nitrate, a fertilizer then smuggled into Afghanistan. The insurgents mixed the nitrate, which acted as the oxidizer, with fuel and packed the gummy substance into plastic jugs. A blasting cap the size of a firecracker was attached to a few feet of wire, with the open end glued to a piece of wood. A wire on another piece of wood was wrapped at one end around a flashlight battery. The two pieces of wood were taped together with the wires facing each other, kept apart by a slice of sponge. The jug, wires, battery, and parallel pieces of wood were buried in the dirt. When the weight of a foot pressed the boards and wires together, a spark leaped from the battery to the blasting cap, setting off ten pounds of nitrate that ripped apart legs, testicles, intestines, and chests.

———————

Abbate unfolded the black tourniquet strap and wrapped it around Johnson's soaked trouser. He threaded the strap back through the plastic buckle, pulled the strap tight, grabbed the knob, and twisted to tighten the strap. The pain jolted through Johnson, who struggled to get up.

"Let me up," he muttered. "Gotta get this shit organized."

A grunt can cinch up a tourniquet in his sleep. It's an automatic reflex. When the blood is gushing and severed legs are twitching and the smoke is blinding and the screaming is too loud to hear—that's when the tourniquet must be applied. Abbate twisted the tourniquet tighter, pushing Johnson's face down so that he couldn't see the blood gushing from his shattered leg.

"Don't look, bro," he said.

Cpl. Jacob Ruiz, carrying the radio for the sniper section, hustled over. Ruiz, twenty-five, from California, was calm and efficient.

"Call for medevac," Abbate said. "Urgent."

After sending the message, Ruiz heard a *pfzz*ing noise and glanced up to see the black shape of a rocket whizzing past. He looked down a corn row and locked eyes with two men, each holding a grenade launcher. One, wearing a brown man-dress and a kapul (flat hat), ducked back, while the other, in a dirty blue man-dress, stood his ground. Ruiz dropped the handset and swung up his M4 rifle. The man was too quick, darting into the corn.

The explosive concussion had knocked two other Marines into the canal. In shock amid the carnage, many did not return fire. That's the killer in a firefight. If you don't keep shooting, no matter how wildly, your enemy moves freely to a spot where he can finish you off. As General Patton put it, "to halt under fire and not fire back is suicide." With scant return fire, the Taliban were dodging safely from spot to spot in the shallow ditches among the tree lines. Amid the smoke and dust, the enemy pressed forward.

Abbate ran up and down the canal road, ignoring the bullets and the IEDs lurking underfoot, urging the Marines to return fire. He grabbed one man after another, pulling each into a firing position and assigning a sector of fire.

"When you see dust," he yelled, "spray it down."

Occasionally he paused to aim in with his Mark 11 sniper rifle, snapping off a few quick shots. Once he had set up a base of fire, he paused and looked around. Two Marines were floundering in the canal, trying to keep Catherwood's head above water. Alec Catherwood, nineteen, from Illinois, had wanted to be a Marine since he was three. He was engaged to be married in July. This was his first deployment and his first firefight.

Abbate leaped in and the three pulled Catherwood onto the bank. Catherwood wasn't breathing and his lips had turned blue. His left arm had been sheared off by the blast and his body had gone into shock. As his blood poured out, his body heat drained away. The sudden drop in temperature prevented his blood from clotting, enabling more blood to spill into the dirt. The lethal combination of lactic acid buildup and lower blood pressure eventually throws the heart out of rhythm. Abbate helped cinch tight a tourniquet and yelled for Marines to try mouth-to-mouth resuscitation, knowing that death hovered a minute away.

Back at Kilo Company's ops center, frustration reigned. A dozen Marines huddled around the radios; there was nothing they could do. Another squad had already left Fires to help, and the 81mm mortars at Inkerman were firing. Amid the background clunk of outgoing mortar shells, those in the ops center could only listen to the screams over the radio.

———

At the scene of the fight, Abbate was checking on the wounded. Ruiz was still aiding Johnson, the chunk of rifle barrel still soldered deep into his mangled left thigh.

"You're going to make it," Abbate said. "We'll get you out of here."

Johnson remembered being thrown into the air. He thought his friend had caught him.

Some of the enemy had forded the canal farther to the north and were attacking the Marines' right flank, trying to cut off their route back to Fires. Abbate ran over to Cpl. Royce Hughie, who was covering the eastern approach with his squad automatic weapon. A SAW spews 800 rounds a minute; that volume of bullets melds into a glowing red laser beam slicing in half anything in its path. As Hughie shifted around, a rocket-propelled grenade (RPG) shot out of the corn, struck the ground in front of him, and spun to a stop without exploding. Hughie shoved the SAW's bipod into the mud and hosed down the fields to the north.

Abbate ran back down the road, with bullets zipping in different directions, to see after Catherwood. Doc Swartz looked up and shook his head.

"I can't revive him," he said. "He's dead."

Shells from the mortars back at Inkerman were exploding to the north. The Taliban responded with RPGs, some direct shots through the corn and most lofted at an angle. Corn stalks were smoldering and the battlefield was thick with smoke. Over the next twenty minutes, under supporting fire by Hughie, all of the Marines moved back across the canal.

Seeking cover, LCpl. Joseph Lopez ran toward a compound designated House 3 on the leaders' photomaps. A concussion wave swept over Abbate and Swartz, followed by a sharp *bang!* and a swirl of black smoke. Lopez, twenty-six, from Rosamond, California, had absorbed the full force of the explosion.

Instinctively, Cpl. Sloan Hicks started toward Lopez. Abbate grabbed him.

"No!" he shouted. "Stay off that goddamn path!"

The Taliban had dug in IEDs along the banks of the canal, on the few trails, and in the courtyards. Marines were screaming back and forth, no one daring to move. Despite what he had just told Hicks, Abbate stood up, ignored the incoming fire, ran at full speed back to Ruiz, and grabbed the handset.

"We have multiple cas from a second IED," he radioed to Fires. "Too many to carry back. Direct the helos in here."

Doc Swartz was running past Abbate, toward the wounded near House 3. Another flash, another concussion wave, another patch of black smoke. Doc was down, with both legs blown off.

"Freeze!" Abbate screamed at the spread-out Marines. "No one else move. Get that Vallon up here!"

The engineer trained to use the metal detector was in shock. Three successive blasts had struck down four Marines behind him and three more in front of him. He refused to move. When Abbate yelled at him a second time, he responded by pitching his Vallon forward.

Abbate crawled over and picked it up. He had no idea how to read a small quiver of the needle. He faked it, standing erect and slowly walking to Doc Swartz, scuffing his feet to leave marks for the others to follow. He kept going for about twenty meters until he reached a spot where the dirt was caked as hard as concrete, safe from any IED. Then he threw the Vallon to Hughie, who was holding the dying Lopez.

Joseph Lopez had joined the Marines to "find his way." He read the Bible daily and Johnson, his squad leader, had trusted his judgment. Before deploying, he told his father, "I know God, and if anything happens to me, I want you to tell my Mom I'm okay."

Together, Sergeant Dy, as everyone called him, and Sergeant Abbate carried first Lopez and then Doc Swartz to the safe ground.

There were now three wounded who urgently needed blood transfusions, plus one dying and one dead Marine.

"Sergeant Abbate," Ruiz yelled, "helos inbound in five mikes!"

Abbate again took the Vallon and walked through the soft dirt for about fifty meters to an open spot where the helicopters could land. As the wounded and dead were carried to the landing zone, he realized the northwest flank was unguarded. He ran back along the path he had cleared, grabbed three Marines, and led them forward to cover the flank.

As soon as the *whump-whump* of helicopter blades could be heard, LCpl. Willie Deel saw a farmer in a brown man-dress dart out of a cornfield, pointing upward with an RPG. Seeing Deel aim in at him, the man ducked back into the corn. From the other side of a minefield, the Taliban could shoot carefully as the helos fluttered down. The enemy intensified their machine gun fire.

There wasn't time to find a route through the irrigation ditches to attack from the flank, and to slowly sweep a path with the Vallon across the field guaranteed being hit. LCpl. Mario Launder, a fire team leader, watched as Abbate picked up his rifle, scrambled up the canal bank, and without looking back headed out into the field toward the enemy position. After advancing several meters, Abbate realized he was alone. He stopped, turned around, and shouted.

"Let's go! We all die together!"

Launder's squad leaped up and moved behind him.

Seeing the Marines running toward them, the enemy slipped into a shallow canal and pulled back. No IEDs exploded. Perhaps none had been set in the field, or maybe the Marines were just plain lucky.

With only a few bullets incoming, two helos landed in fast succession and took off with the casualties. One helo was diverted to pick up the body of LCpl. Irvin Ceniceros, twenty-one, from Alaska, killed in another fight a few kilometers south.

After the medevac birds left, Abbate grabbed a machine gun and took up post as the rear guard. He was the last man to reenter the wire back at Patrol Base Fires.

That wasn't the end of it. The Taliban had blown a sluice gate a few hundred meters to the west, allowing a tributary from the Helmand River to flood in. The fields outside PB Fires were chest-deep in water. By late afternoon, the rising water was lapping inside the wire. With the fort almost underwater, the Taliban crept closer, shooting from all sides. The Marines furiously returned fire. They sent out a patrol to flank the enemy to the east. The Taliban easily avoided them, while maintaining constant fire. When the patrol returned to Fires and ammunition was redistributed, the defenders were down to one magazine per rifle.

Back at Inkerman, Capt. Nick Johnson organized an emergency working party.

"Everybody not on watch," LCpl. Jaspar Jones, who was at the headquarters, said, "went on that working party. We had to get ammo out to Fires. All of us wanted to help."

They loaded the munitions into a truck and drove until it mired down. Then they strapped ammo boxes on their backs and trudged forward. Captain Johnson toted one hundred pounds of .50 caliber ammo by himself. By the third trip, he was exhausted. For three hours, the working party staggered, slipped, and slid in thigh-deep mud from the truck to the fort. When they could carry no more individually, they slung the ammo boxes on poles, shouldered by two of them.

After the pile of ammo was waist-high, Johnson called together the sopping Marines.

"I know what you're feeling," he said. "Losing buddies to IEDs sucks. The Taliban believe they've cut you off and that we'll leave. No way we'll do that. In 1950, this battalion broke out of the Chosin Reservoir, in temperatures twenty below, surrounded by thousands of Chinese. We can't fail them. You have to stay and break out."

Gunnery Sgt. Christopher Carlisle, imposing in stature and voice, stomped around the fort, clasping the shaken Marines by their shoulders.

"The Taliban think that flooding is going to stop us," he yelled. "They have no idea the hell we're going to unleash. I got your back, little brothers!"

Carlisle was enraged.

"The enemy doesn't kill," he screamed, "or take the limbs of any of us without paying tenfold. No one fucks with our family. We'll drop the sledgehammer on their ass."

Within two days of pushing into the Green Zone, Battalion 3/5 had suffered eight killed and two dozen wounded. A British officer later said, "We warned you." He wasn't being mean-spirited; the British had learned that the enemy fought for every foot of ground. If you left the perimeter, you took casualties.

The Kilo Company first sergeant, Jorge Melendez, was wiry and meticulous. To him, everything had a place and an order to it. Each casualty somehow fitted into an unseen pattern.

"God," he said, "doesn't give you burdens you can't carry."

The Marines were carrying a heavy burden, their morale challenged by an enemy that was unafraid. Eventually either the Taliban would pull back or the Marines would cease to patrol. The outcome depended upon whose will broke first.

Chapter 2

LEADER LOST

"The public doesn't know what goes on out here on the front lines."

—KYLE DOYLE, CALIFORNIA

While the fight and the waters swirled around PB Fires, a mile to the north Kilo's 3rd Platoon was gingerly reconnoitering the terrain. The British had warned that the shrub growth on both sides of Route 611 was littered with mines. All day the platoon had exchanged shots with enemy skirmishers hidden in the cornfields and irrigation ditches. The technical term is "skulking"—shoot, slip along a ditch to another corn patch, wait half an hour, take a random shot, and scoot away. This was the American Indian way of war in skirmishes against the settlers in the eighteenth century.

At the end of a frustrating day, 3rd Platoon had briefly glimpsed only two men with AKs.

The platoon moved into an abandoned compound for the night

and Lt. Cameron West, the platoon commander, called the men together. A strapping outdoorsman who grew up on a cattle ranch in Georgia, he pushed his Marines hard. But on long marches when some straggled, he joked rather than yelled at them. West's love of the land and outgoing manner had earned him the nickname "Big Country."

"We lost two Marines near Fires today," he said. "IEDs are everywhere. Be damn careful. Watch out for each other. Third Platoon is out here by itself."

A rifle platoon of forty-four men, 3rd Platoon was augmented by two machine gun crews, two mortar crews, a forward observer, and a few snipers. The total number was fifty.

Third Platoon was not a cross section of American society. Back in World War II, Korea, and Vietnam, the draft guaranteed that a platoon resembled the face of America, diverse in backgrounds, tastes, and ambitions. In contrast, today's military is self-selected, educated, and middle-class. Three out of four American youths cannot qualify mentally or physically for today's military. Nevertheless, the Marine Corps has a one-year waiting list.

The young men in 3rd Platoon were smarter, wealthier, fitter, and more committed than the average American. Most had joined the Marine Corps because of its tough, disciplined standards, and believed the Corps had changed them. They were well trained, but not to the degree of career professionals like the SEALs or Army Special Forces. Most planned to serve for four years and return to civilian life. Only four believed they would learn a trade in the Marine Corps.

Everyone in the platoon had graduated from high school. Seventy-five percent came from a two-parent family, a strong indicator of emotional stability. The average age was twenty-one, and one in three was married, with at least one child. Most considered their tastes in music and movies to be the same as that of their civilian friends. They thought their civilian counterparts were softer than they, but most said that made no difference. Sixty-five percent "believe in God, his rules and heaven," while only a few believed God was a myth. Eight out of ten were more caring or appreciative of life due to combat, while only one in ten thought combat had made him harder.

Overall, 3rd Platoon was made up of well-adjusted, self-confident, middle-class young men who liked each other and had confidence in their leader, Big Country.

Day 3. 18,000 Steps

On the morning of October 15, 3rd Platoon resumed scouting for safe paths by the trial-and-error tactic. They walked along, and if no one was blown up, that trail was safe, at least until dark. The Marines had night-vision devices, but they couldn't shoot someone for being out at night. The sun was scorching, and many farmers tended their corn and poppy after dark—or dug in IEDs.

Second Squad was at point, led by Sgt. Alex Deykeroff, twenty-three, who had two previous combat tours in Iraq. He had joined 3/5 to experience the fight in Afghanistan. Sergeant Dy read a book a week and was a walking encyclopedia of Marine history. He had enjoyed the battalion's six-month work-up. The command didn't have screamers at the top and he had free rein to shape the dozen Marines in 2d Squad.

The instructors back in California had trained the battalion based on lessons from Iraq, where patrols used vehicles and IEDs were buried in trash piles next to hard-paved roads. But no one in 3rd Platoon ever patrolled in a vehicle. Marines walked off to the sides of dirt paths, encased among thousands of corn stalks. Herds of sheep and cows, tended by barefoot boys with long sticks, grazed in the few open fields. Thick undergrowth and rows of tall trees lined the irrigation ditches and canals.

The day before, Sergeant Dy had heard the firing when Abbate was engaged near Fires. Dy had climbed onto a roof and watched groups of what he assumed were unarmed farmers scurrying around. Later, he watched the helicopters roar by with dead Marines on board. There were no garbage pits out in the fields. Where were the IEDs hidden?

Slowly, slowly, 2d Squad moved in single file, only a few hundred meters off Route 611. They were walking on an embankment next to a waist-deep canal when LCpl. Tim Wagner, nineteen, saw the edge of a board sticking out of the dirt. Wagner, from Nebraska farm country, needed no prompting. He raised a clenched fist and froze. A few feet away, another Marine stopped, took a careful look around, and pointed at a mound of freshly turned earth. They both backed away.

Sergeant Dy called back to Big Country, about sixty yards behind them.

"We got IEDs up here."

Lieutenant West was already on super-alert. A farmer had just signaled from his field, shaking his head in a warning not to go farther.

"Don't advance," West said.

Big Country then did what he was expected to do, and why the loss rate among Marine second lieutenants is so staggering: he walked up to the front. Platoon sergeants often complain about their young officers being headstrong, but no sergeant wants a leader who holds back. Big Country walked the few meters toward Dy, staying in a swept lane marked by squirts of shaving cream.

He moved carefully around LCpl. Aaron Lantznester, twenty-one, from Ohio. Lantz had bright blue eyes that looked so innocent that the squad called him Bambi. He had found boot camp to be too easy, but later, in infantry training, had paid close attention during the Combat Life Savers course, learning how to treat sucking chest wounds and massive hemorrhages. The instructors shouted at the recruits when they were least expecting it—during a ten-mile march, or in a classroom, or in the squad bay.

"Jones, lie down! You've lost your leg! The rest of you—save him!"

Lantz was carrying eight tourniquets.

As West walked by, he gave Lantz a friendly tap on the helmet.

"Get an engineer up here," West said.

LCpl. James Boelk, on his first combat patrol as the radio operator, was a few meters behind, scrambling to catch up to his lieutenant. The largest man in the platoon, his squad nicknamed him "Baloo," after the gentle bear in *The Jungle Book*. Less than a foot away from where a dozen other Marines had walked, Boelk slipped on the bank. An explosion hurled his body into the canal, killing him instantly.

West felt a truck hit him. The force threw him thirty feet backward. He landed with his back against a tree, his leg lying next to him.

The shock wave drove Lantznester's face into the dirt. For several seconds, he couldn't hear or focus his eyes. When his vision cleared, he crawled to West, ripped off his shredded armor, and cinched two tourniquets around the gushing stump.

"Tell everyone not to move," West said. "We gotta . . ."

West tried to raise his right hand, but it too had been mangled. His face was twisted at an odd angle, a chunk of shrapnel jutting from his left eye.

"You're okay, sir," Lantz said. "Everything's going to be okay."

West felt no pain, only frustration.

"Shut the fuck up, Lantz. Nothing's okay."

The blast had scythed down the command group. Burning metal had smashed into LCpl. Zach White's face, breaking his jaw. Other shards snapped the arm of the corpsman, HM3 Stephen Librando. Two other Marines were holding their torn faces, while a third lay dazed with a concussion.

With the explosion echoing in their ears, no one could hear. An engineer scraped the ground around the blast area, found another IED within arm's length of Lantz, and snipped the wires. Lantz continued to look after West.

Sergeant Dy, a few feet away, felt like he had been hurled underwater. Everything looked white and faded out, with pieces of corn and dirt swirling and bobbing. With both radios blown, Dy fired off red signal flares.

Staff Sgt. Matt Cartier, the platoon sergeant, made his way up from the rear, staying inside the gobs of shaving cream. He organized first aid and used his radio to call in the disaster. Back at Inkerman, Gunny Carlisle ran to the nearest vehicle, hopped in, and told the startled driver to get up the road. Within minutes, the armored vehicle had skidded to a stop near the red smoke signal marking the casualties out in the field. Carlisle ran down the path, took one look at West's pale face, hoisted him over his shoulder, and lumbered back to the MRAP. Sergeant Cartier directed the movement of the other litters, and within half an hour all the casualties had been flown out of Inkerman.

The next day, David Boelk, a retired Air Force master sergeant, was sitting at his desk in Washington, D.C. He read of a massive explosion that had killed and wounded several Marines in Sangin. He thought, "Wow, my son's unit, somebody died, that really hits close to home." His office phone rang a few minutes later; then two somber Marines were at his house.

LCpl. James Boelk, twenty-four, left behind his parents, five sisters, and a brother. Matt Cartier, the platoon sergeant, had a soft spot for Boelk, who immediately did everything he was told, with a loopy grin on his face. He was the sort of Marine every sergeant liked to have in his unit—obedient, eager, and good-natured.

Elsewhere in the battalion, an IED explosion killed Sgt. Ian Tawney, twenty-five, of Oregon. His wife, Ashley, was expecting a baby girl in January. Tawney was the top student in squad leader school and graduated as the class honor man. 3/5 had lost ten Marines and more than thirty-five wounded. At Camp Bastion, the main coalition base in southern Afghanistan, the Personnel Retrieval and Processing Company prepared each body for transit to the States.

"If it was a Marine [body] coming in," Sgt. Thor Holm wrote to me, "we assumed he was coming from 3/5. We tried to take care of him for his buddies. We ironed every flag."

Lieutenant Colonel Morris sent a long email to the families of those serving in the battalion.

"I have decided," Morris wrote, "not to announce casualty information via the Battalion's webpage, because I think it will be less mentally draining on families over time than announcing every casualty we sustain as soon as it happens."

He had a tough time composing that letter. He knew every family was poring over the daily news bulletins. Names of the fallen, however, were not released until a full day after the next of kin had been notified. Even then, in order not to provide intelligence to the enemy, the location of the incident was not revealed. This meant hundreds of families held their breath for two to three days, not knowing who was ringing the doorbell.

The families stayed constantly in touch. Patty Schumacher, whose son Victor had been killed on the 13th, talked with Mark and Teresa Soto. Mark had been Victor's high school football coach. Together, the three launched a Facebook page entitled "The Boys of 3/5." A news story about each fallen Marine in 3/5 appeared on the page.

"At the time," Morris later told NPR, "I was wondering, what were we doing wrong?"

Chapter 3

WITH THE OLD BREED

"We fight, bleed, lose buddies, and get shit done."
—JEREMY MORENO, CALIFORNIA

What shocked 3rd Platoon was that it happened so fast. Ten percent of the unit was gone in one thunderous clap, blood and limbs strewn about. Big Country, their cheerful platoon commander, had left them. One day they were intact, and the next day they were leaderless, with holes blown in their ranks.

"We lost so many so fast," LCpl. Trevor Halcomb, twenty-two, said. "I wasn't sure I'd get back to Texas to have a happy, healthy family and a house with a white picket fence."

Captain Nick Johnson knew 3rd Platoon's morale had sunk. A student of history, Johnson had devoured Cpl. E. B. Sledge's harrowing book, *With the Old Breed*. Sledge, who had served in Kilo

Company during World War II, depicted battle as a pitiless monster. The "old breed" of Marines, expecting that many among them would die, bottled up their emotions and fought stoically. Kilo's radio call sign was Sledgehammer. Knowing 3rd Platoon needed a man like Sledge, Captain Johnson reached for the hardest lieutenant he knew.

Second Lt. Victor Garcia looked like a walking rock. If you saw him with a scowl on his face, you'd cross to the other side of the street. He spoke softly and with excellent diction. At thirty-six, he was the oldest lieutenant in the battalion. His parents had immigrated from Mexico to the Salinas farming community in California, where his father was a mechanic. His older brother had served in the Marines, and his two sisters were computer designers.

In high school, Garcia was a champion heavyweight wrestler with mediocre grades. He had joined the Marines in response to a recruiter's classic gambit that he couldn't hack it. He liked being a grunt, and did three combat tours in Iraq, progressing from squad leader to platoon sergeant to company gunny. Officers, though, gave the orders, and he wanted to make his own decisions in battle. Selected to attend college as part of the officers program, he enrolled at San Diego State, where he weekly wore his uniform to class. He found the students to be friendly, if a bit intimidated by a Marine gunny. He graduated in two years with straight As, except for a B in Women's Studies.

Assigned to Kilo Company, he had hoped to command a platoon. But after five years of deployments, he knew how to control mortars, rockets, artillery, and air. That experience landed him at company headquarters as the Fire Support Officer. Now Johnson needed an experienced leader in the field.

"Pack your gear," he told Garcia, "and take over 3rd. Keep the platoon here at company until you get your feet wet."

That was it. No rah-rah speech, no pep talk.

Day 4. 24,000 Steps

Garcia called together 3rd Platoon for the first time. The numbed Marines knew he had served as a platoon sergeant in Ramadi, where IEDs, snipers, and rocket-propelled grenades were daily occurrences.

"We're going to get those sons of bitches," he said. "We'll honor our dead by going out again today and every day."

Staff Sergeant Cartier took Garcia aside.

"I'm the platoon sergeant, sir," he said. "Lieutenant West and I trained this platoon together. With him gone, I have to show I'm still here for them. Let me take out this patrol without you."

Garcia knew that Cartier had torn the ligaments in his right knee and, in order to stay in the field, was avoiding the battalion doctor.

"You got it," Garcia said. "Take it slow."

"I can't do it any other way."

The patrol left the wire, exchanged small arms fire for a few hours, and returned with no casualties. After that first step, Garcia and Cartier agreed to a division of labor. The platoon sergeant set the patrol and guard rotations, supervised camp cleanliness, listened to everyone's gripes, and took care of problems that shouldn't reach the lieutenant. Lighthearted where Garcia was saturnine, Cartier fitted into the role of counselor and ombudsman for the troops. Garcia didn't want to come across as the hardass that he was.

"After taking so many losses," he said, "the platoon was ignoring the little things. They weren't blousing their trousers, wearing Marine-issue boots, shaving every morning. They were losing the habit of discipline. So each day, I'd suggest one correction to Matt Cartier, and he'd get the point across to the platoon."

Garcia understood the Marines, but he wasn't their buddy. As the new platoon commander, he made no effort to mix in. He let the squad leaders do their jobs, while Cartier kept his finger on the pulse of the unit.

Garcia's quiet separateness suggested he had seen this all before. Actually, he had no more understanding of village warfare than did the platoon. The Iraqi city of Ramadi had been the classic urban fight. The concrete streets and sidewalks made it impossible to dig in IEDs; the Marines learned to avoid garbage heaps and abandoned cars. Shots came from the upper windows of apartment buildings, not from distant tree lines. Once the Marines gained control of a city block, concrete barriers were erected at the entrances. There were no open spaces inside a city.

The Green Zone was a leap in time back into the paddies and bush of Vietnam. No hard roads, no cars, no bright lights, no Quick Reaction Force mounted in armored vehicles. In Sangin, the local Taliban—about 200 full-time and twice that number as part-time help—simply had to prevent the Marines from pushing outside the lines established by the British. The hated occupiers—the infidels or jafirs—were too powerful to assault head-on. But as long as they were penned in close to their forts, they were no threat. Sooner or later, they would leave. The infidels had the watches, but the Islamist resistance had the time.

Day 5. 30,000 Steps

Shortly after breakfast, 3rd Platoon heard the distant thumps and rattles of a firefight to their north, up near the Kajacki Dam, guarded by India Battery of the 12th Marine Regiment. LCpl. Francisco Jackson had been killed by an IED and his squad was pinned down, unable to recover his body. After a second Marine was shot, the Taliban closed in to prevent the squad from withdrawing. Back at 3/5's op center, the air officer, Capt. Matt Pasquali, called for an air attack. Two F-18s responded by dropping two 500-pound bombs, followed by several gun runs.

Low on fuel, the F-18s had returned to base before Garcia left Fires with the morning patrol.

Third Platoon had not moved 500 meters outside the wire before bumping into a Taliban gang. Both sides were moving parallel along thick rows of eight-foot-tall corn when they heard each other. In the ensuing firefight, thousands of bullets scythed down the cornfield. When the shooting ended, the Marines found two dead Taliban and a dead farmer. Nearby another farmer lay moaning with bullets in his leg. The Marines attached a tourniquet and the wounded man was taken by tractor to the district market.

This pattern of fighting—two enemy fighters dead at a cost of one innocent farmer and another badly wounded, plus repeated bombing runs to the north—deeply disturbed the high command. In fact, no army in history ever fought with more restraint than did the Americans, Danes, Dutch, and British in Afghanistan. Seven out of ten civilian casualties were caused by the Taliban, who insisted that every Pashtun sacrifice for jihad. President Hamid Karzai never complained about Pashtun Taliban killing fellow Pashtuns. But he railed about every casualty caused by the foreigners. Karzai had pointed an accusing finger at civilian casualties in Sangin just a few months before 3rd Platoon arrived. The high command was determined to increase restrictions until almost no civilian was killed by coalition fire.

Shortly after taking command in mid-2009, Gen. McChrystal had issued an extraordinarily specific order, called a "Tactical Directive," all the way down to the platoon and squad level.

"The ground commander," the Tactical Directive read, "will not employ indirect weapons against a compound that may be occupied by civilians, unless the commander is in a life-threatening position and cannot withdraw."

The high command, civilian and military, was preaching a theory of benevolent war. The standing order was to ensure PID, Positive Identification, which meant identifying a clear, hostile target before returning fire. But most firefights were exchanges of burning lead and explosives between two tree lines, or between Taliban inside a compound and a coalition patrol in an open field. In 3rd Platoon's case, within a day of arriving in Sangin, they had seen their friends blown apart, and they carried the bloodstains of their comrades on their cammies.

Each day, a patrol took fire from somewhere out in the corn and bush. How do you convince them *not to shoot back*? What strategic rationale, what spiritual commandment, what sorcery would convince these young men to reject what their drill instructors had drummed into them—*kill before you are killed*? With the enemy wearing civilian clothes and hiding among compliant villagers in flat fields where bullets traveled far distances, the moral choice confronting the grunt—shoot back or hold your fire?—was never clear-cut.

Third Platoon could not advance a kilometer in any direction without receiving fire from a compound. Since no one can see through walls, civilians may have occupied every compound. The odds were heavily against it, but odds are never perfect. In every battalion operations center, a lawyer monitored all calls for artillery or air support, constantly weighing who might face court-martial or be relieved of command for making a wrong call. General George Marshall, the top commander in World War II, believed two qualities were common to every battlefield victor: energy and optimism. Having to check with lawyers before employing indirect fire hindered both energy and optimism.

One night at a remote outpost, I sat opposite a visiting Marine brigadier general. I asked him about the Tactical Directive. He looked at the candle flickering between us and said not one word.

The following day, it was more of the same for 3rd Platoon—a running gunfight in sector Q1E for six hours. Nothing much to report in the logbook—a few bursts of AK or PKM fire each hour forcing the Marines to flop down and peer at green corn rows, green tree lines, and green grass fields, all shimmering in sweltering, humid heat. No wisps of dust, no tiny red flickers as bullets left the muzzles, no shouts, and definitely no PID. In a day of desultory sniping under the oppressive sun, four enemy were seen, each for only one or two seconds.

Three IEDs were uncovered and blown up without damage. At least that was a plus.

Garcia was learning the fight by walking the ground. But 3rd Platoon didn't want to lose two commanders in a row. Throughout the patrol, the Marines called him "Garcia," not out of disrespect but so that the locals couldn't single him out. Garcia was having none of it.

"Here's how it is," Garcia told the platoon. "We step off together, and come back together. I take my chances equally with you. But I'm not 'Garcia' to any of you. You call me Lieutenant regardless of where we are."

Day 8. 48,000 Steps

Captain Johnson sent the platoon north to work out of Patrol Base Fires. PB Fires was an isolated, disintegrating farmhouse enclosed in barbed wire, located in sector Q1E in the center of the Green Zone. Third Platoon was expected to control the Green Zone from the Helmand River in the west to Kilo Company's headquarters at Inkerman in the east. First Platoon would operate from Inkerman, while 2d Platoon eventually moved up to Outpost Transformer, a mile north on 611.

As soon as they arrived, Garcia took most of 3rd Platoon out on a large patrol. Amid the thick corn stalks, the Marines could see only a few feet. So Garcia adjusted by splitting the patrol into two sections. One hacked down fighting positions in the sedge and lay ready to fire whenever the other crossed an open spot. Within two hours, the Taliban had sneaked up behind the large unit and opened fire. In the ensuing melee, the Marines killed two men with AKs and two farmers, and Cpl. Hughie, a sniper, took a bullet in his left arm.

Again the inevitable had happened. Panicked farmers had stood erect and tried to run away, unaware they were caught inside the kill zones of the invisible lines of bullets unleashed by both sides. The only way to avoid enfilade fire is to dig down and never stand up, a technique the farmers didn't understand. On the platoon's way back to Fires, survivors came forward to complain bitterly about their dead, their terrorized families, and the damage to their crops. Stay out of the fields, they urged the Marines, use the paths. We must know where you are to avoid this.

Garcia shook his head no. The Marines would not walk where they could be easily seen or tracked. They would not go where they were expected. Instead, they would move through the corn every day. When the shooting erupted, some crops would be destroyed and some workers in the fields might die.

The Marines were extra-careful when they were returning to Fires. A circle of barbed wire enclosed their farmhouse. The Marines varied where they exited the wire, and the Taliban didn't dare set up fixed positions to surround the fort. The platoon mortar teams would gleefully destroy such occupied positions.

Out in the Green Zone, every patrol was eventually seen. The farmers told the spotters, or dickers, who carried the Icom handheld

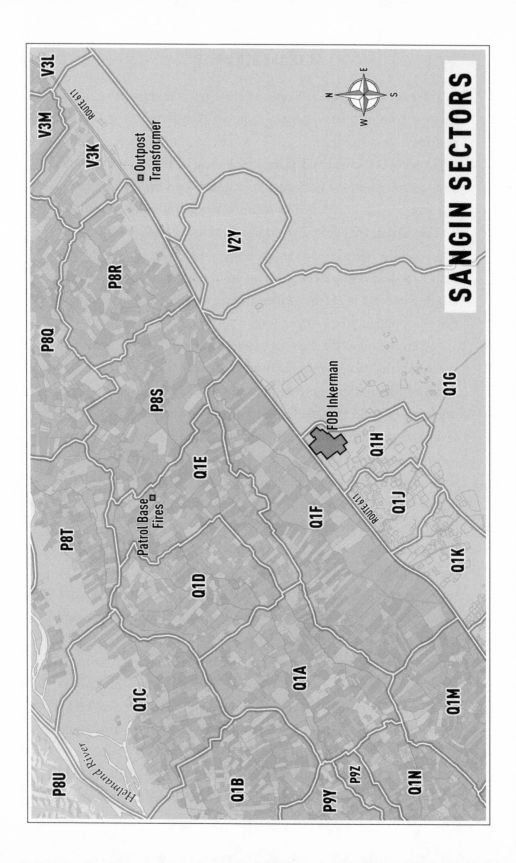

radios sold in Pakistan for thirty U.S. dollars. The patrols zigzagged unpredictably, but at the end of the day they all returned to base dripping sweat and exhausted. The Taliban learned to lurk near Fires in order to shoot at the backs of the Marines as they trudged across the open space in front of the barbed wire. Sometimes the sniping was so good that the final few Marines had to crawl back inside the wire. No one was hit during the first week, but the reverse siege was unnerving.

Day 9. 54,000 Steps

Cpl. Jeff Sibley, a twenty-three-year-old sniper from California, was strapping on his kit for a patrol when a shot rang out. The sentry in a nearby guard tower stumbled down, a bullet had smashed his left forearm, with a piece of white bone sticking through. Abbate grabbed Sibley and three other snipers and left the fort, pursuing the sound of the shot northwest.

Sibley, carrying a 7.62mm semiautomatic sniper rifle, was thoroughly trained. He had been drilled in keeping a daily shooting log, sketching a diagram of the terrain, recording the trajectory of bullet drop and drift over varying ranges. He could call shots by watching the bullet's vapor trail, calculating milliradians to compensate for the pull of gravity, estimating windage and mirage, glassing systematically, employing a noise suppressor, giving clear directions to orient on a target, and practicing rapid fire at multiple targets. Over the past week, he had killed two Taliban.

He wasn't worried about this sudden mission. He was on his second combat tour, and was convinced that five snipers could decimate any Taliban gang. Once he had walked a few hundred meters into the cornfields, Sibley called in mortars to their front. He assumed whoever had shot the sentry was pulling back. Maybe a mortar shell would get lucky. It was a "danger close" mission, meaning the shells would land within a hundred meters of the patrol. To adjust the rounds, Sibley walked to the edge of a corn row and was looking out when he felt a hard punch under his left armpit.

"Fuck," he yelled, "I think I've been shot."

He stumbled back a few feet and sat down heavily. Abbate pulled off Sibley's armor and peered at the bullet hole.

"Holy shit," Abbate said, "this looks fucked up."

The other snipers peered at the entry wound in Sibley's side and nodded. Abbate reconsidered his words.

"Nah, you're fine," Abbate said. "Don't worry about it."

Sibley laughed, the pain doubling him over.

"Could be a sucking chest wound," Cpl. Jacob Ruiz offered helpfully.

None of them had any idea whether that was true, but it sounded serious.

"Can you breathe?" Abbate asked.

"What do you think I'm doing?" Sibley said.

"Then you're okay," Abbate said. "We'll push ahead. You go back."

Supported by Ruiz, Sibley hobbled back. At one point, harassing fire forced them into a ditch. From Fires, Sibley was flown to Camp Leatherneck, where a surgeon removed a small caliber bullet that had caused no major damage. When Sibley woke up in the hospital, he saw Lance Corporal Kane, the sentry who'd been shot in the forearm, lying in the next bed.

"How'd it go out there?" Kane asked.

"Not too fucking good, man," Sibley said, "or I wouldn't be lying next to you."

Day 11. 66,000 Steps

Sgt. Clint Thoman, thirty-four, from Colorado, led the 3rd Squad. He was on his third combat tour, having served both in the elite Fleet

Anti-Terrorism Security Team and in the 2004 bloody assault against the city of Fallujah. His street-fighting experience didn't help in Sangin. He judged the mood inside his squad and inside the platoon as nervous and fatalistic.

"The platoon felt everyone would be blown up eventually," he said. "Made no difference if you were a boot on your first tour or an experienced NCO. You'd walk and walk until an IED got you. It was a matter of time. Not if, but when. That didn't stop us from patrolling, but everyone thought about it. You were going to get blown up."

That was the worst feeling a small unit can have—the foreboding of death, imminent and impersonal, overwhelming anything you do to protect yourself. That conviction leads to a dread of patrolling. What follows is the construction of forts and colored dots on a map designating the "Forward Line of Troops." Everything beyond the FLOT is conceded to the Taliban. When that happens, the enemy has won: game, set, match.

Knowing that attack helicopters and Predator drones lurked overhead, the Taliban avoided massing in large numbers; they preferred to maneuver in groups of three or six. Lacking the marksmanship of the Marines, they had to shoot hastily and run quickly to another position, or fired from so far back that the trees spoiled their aim. In any fight decided by bullets rather than IEDs, they became the hunted rather than the hunters, provided the Marines had the confidence to advance across the IED-laced fields.

On October 23, Garcia was accompanying Thoman and his squad on a patrol northwest of Fires. On his photomap, each thousand-meter square was outlined in yellow and marked alphanumerically, such as P8Q or Q1D. Inside each square, every compound was numbered. That way, a pilot or mortar crew could be quickly told the location of a target.

Normally, about 8,000 people lived in the 500-odd compounds in

3rd Platoon's area. But since the shooting that erupted following the arrival of the Marines, most compounds to the north of Fires were abandoned. Walking in the middle of the patrol, Garcia noticed that the point element was veering toward empty Compound 17 in sector Q1E. Everyone in the patrol had listened to the same brief. Months earlier, a friendly squad had used #17 as a lookout post. Be careful; it could be mined.

Garcia felt uneasy, but what was he to do? He was new to the platoon, and every grunt has occasional feelings of impending doom. The point element was following a trail of beaten-down grass around the compound wall. Garcia thought they were edging too close, but he didn't butt in. Sgt. Clint Thoman felt the same way, keeping steady, not showing any nervousness.

Both leaders had combat experience, but didn't know this territory, or how the enemy acted. They did know that taking counsel of your fears was the surest way to spread doubt and hesitation. If the men at point believed their leaders had lost faith in them, that word would spread and this was only their eleventh day.

The sudden shock wave rippled past Garcia, followed by a high-screeching echo in the ears, stinging in the eyes, and a sucking for breath that left an acrid taste. Oh shit, not again. Three Marines were staggering around, groggy from concussions. Lying near them was LCpl. Juan Dominguez, who always had a quip and never hesitated to walk at point. The IED had ripped him apart, severing a leg, an arm, and mangling his other leg beyond repair. In an instant, a triple amputee.

After the evacuations, Sergeant Thoman took aside his 3rd Squad back at Fires to reassure them as best he could. It was tough. Third Squad had seen Lieutenant West and Corporal Boelk go down, and now it was Dominguez.

Garcia was shaken. Here he was, the new platoon commander, and he had done nothing. Could he have prevented it by yelling out from a hundred yards in the rear? How would the squad leaders react in the future, if he interfered whenever he felt something was going wrong?

In Vietnam in the summer of 1966, I was on patrol in a bad area called Hill 55. For hours we had been on the move in scorching heat, harassed by snipers. Warned about mines, we walked in the tracks of an amphibious vehicle that chugged along at point, its tense crew sitting on sandbags.

As we crossed a dry paddy, *Wham!*, a pressure wave buffeted me from behind. I turned around and saw three Marines down in the dust. Exhausted from the heat, they had wandered out of the tracks and been blown off their feet by the mine. Two lay dazed, with non-life-threatening lacerations. The third was screaming, with red-hot shrapnel seared deep into his thighs and blood spurting out. A double amputee.

Our corpsman, Doc Robert Perkins, swiftly wrapped elastic cords around both stumps and injected morphine. Platoon Sgt. William Cunningham, anguish and frustration in his eyes, called for a helo.

"Stay in the tracks," he screamed at the wounded, pointing down at the tread marks. "I told you. The goddamn tracks! I told you!"

He was angrier at himself than at his men. A commander can't protect everyone or prevent everything, but that's not how he feels when things go wrong. What if he had done something differently?

Garcia felt the same way.

"Dominguez was my low point," Garcia said. "I felt like crap. I went back to Inkerman and emailed a commander I had served with in Iraq. He wrote back that if I hadn't been there, it still would have happened. His tough-love message was to suck it up and get back in the fight."

The enemy had won the first round. On October 13, an IED had taken the lives of four Marines. On the 14th, three more died, with far worse disaster prevented only by Abbate. On the 15th, Boelk was blown up and Big Country West lost his leg. On the 21st, Kane and Sibley were shot. On the 23rd, Dominguez was cut down.

The nights were hardest for 3rd Platoon. As they dropped off to sleep, it seemed mines lurked everywhere, waiting to rip the life or the legs from one Marine after another, until no one was left.

Day 16. 96,000 Steps

The Taliban plan was battle-tested. They had kept the British hemmed in by IED belts that sealed off the Green Zone and allowed the Taliban to travel freely on back roads and rest securely in compounds until they chose the next fight. There was no way they were allowing 3rd Platoon to stay at Fires, right in the middle of the Green Zone.

"In Iraq, the danger was the RPG," Garcia said. "In Sangin, it was the IED. The British had this mind-set about establishing a forward line of troops. So the Taliban buried mines outside the British line. I had to show my platoon that once we broke through the mine belts, we'd fight them on our terms. We had to get in their rear to dislodge them."

So on the morning of October 28, Garcia packed up the entire platoon and headed southwest into sector Q1A on a three-day operation. At point, two engineers swept their Vallons back and forth, stopping to prod the dirt with their knives. The Marines walked carefully in a long single file, covering less than a hundred meters in the first hour. Garcia didn't care how long they took.

The white flags of the Taliban flew above the walls of abandoned compounds, taunting the Marines, daring them to approach. Dickers on motorbikes puttered along on the flanks, tracking the platoon's movement. There was not a thing the Marines could do about them.

Avoiding the obvious trails and crossings at the canals and irrigation ditches, the patrol plunged through acre after acre of sweltering corn. Occasionally from an adjoining field a few hundred meters away, someone would randomly shoot off a few rounds, hoping to attract return fire that would give away the platoon's position.

When the Marines entered a field, the Taliban scooted out the other end. Skirmishers instinctively hate being trapped. In the Vietnam battle for Hue City in 1968, the North Vietnamese would run out the rear of the houses when the Marines approached from the front. It was the same in the Sangin cornfields.

Around noon, the platoon crossed an untilled field. LCpl. Tim Wagner, nineteen, was again at point. He had performed well when Lieutenant West was hit, and Sergeant Thoman, his squad leader, had confidence in him. Wagner planned to go to college back in the Midwest and live there for the rest of his life. Tall, skinny, and smart, he knew when things were off-kilter out in the fields. Once the platoon stepped into the open, he took note of several trees, about fifty meters apart, with the lower branches hacked off.

"Aiming stakes," he shouted, meaning the trees were markers for weapons fired from a distance.

Sure enough, a burst of PKM bullets zipped past. One bullet knocked the night-vision goggles off Wagner's helmet. Farther back in the file, LCpl. Brandon Weese took a round through his right hand. It took an hour to drive off the Taliban. By that time, a dozen sheep had been slaughtered in the crossfire, marking the landing zone for the medevac helicopter.

After that, the pace of the platoon slowed to a crawl. The engineers with their Vallons were tired and felt they had done more than their share. Not one IED had been found, confirming Garcia's suspicion that the enemy didn't mine their own territory. As clouds and fog moved in at twilight, the platoon set up defenses inside an abandoned compound. Two donkeys were foraging in the courtyard with all their legs still attached, a sure indication that IEDs did not lay in wait.

But soon, small enemy groups were shooting from behind the outer walls of neighboring compounds. Two motorcycles drove rapidly up to a nearby compound. Three men ran inside, and minutes later a few RPG rockets arced toward the Marine position and exploded short of the target. Garcia felt a twinge of doubt. He had brought his platoon two miles inside enemy territory. If he took a casualty, evacuation after dark was doubtful. He needed help, something to shake up the Taliban before they gathered enough force for a night attack.

"Driftwood, this is Sledgehammer 3," he radioed to Kilo's ops center. "I'm in compound 13 in Quebec One Alpha. Under fire from Compound 12 due west. Got anything on station?"

Driftwood was the call sign for Capt. Chuck "Spokes" Beardsley, whose lifetime dream had been to be a pilot. Motivated by 9/11, he had joined the Marines and for three years flew the KC-130 transportation workhorse. Then he volunteered to serve as an air controller with the grunts and was assigned to Kilo Company.

Spokes told Garcia that two F-18s were on call. Marine squadron VMFA-232, "Red Devils," was stationed at Kandahar air base, a hundred miles to the east. Whenever Red Devils were airborne, Kilo and the other companies were alerted via a digital chat room.

Garcia turned the air mission over to Staff Sgt. Nick Tock, a forward observer. Tock radioed to Beardlsey the standard 9-line brief, describing the target location, nearest friendly troops, direction for the bomb run, and other vital information.

Spokes passed the data to the pilots and to the battalion senior air officer, who consulted with the battalion lawyer. Both authorized a strike and notified the pilots that rules 421 to 424, set down by General McChrystal, had been satisfied. This meant that Garcia could not retreat safely, that no civilians were observed, and that hostile fire was coming from the target compound. Gen. David Petraeus had taken over from McChrystal in July. He had left the rules in effect, but also let the Marines employ Marine air without interfering.

Although a videotape of every bomb run was later reviewed by a lawyer, the pilots dropped bombs based on faith in what the grunt on the ground reported. During their six-month deployment, the twelve F-18s in VMFA Squadron 232 dropped 80,000 pounds of high explosives. Across Afghanistan, nine out of ten strike aircraft returned to base with their full load of ordnance. For the Red Devils squadron down in Helmand, nine of ten aircraft expended their ordnance supporting the ground patrols.

Hovering 10,000 feet above 3rd Platoon were Capts. Jimmy "Postal" Knipe and Taj "Cabbie" Sareen. Cabbie rolled in first.

"Sledgehammer, this is Stoic 74," Sareen radioed. "Off safe. One away. Lasing."

Lasing meant that the bomb was following a laser beam from the aircraft to the compound.

Third Platoon kept their heads down. They were inside the "danger close" radius of shrapnel from the GBU-12 500-pound bomb. The compound shuddered under the explosion, but did not collapse.

"That's a shack," Tock radioed, meaning a direct hit.

The two F-18s circled, waiting. Both were equipped with day and night cameras that could distinguish between a man and a woman from 10,000 feet. Watching the video feeds at 3/5's ops center, the air officer, Capt. Matt "Squeeze" Pasquali, had often seen men running from the rubble. The lead F-18 bombed the compound, while the second F-18 trailed behind and twenty seconds later delivered another 500-pounder that burst in the air to scythe down any squirters. This was called "shake and bake."

Knipe, trailing in Stoic 73, was poised to roll in when a secondary explosion rocked the compound, probably RPG rockets cooking off. No squirters emerged. The aircraft loitered hawklike above 3rd Platoon for the next fifteen minutes. No enemy fired at the 3rd Platoon. The F-18s returned to base.

After it was dark, Garcia occasionally called for illumination rounds above the platoon's compound, demonstrating that the 60mm mortar crew back at Fires would respond quickly. The next day, no enemy fire was received, while several farmers came forward, curious about the strangers. No British or American soldiers had been in the area before. The farmers seemed tolerant but wary. Would the foreigners be staying long?

When the platoon went back to Fires two days later, they took back with them a white Taliban flag they had ripped from a tree. It wasn't much, but it gave Staff Sgt. Matt Cartier, the platoon sergeant, something to build on.

"I told them," he said, "we'd gone into Taliban territory and they couldn't protect their own flag."

Garcia had no intention of lugging the entire platoon around the battlefield. He had eight sectors to cover, 500 compounds to search, and a thousand irrigation ditches to cross. If the platoon stayed together, it could never dislodge the Taliban. He had to send out two to three squad patrols a day, often going in different directions.

"The Taliban will swarm a squad," he said, "unless they fear indirect fire. My squad leaders had to believe they could call in fire anytime they wanted. The whole platoon had seen the air support Spokes Beardsley delivered. That made a difference."

While 3rd Platoon was out on their operation, Lieutenant Colonel Morris emailed back to the families, "Despite taking tough losses in the first days in their area of operations, the Battalion has dusted itself off and continued to move forward. . . . I just conducted a memorial service for LCpls Catherwood, Boelk and Lopez from Kilo Company . . . will send you another update. In the meantime, we'll be 'getting some'!"

"Get some" means kill the enemy, and it was 3/5's motto.

Sometimes IEDs struck unwary children in the fields, although for the most part the farmers knew which areas to avoid. The villagers allowed the Taliban to use children as shields. Out of fear and/or tribal loyalty, they kept quiet about the locations of the IEDs and the Taliban gangs. The tribes accepted callousness from the Taliban.

American firepower, on the other hand, angered and distressed the people. The image of Americans rolling about in large armored convoys or swooping in to burn an enemy village was a caricature. The people weren't forcibly moved, as happened in Vietnam. Nor were there free fire zones or indiscriminate bombing.

The reality was more complicated. The Marine approach was to spread out a battalion across a district, clear it, and then turn it over to Afghan forces to hold. In Sangin, the tribes were firmly controlled by, and contributed to, the Taliban. And so the clearing operation became a brutal fight between the Marines and the insurgents. Usually, the Marines didn't see the Taliban, and shot back after they were fired at. They struck the compounds, tree lines, and fields from which they received fire. Naturally, the farmers fled in fear and resentment.

This wasn't happening just in 3rd Platoon's area. A dozen platoon commanders in 3/5 were reacting like Garcia. A Marine spokesman claimed, "There is nothing out of the norm in terms of operations in Sangin." But it wasn't true. October marked the highest number of air strikes in two years, led by 3/5 in Sangin. And Kilo called in the most air strikes of any company, led by 3rd Platoon.

———

Sangin was a war of attrition, not counterinsurgency. Controlling the farmlands was psychological, not physical. Neither the Taliban nor the Marines could be everywhere. Each side has to send out small groups of men willing to fight when they bumped into the other side. Once one side flinched and avoided entering certain areas, the other side had won. When the Taliban could not sustain their losses, they would withdraw. To break the grip of the Taliban, Garcia's challenge wasn't so much the enemy; it was convincing his own Marines that they could survive seven months without being blown up.

Chapter 4

LEADERS FOUND

"We are battle-hardened, but still ordinary goof-offs."
—MATTHEW CARTIER, ILLINOIS

With the platoon back at Fires, Staff Sgt. Matt Cartier was beginning to feel a bit more upbeat. The fear of the IEDs gave the Taliban a mental edge, but he sensed that the gloom enveloping the platoon had lifted slightly. The operation had proved an elementary point: the enemy could not plant mines everywhere.

Garcia was putting it together. The Iraqi experience had led the Marines astray. In Iraq, a dozen or more civilians lived in a concrete house encased by a stout concrete wall that separated it from the next house. Fifty or sixty houses made up a block, several dozen blocks constituted a neighborhood. The neighborhoods were bounded by broad streets. Sunni insurgents and Shiite militias fought for every inch of turf. As soon as a family on one block was frightened into fleeing, the other side moved in one of its own families. Both Shiite and Sunni fighters planted IEDs along the roads used by the U.S. military, but not inside recently vacated houses families from their own side would occupy within a day or two.

In Sangin, the Taliban were placing their IEDs inside the courtyards and rooms of abandoned compounds. On their forays over the years, coalition troops occasionally stayed overnight in a few isolated, easily defended compounds, abandoned due to the fighting. After they left, the Taliban set pressure plates in the rooms, walls, courtyards, and adjoining pathways. Unlike in the fields, the Taliban didn't keep track of where they placed them.

Once a compound was rigged, no locals would go near it. A family lost their home, but the Taliban didn't care. They set the rules, and everyone was supposed to contribute to the jihad against the infidel foreigners. Abandoning his farm was the least a farmer could contribute. Hundreds of compounds stood empty for months. The Taliban reserved a few for their intermittent use. The others were death traps awaiting a fresh set of foreigners.

In 2010, Sangin wasn't ready for economic development, local government, or farm granges. It might never be ready. The Taliban were embedded among the people. Some were auxiliaries—young men living at home with AKs hidden nearby. Most were roaming about in gangs of four to six, staying in one abandoned compound for several days before moving to another. Whenever the Marines left the wire, farmers and Taliban alike grabbed their cell phones and Icoms to report their movement.

Sangin was like France in late 1944, a battleground where the civilians hid or ran away while the two armed sides slugged it out. The practical definition of control is the confidence to walk where you please, without being shot at. A dog pisses on trees to mark his territory. Similarly, young insurgents cannot resist taking potshots at government soldiers. The same was true in Vietnam and Iraq. Judging by the daily sniping at every patrol, the Taliban were firmly in control.

Back at Fires, Garcia called together his three squad leaders. Lieutenant West was immensely popular and his spirit hung over the platoon. Garcia knew he had to tread carefully.

"Here's the deal," he said. "Our routine will be two squad patrols each day, with a third squad as the QRF"—Quick Reaction Force.

Sgt. Dominic Esquibel, thirty-three, led the 1st Squad. Esquibel wore the ugliest black-rimmed glasses known to man, with shatterproof lenses thick enough to stop a bullet. Slight of frame and diffident in demeanor, he would blend in among the geeks manning the Genius Bar at an Apple Store.

On Thanksgiving Day back in 2004, Esquibel's platoon was completing its twenty-first day of house-to-house fighting in the Iraqi city of Fallujah. Suicidal jihadists were hiding amid the city's 10,000 houses. In three weeks, the Marines had engaged in more firefights inside rooms than the combined total of all police SWAT teams in history.

Esquibel's platoon was assigned to a sector called Queens, a slum neighborhood of one-story concrete buildings. His job as a scout-sniper was to climb onto a roof and cover the alleys while the squad below him searched room to room. As the squad entered a courtyard, five were struck down by firing from inside the house. Esquibel ran to the lip of the roof and hurled a grenade through a window, killing two insurgents and destroying a machine gun. He then crawled across the roof and threw down a second grenade, killing two more and taking out another machine gun. When a tank moved in and began bashing a hole in the courtyard wall, Esquibel took advantage of the dust and noise to drop off the roof and drag a wounded Marine to safety. He then waited until the tank gun fired and darted back into the courtyard, dragging out a second Marine. When the tank again fired, he raced inside a third time, beat out the flames on the body of a mortally wounded Marine, and dragged him outside.

Awarded the Navy Cross—second only to the Medal of Honor—Esquibel refused to wear the medal or to discuss his valor. He was so self-effacing that he requested the Marine Corps to delete the medal from the records (which the Marines refused to do). When I mentioned other Marines I knew during the Fallujah battle, he readily reminisced about them. When I asked about his actions, he waved me off.

"I'm not going there, sir," he said. "This is my last rodeo. I'm getting out once we're back in the States. It's not about me. I'm here for my men, and that's all."

Esquibel was as old as Garcia. He respected the former gunnery sergeant, but didn't hold him in awe. Esquibel accepted every patrol order and carried out the mission to the letter—his way. Determined to bring every member of his squad back in one piece, he maneuvered 1st Squad firmly and with great caution. He assumed an IED lurked on every cow path, every opening in a tree line, and every irrigation bank. If it took an hour to move 1st Squad one hundred meters—and it often did—that was fine with him. In fact, he took pride in his deliberate approach.

"I take the most miserable way," Esquibel said. "We wade across every canal. My nickname is 'Wet Bridge.' I go wherever Lieutenant Garcia wants, and I don't care if it takes me all day. I like open fields. When we take fire, we can outshoot them. Sure, we're lying in mud, wet and shivering. But that's better than getting blown up."

Garcia considered Esquibel as stubborn as a mule and as reliable. He wouldn't be hurried or badgered into altering his pace. Believing that any straight path led to perdition, Esquibel invariably took a circuitous route. Despite grumblings from his squad, he chose to hack through thickets rather than trust a cow path. No matter how many footprints showed that farmers routinely crossed over log bridges, 1st Squad sloshed through chest-high muddy water.

From the start, Esquibel made it clear to 1st Squad: he decided how they ran their patrols. He sought no friendships. He viewed his mission as bringing his men home. If that meant hurt feelings or resentments over his cautious exactitude, so be it. After each patrol, he hand-printed in the platoon log a succinct summary, naming those who performed well and those who bitched or hesitated.

"The Taliban were learning too fast," Esquibel said. "At first, they fired from in close in the cornfields. But we were too good at trading lead. Once they stayed 300 meters away on the other side of a tree line, it was a lot harder to kill them."

The tactics of 1st Squad were typical of the platoon. Cpl. Darin Hess, the engineer, went first, sweeping with the Vallon. Despite being hit three times by IEDs, he found the will to go back out, moving at the ideal cautious pace Esquibel wanted. Behind him usually came LCpl. Juan Palma, aggressive and sure of himself. The battalion had almost left him behind in the States, due to his "too cool for school" attitude and intolerance of regulations. Esquibel, though, liked Palma's cockiness.

"On one patrol," Esquibel said, "I caught him stomping on the ground to show Hess that it was safe to move on. I told Palma, 'Man, you're the eyes of the squad. You get yourself blown up and we're all screwed.'"

Esquibel was third in line, followed by a SAW gunner, ready to suppress any tree line with 800 rounds in a minute. Next came a sniper, and then the other Marines. Each patrol had two riflemen with 203s, stubby tubes that lobbed 40mm grenade shells in arcs out to 300 meters. Farther back in the file a Marine carried a second Vallon. Half the squad would move forward or flank the enemy, while the other half provided covering fire.

"Lieutenant Garcia tells me what he wants," Esquibel told me, "and I get it done my way."

———

Sgt. Alex Deykeroff had transferred to 3/5 because he wanted to fight in Afghanistan and arrived in Sangin expecting to see bare, open country. On large-scale maps, the blue line representing the Helmand River and the tiny slice of green called Sangin were dwarfed by gobs of bare brown desert on either side. Sergeant Dy had pulled three combat tours in the desert of western Iraq near Syria, where centuries of wind had scoured away the sand, leaving thousands of kilometers of hard-packed earth. Burying IEDs in the desert was backbreaking and fruitless work. The Marines, in armored vehicles, drove wherever they pleased across the desert. The odds of a vehicle driving over the exact spot of an IED were one in a thousand.

But Sangin's Green Zone, with its expansive, soggy fields of tall corn and low visibility, meant close-in fighting. To Dy, that was fine. He and Sergeant Thoman, the leader of 3rd Squad, weren't concerned about crossfires. While watching YouTube together back in California, they'd laughed when Bill O'Reilly had lost his temper and yelled to his camera crew, "We'll do it live! Fuck it!" Now they enjoyed harassing each other before a patrol by yelling the same thing: "Do it live!"

The squad leaders knew how to adapt in firefights, but the IEDs rattled them both. The day after Abbate's fight, Dy saw four members of his 2d Squad blown up along with Lieutenant West. Farther back in the column with 3rd Squad, Sergeant Thoman helped to carry out the casualties. Neither wanted to lose anyone else to an IED, but they seemed to be everywhere, on every canal bank, at every break in a tree line, at the edge of every field. Dy and Thoman talked it over and agreed not to push their men. They would stall for time until they could figure out the IED threat.

"We weren't shutting down," Thoman said. "But we had slowed the pace to get a grasp on the enemy tactics."

When Garcia gave 2d Squad a sector to check out, Dy marked its edge on his map, moved forward until his GPS touched that line, spread out his men, and watched for movement in the far fields. Technically, he was accomplishing the mission.

Shortly after Dominguez was blown up, Dy's squad was approaching an abandoned compound when a boy ran up, warning that an IED was buried up ahead. Then he ran off, leaving a rattled Dy to decide whether the boy was telling the truth, or wanted the squad to use an alternate route that was mined. Garcia, who was accompanying the patrol, said nothing.

"Every squad leader," Garcia said, "had to find his own comfort level. The worst thing I could do was pressure someone into a hasty mistake."

That night, he took Dy aside.

"He said my squad had been hit the most," Dy said. "But we all had to run the same risks every day, no matter who had been hit the hardest. I got the message. He never said a word in front of anyone else."

Garcia's fix was simple. Before a patrol, he picked out a compound numbered on the map and told Dy to report back what he found inside the compound. When no IED was triggered on patrol after patrol, Dy and 2d Squad would start to feel surer of themselves.

"Deykeroff was best with the people," Garcia said. "He loved to talk, easygoing, smiling. Sometimes a kid would even lead his squad across a few fields."

Pushing north one day, 2d Squad reached the edge of the large open area called the Golf Course. Nearby, three men were digging an irrigation ditch. One of the diggers started waving his shovel back and forth, and within a minute several AKs and a PKM opened fire from the opposite side of the field. The Marines shot the digger. A battlefield was not a court of law.

Dy radioed in the shot before returning. When Garcia plotted the position, he saw that Deykeroff was 500 meters beyond his assigned compound. Confidence regained.

After two tours in Iraq, Sgt. Clint Thoman, the 3rd Squad leader, had ample combat experience. Initially, Thoman would lead his 3rd Squad deeper into the sector than Deykeroff, but if the Taliban shot at them, he pulled back rather than risk striking an IED by pushing forward. It was obvious to Garcia that Thoman too was constantly remembering Dominguez, and was loath to put his point element at risk again.

Thoman noticed that the platoon commander didn't say much when he accompanied 3rd Squad. But he knew Garcia was evaluating him. One day when Garcia was back at Fires, a call for mortar support came in from Thoman.

"What do you have?" Garcia radioed.

"Taking fire from our north," Thoman said. "Two to four shooters."

Garcia expected Thoman to break contact and pull back to base.

"Roger. Are you disengaging?"

"Negative. I'm pushing forward."

Thoman told one four-man fire team to flank the enemy from the east. When a larger Taliban gang turned toward them, the team pulled back. This wasn't unusual. Contrary to public image, Marines do have some common sense. The sniper with the fire team was LCpl. Willie Deel, twenty, from Kansas. His wife was waiting back in California. Willie had this vision: they would have a good life in California, and one day when he was old, his children would ask what he did in the war and he would say, "We made a difference."

Willie Deel's difference was his shooting skill. As the fire team pulled back, he settled in his bipod, peered through the scope, and shot the lead Taliban in the chest. The others fell back to an adjoining tree line, and the two sides exchanged fire for an hour without another casualty.

Thoman kept sliding 3rd Squad forward inside the concealment of the trees, looking for a chance to trap the enemy. The Taliban were yelling back and forth to each other, trying to figure out where the Marines were. When they sent children out from a compound to look, Thoman told his men not to fire or move. By the time the children went back inside, the Taliban had pulled out.

Thoman called back to Garcia at Fire.

"Sledgehammer 6, this is 2. No joy. The fuckers have disappeared. We have one Taliban body."

"I knew then," Garcia said, "that Thoman had broken through his fear of the IEDs."

Thoman appreciated Garcia's style.

"I talked with the lieutenant before each patrol," Thoman said. "He explained what he wanted done, but didn't tell me how to do it. I didn't second-guess myself when he came out with me. I was in charge."

While 3rd Platoon now had three solid squad leaders—Esquibel, Deykeroff, and Thoman—supported by two accurate 60mm mortar crews, they had taken so many casualties that the patrols went undermanned. Garcia didn't have sufficient grunts, until the snipers volunteered.

Sgt. Matt Abbate commanded two sniper sections, totaling ten men. The snipers brought more skills than expert shooting. Before a sniper received the symbolic HOG (Hunter of Gunmen) bullet, he had to prove he could plan and carry out a mission from start to finish—select the routes, choose the gear, arrange the comms, evaluate enemy countermoves, accomplish the kill, and return safely. Each sniper was expected to have the decision-making skills of a squad leader.

Before arriving in Sangin, the snipers had been wary of joining Kilo Company, after some troops had grumbled about "Boot Camp Kilo." Of the four services, the Marine Corps teetered the closest to that thin line separating discipline from rote harassment. Some Marine units were too rigid. In mature commando units like the SEAL and Special Forces teams, officers and enlisted were on a first-name basis. In the Marines, a corporal was called "Corporal."

Gunny Sergeant Carlisle was a terror in training. You did it his way, or you did it again and again until it was done his way. The skipper, Capt. Nick Johnson, believed in traditions. He wanted things done "the Old Breed way," meaning sweat, grunge, and order. But once Kilo arrived in Sangin, the company was all about fighting. "Old Breed" meant everyone was expected to be a fighter, and even Gunny Carlisle, senior as he was, went on patrols. It was all about the job.

The snipers were supposed to stay at Inkerman. But every patrol from Fires was making contact, so in early November Abbate brought his snipers over to 3rd Platoon to work for a few days. Once there, they never left. The action was too constant. Technically, they were "in support," meaning they reported back to battalion, not to Garcia. Practically, they fitted right in, having their own fire pit and caves, attending the daily briefs, and pitching in where needed.

According to doctrine, sniper teams weren't supposed to integrate into regular grunt patrols as though they were additional riflemen. That would take away their special skills. Third Platoon and Abbate, though, were flexible. Together they learned that leaving snipers behind in hide sites rarely worked. Every tiller in the field—woman, child, or man—was potentially a spotter. Most times, snipers in a hide site never saw a man with a weapon.

The patrols were a different story. Two or three snipers accompanied each squad patrol. The snipers practiced close-in snap shooting as well as long-distance accuracy. Where the average grunt may have

300 hours rifle practice, a sniper had 3,000 hours. After first shooting at a patrol, the Taliban liked to dog the flanks for a second shot. The snipers, with the call sign Banshee, waited for that moment. When a man with an AK broke cover and ran twenty yards across an open field to stay abreast of the patrol, that six-second run became a trip to eternity. About every other day, a sniper killed a Taliban fighter.

The Taliban hung in there, trying to even the score. Abbate and Cpl. Jordan Laird, twenty-four, from Idaho were standing beside a tree when a bullet zipped between their two heads, struck the wood, and sprayed splinters into Laird's face. Both burst out laughing at what Laird called "the surreal feeling of being alive when you should be dead."

The next day, Laird was acting as the cover man for a patrol crossing a large open field. Through his telescope, he saw a man in the far tree line talking on an Icom. After watching the patrol, the man scurried through the shrubbery, opened a sack, and began to hastily dig a hole. Laird dialed in the range of 285 meters and shot him in the chest.

A few days later, an enemy machine gunner caught the snipers climbing out of their hide in a ditch 500 meters north of Fires. A three-round burst of PKM fire sent a round through Abbate's trousers, knocked the flash suppressor off another Marine's rifle, and left a red crease along the leg of a third. With a slight adjustment, the machine gunner would have hit all three. Instead, the snipers returned fire and killed two Taliban. Searching the bodies, the snipers found a wad of Pakistani money, a high-frequency Chinese radio, and a bag of white powder that they poured into the dirt.

Nothing is worse for morale than losing lives and limbs to mines and never engaging an elusive enemy. The snipers provided 3rd Platoon with the satisfaction of payback.

———

Sgt. Matt Abbate showed no fear of death, but when not on patrol he was everyone's big brother. At night, he circulated among the squad campfires, appending "dude" to his remarks in surfer style. He walked around, pointing his finger like a pistol and quoting absurd lines from the cult film *The Way of the Gun*.

"I promise you," Abbate slowly drawled, "a day of reckoning that you won't live long enough to never forget."

He shared his homecoming plan of packing his wife and two-year-old-son, Carson, on the back of his Harley and roaring around Big Sur. When he talked to his family every few weeks, he never mentioned the fighting or his wounds. Recommended for the Navy Cross for pulling the squad out of the minefield, he refused to discuss the incident.

"I don't fucking want it," he said. "We all didn't make it back."

When someone was down, he'd share his stories about drifting homeless in Hawaii and serving as a waiter on a cruise line. "Lot of things worse than serving in the Corps, bro," he'd say. "You die when it's your time. Until that day."

Matt refused to have a bad day, and the platoon fed off his energy. He made sure at least two snipers hopped on any patrol likely to make contact. He was up for any scheme to kill more Taliban. In one month, he had twelve kills and had charged across a minefield. Garcia was the mind directing the platoon; Abbate was its heart.

"Matt gives heart-to-heart talks that end with a joke," Lantznester said. "On patrol, he'll shout at me, 'Bambi, keep your SAW up! We're killing those bastards!'"

Matt reminded me of Doug Zembiec, a Marine I embedded with during the 2004 Fallujah battle. You couldn't beat Doug's enthusiasm down with a stick. He wore a perpetual grin, and was always grabbing you to tell a funny story. One time, Doug led part of his company way too far forward of the lines. They set up inside a block of apartment buildings and were promptly attacked by dozens of insurgents who were smashing down adjoining walls to get at them. So many bullets were flying that the houses were disintegrating.

As the Marines pulled back, Doug brought up the rear with Master Sgt. Donald Hollenbaugh, the leader of a hush-hush Army commando team. Doug wanted to be the last man to leave. But Don had a special grenade, called a thermobaric, and was determined to throw it after all the friendlies had left, including Doug. The two argued so long they almost didn't make it out. Doug was later killed in a special operation in Baghdad. Marines still talk about him.

Possessed of that same oddball spirit, Abbate one day approached Lt. Tom Schueman with a crazy scheme. Schueman, a friendly sort with an understated manner, was working out of Inkerman with 1st Platoon. For several days, his platoon had been shot at when they walked past a certain canal. Abbate proposed that Schueman lead a patrol up one side of the canal. Abbate and Laird would move along on the other side, trailing a few hundred meters behind. When the Taliban sneaked up to the bank to shoot across at the patrol, the snipers would bag them. This was risky business. If there were friendly casualties, Schueman was sure to face an investigation.

"What if you get cut off?" Schueman said.

"Sirrr!" Abbate said, looking offended.

Schueman agreed with a laugh. Abbate and Laird killed two that day.

"You should see this one dude," Abbate radioed to Schueman. "Brains all over the place. They'll stay away from your platoon for a while."

In addition to the snipers, a squad of Afghan soldiers lived at Fires. They had their own caves, fire pit, and food. Two or three soldiers, or askaris, usually accompanied a Marine patrol. They stayed in the middle of the column and were the first to enter any compound occupied by villagers. None had volunteered for Fires. If an askari is killed, his family receives scant compensation.

Fires provided a comfortable base. A few ropes were stretched across the small, dirt courtyard to dry out sopping cammies, and a rickety wooden table was loaded with Pop-Tarts, snack foods, and hot sauces. A hand pump in the corner provided cold water for daily shaves and weekly haircuts. Wading across the creeks substituted for showers. For breakfast, the men dipped into oven-sized trays of powdered eggs and ground meat, heated by chemical tabs. Dinner consisted of luckless farm animals or dried foods mailed by the families. Drinking water in plastic bottles came in via resupply from Kilo Company. The biweekly phone calls home followed a ritual. Mothers and wives, reading every day about 3/5's casualties, would cry, while the grunts claimed they were safe and asked about sports scores.

Each squad had its own block of three or four caves, hacked out of the thick mud walls. To the Marines, these man-caves were luxury condominiums, furnished with cots, notes from third-graders, and piles of goodies from home. Three to five Marines shared a man-cave, decorated in quirky fashion. The days were warm, but the November nights had turned sharply cold in the desert climate, which shed its heat as soon as the sun went down. Third Squad luxuriated in fleece blankets wrapped inside their sleeping bags, while the snipers decided to install wood-burning stoves inside their caves.

Every farm had a mud oven for baking flatbread. After studying the design, Laird's sniper team spent all day mixing mud and straw with a dash of sand, then carefully packing the mixture in layers inside their cave. By dinnertime, they had built their small furnace, complete with a square chimney for ventilation. Quite proud of themselves, they shoved dry sticks inside, started a fire, and sat back to eat their MREs.

"Let's test the chimney for leaks," one Marine said.

Before the others grasped what he had in mind, he pulled the pin on a smoke grenade and tossed it into the furnace. The grenade cooked off, shattering the furnace and filling the cave with red smoke so thick it permeated into every crevice and piece of clothing.

Each night, the squads sat around their fire pits, eating and talking tactics. Once off duty, they shucked their armor and wore whatever they wanted. The small generator for the military radios provided enough juice to charge the batteries for a few iPods and laptops with DVDs. After dinner, the Marines socialized from campfire to campfire amid a cacophony of blaring hard rock music. Abbate was forever repeating his favorite movie quote, *"You die when it's your time; until that day."* Eventually the platoon greeting became *Until that day.* To keep their sanity, Garcia and Cartier slept in the inner courtyard next to the radio room, well apart from the squads and their music.

The grunts took pride in their primitive living. They had water and chow and, far from the first sergeant and garrison chores, were left alone to fight in peace.

On an outside wall, the snipers kept count of their kills. They had carved into the hardened mud a symbol of the cross of St. George. Next to it was a line of stick figures that grew longer each day. The deaths of some stick figures made for fine stories around the campfires; others perished without remark, like the skins of the coyotes killed and hung on the walls.

The grunts mocked, laughed, and marveled about how enemy soldiers react when hit. Only in Hollywood does a bullet blow a man off his feet. A one-ounce bullet cannot cause a 150-pound man to fly through the air. Even a .50 caliber knocks back both shooter and target by only several inches.

When hit, some men stand frozen for a second until the brain registers the intense pain and they collapse. Or the concussive shock from that tiny piece of metal traveling at a thousand miles an hour sends an instantaneous pressure wave to the brain, shutting down all nerve endings. The target withers and deflates, like the air suddenly rushing out of a balloon. Often the adrenaline is pumping so hard that a man, after being hit, keeps on running until out of sight, eventually dropping unconscious from blood loss. Others stand in place, twitching and shaking as if having an epileptic fit.

Abbate hammered a piece of plywood onto the wall of his cave and printed his "Rules of War":

1) Young warriors die
2) You cannot change Rule #1
3) Someone must walk the point (where you are sure to die)
4) Nothing matters more than thy brethren . . . thou shall protect no matter what
5) Going out in a hail of gunfire . . . pop dem nugs until thy body runs dry of blood
   . . . AND LOOK HELLASICK

Matt's rules reminded me of the grunt in 3/5 who printed a message on a bridge after the battle for Fallujah in 2004: "This is for the Americans murdered here." In both cases, the idea was the same: *Thou shall protect no matter what.* We all look hellasick in death. What counts is why we die.

Chapter 5

TOE-TO-TOE

On November 3, Cpl. Jordan Laird was lying on top of a roof as a patrol pushed north of him in sector P8Q toward the Helmand River. The Taliban routinely camped on the far side, indistinguishable from civilians when they rowed across. This day, three of the enemy broke their standing rule and, grasping their AKs, hopped onto a raft. In quick succession, Laird shot two. The third leaped into chest-deep water and splashed at incredible speed into the underbrush.

With the snipers producing kills, Esquibel, Deykeroff, and Thoman led their squads deeper into enemy territory. At the same time, radio intercepts identified Outpost Fires as the key outpost the Taliban were determined to shut down. Until that battle was decided, the farmers were staying out of the way. It would have been crazy of them to do otherwise. The areas north and west of Fires were ghost towns. A few families still lived in one set of compounds called Hi-Mars, so named because the homes there had been blasted apart by High Mobility Artillery Rocket Systems, or HIMARS. But most farmers moved in with relatives along Route 611, venturing back into the Green Zone only to tend their crops and scooting away when a Marine patrol appeared.

The platoon developed a rhythm of two patrols a day, with the third squad back at Fires ready for quick reaction, in addition to an assortment of standard chores. Every patrol moved Ranger-style in single file, with the point man dropping bottle caps that guided the others and were picked up by the last man in the file. The engineer at point swept a narrow path with his Vallon. More IEDs were detected by alert eyes than by the Vallon, but the device had its place. Sometimes it did signal the presence of a D cell flashlight battery, and in any case it suggested that the coalition had a magical edge in technology.

That was partially true. Secretary of Defense Gates was immensely proud of ramming an MRAP armored vehicle through the sclerotic Pentagon bureaucracy. Costing $500,000 each, the MRAPs saved the lives of many coalition soldiers on the roads.

In the Green Zone, though, there was no comparable technical wonder. The $500 Vallon helped our grunts less than the equally inexpensive Icoms helped our enemy. Radio chatter lit up whenever a patrol left the wire at Fires. Spotters boldly squatted at the edges of fields, knowing they were safe provided they didn't show their radios. The standard Taliban pattern was to shoot a few rounds in hopes of enticing the Marines to attack directly forward and cross into an IED belt. If one Marine went down, then the Taliban edged in closer while the Marines were diverted.

Third Platoon developed a standard counter. The instant a Taliban fired, the machine gun crew on the patrol sprayed the suspected area. The chances of hitting anyone, or even striking the right general area, were low. The hope was simply to spoil the enemy's aim. The squad leader used that interval to orient himself, direct the aim of the Marines, and call back to Fires, requesting mortars or a reaction force.

If the Taliban had only a few shooters, they quickly pulled away. If they had four or more, they lingered until they heard the snaps of Marine rounds overhead before dropping back. The patrol would push on, with the Taliban dogging their flanks. As the patrol passed through some hedges or undergrowth, the snipers would lie down, extend their bipods, and glass the adjoining fields, waiting to glimpse an enemy darting forward. Within three weeks, the enemy was already adapting. Sightings were fewer, most 300 to 500 yards away and lasting only three to five seconds. The Taliban now ran at full speed across openings. Maybe time enough for one shot. Rarely was a man dropped in the open and counted as a definite kill.

The Taliban were poor shots. But during one routine patrol, two snipers—Sgt. John D. Browning and Corporal Laird—had climbed onto a roof for a quick glance around. As Browning brought up his binoculars, he heard a firecracker pop next to his ear. Behind him, a branch snapped off. Flopping down, Browning lay still and waited for his heart to stop racing. *The sniper had perfect elevation,* he thought. *His windage was just a click off.*

A disciplined sniper was the surest way for the Taliban to disrupt Marine patrols in the Green Zone. Yet this enemy sniper did not strike again. No intelligence ever followed about whether he had been killed, moved on, or taken up a safer profession.

When going to the sectors where a firefight was certain to break out, Garcia's pattern was to send two patrols at different angles to hem in the Taliban shooters, so that mortar shells could drop on them or force them to run across an open field. The Marines were superior marksmen. But unlike Abbate's sniper section, they hadn't fired the thousands of bullets needed to hone the skills to hit fleeting targets. Four out of five firefights erupted, dazzling like a match dropped into a box of firecrackers, and sputtered out without damage to either side. At the end of three weeks, the Marines and Taliban were slugging it out, toe-to-toe. Both sides were adapting, but it wasn't clear who was gaining the psychological advantage.

On the morning of November 4, 3rd Platoon heard deep rumblings, as though a powerful thunderstorm had struck unseen. The 3rd Battalion of the 12th Marine Regiment was guarding the approaches to the Kajacki Dam. For weeks, the Marines on duty atop that huge concrete structure had watched through powerful telescopes as the Taliban methodically stored weapons and munitions in a set of compounds. The coordinates of each storage point were checked and rechecked, as were the daily movements of enemy and civilians in the vicinity.

The data were shared with Lt. Col. Dan "Knuckles" Shipley, who commanded the Red Devil squadron of twelve F-18s. When 3/12 alerted him that the civilians had left the area, he ordered a strike by seven F-18 Hornets carrying 14,000 pounds of laser-guided bombs.

Satisfaction about the air strike was short-lived, however. In the afternoon, tragedy struck. A Taliban in an Afghan uniform shot and killed two Marines at 3/5 headquarters. LCpl. Brandon Pearson, twenty-one, was an outdoorsman from Denver. LCpl. Matthew Broehm, twenty-two, left behind his wife, Liana, who was eighteen.

"He is with God now," Liana said. "He will always be my husband."

The killer escaped, and the Taliban crowed. Distrust of Afghan soldiers rippled through the Marine ranks. Only three weeks into their deployment, the grunts of 3/5 began to harden against the Afghan soldiers they were supposed to treat as brothers. On patrols, a few Afghan soldiers contributed little. They did not speak Pashto and generally were mediocre marksmen. But their presence did allow senior officers to report "joint operations" that pointed toward the total turnover of responsibility to the Afghan army.

Third Platoon, however, was not training the askaris. Although most tagged along willingly, it wasn't clear what tactics or methods they were learning to apply on their own. They could not read maps; they had no mortars or air support; and they had no intention of absorbing casualties by patrolling in the Green Zone once the Marines departed.

"None of us trusted them," Sergeant Browning said. "We kept our weapons loaded."

The Afghan battalion commander working with Lieutenant Colonel Morris and the Afghan company commander with Captain Johnson were trying their best. Most of the askaris, though, were from the northern part of the country and spoke Dari. They weren't welcomed by the locals. Third Platoon tolerated but generally ignored them.

Worse, since Fires was remote and constantly under pressure, the Afghan officers used it as a penal colony, sending soldiers there as punishment. This included one Pashtun lieutenant who became incensed whenever mortars and bombs were called in. The Marines responded by daring him to lead his men across the fields without fire support. When he refused, he was removed from Fires. The platoon gradually took less interest in the Afghan soldiers. Two or three askaris were expected to accompany a patrol—no more, no fewer.

Sergeant Esquibel had a high degree of maturity and thus empathy for the unfortunate askaris banished to Fires.

"If you act like you don't expect much from a guy," Esquibel said, "you won't get much."

———————

Almost a half century earlier, I had served in a Combined Action Platoon consisting of a dozen Marines and two dozen Vietnamese farmers. We lived together in a ramshackle fort inside a village of 5,000 Vietnamese. For the first three months, every night we clashed with local guerrillas who were infuriated that we had the gall to move in. To stay alive, we had to train and get along with the farmers, called Popular Forces, who fought alongside us. Gradually, the villagers not only accepted our presence; they actually liked us.

Of the 300 rifle squads in a Marine division, 118 were deployed independently in Vietnam villages. The Marines had hoped to apply the same model in Afghanistan. It didn't work. In Vietnam, we were truly integrated. The same squad stayed in a village for a year with the same local militia. In Afghanistan, outposts were shared but not integrated; both Afghan and U.S. squads rotated in and out, moving on after a few months.

The chance of betrayal was high. No American squad dared to live for a year in a compound among the people. Several battalions did establish outposts manned by a mix of Marine and Afghan squads. And the Army Special Forces set up over one hundred local police units, although Americans did not live among them. These efforts, with mixed results, were small in relation to a vast country containing millions of xenophobic tribesmen and suspicious mullahs.

The Americans patrolled on foot in the Green Zone, with indirect firepower and helicopter medevac on call. Left on their own, the Afghan soldiers would remain in fixed posts guarding the roads. They had no such firepower or evacuation means. The high command referred to the placement of Afghan soldiers at U.S. outposts as "partnering," erroneously implying benefits for both sides. Senior commanders claimed that by this technique the Afghan army would mature into a credible stand-alone fighting force. Although daily observation of American combat routines was helpful, the Americans remained the fighters and the Afghans the onlookers.

Day 25. 150,000 Steps

The most dangerous sector in Sangin was P8Q. The canal system forced the Marines to pass through a long defile that provided the Taliban with a clear field of fire. P8Q was the ideal spot for an ambush, a place of peril that would challenge the Marines for the next six months.

On November 6, a patrol, including Sgt. J. D. Browning and two other snipers, cautiously moved across a deep canal on the outskirts of P8Q. Browning was on high alert, constantly scanning the terrain to cover their movement. But he never saw the machine gun that fired from deep in the bush. LCpl. Randy Braggs, twenty-one, of Sierra Vista, Arizona, was struck and killed by a burst from a PKM machine gun. Both of his parents had served in the Army and his younger brother was also in Afghanistan, serving in the Air Force.

Back at the company ops center, Capt. Spokes Beardsley, the air officer, called in two F18s. After they dropped four 500-pound bombs on the suspected tree line in P8Q, enemy firing ceased. One bomb touched off secondary explosions from IEDs inside a compound.

The angry Marines returned the next day. First Squad shot one man talking on an Icom and looking at the passing patrol. His two comrades dragged his body into a herd of goats, using the animals to screen their escape.

On the next patrol into P8Q, a poor goat suffered the wrath of the frustrated Marines. First Squad was moving north near the river when LCpl. Chatchai Xiong shot a man with an AK running from one compound to another. The electronic intercept team at Inkerman warned that the Taliban were talking on Icoms inside different compounds. Within seconds, the patrol came under fire from three directions, while two men dragged away the body.

While shooting from the prone position, Xiong heard a snort and looked up to see a goat standing over him. Xiong, twenty, from St. Paul, planned to design computer games. This scene, though, provided material too bizarre to use. Grabbing the goat's halter, he pulled it down next to him as bullets zipped by. When the firing ceased, the patrol headed back toward Fires, with the goat tagging along. Even when stones were thrown at it, the animal stuck with the patrol. It took over an hour to reach the wire. By that time, the Marines were calling the goat Stacy.

"I told them you shouldn't name anything you might kill," Esquibel said. "The squad thought otherwise."

That night, the Marines ate Stacy.

At the end of the first week in November, two squads of Marine reservists arrived at Fires. Although they weren't trained for Sangin's grunt work, some lobbied Garcia for a chance to fight, and he inserted them into the patrols until Captain Johnson found out.

"Vic," Johnson said, "we can't train them properly out here. On patrol, they'll eventually die. That reserve unit took heavy losses in Iraq. We can't let that happen again."

So the reservists took over the tasks of guarding post and standing the watches. This comparatively safe duty stirred no resentment inside 3rd Platoon. For six weeks, the platoon had functioned on five hours of sleep a night. A Marine was either on patrol, standing watch, or clearing the underbrush around the fort. Now all they had to do was patrol, eat, and sleep for eight hours at a stretch! Third Platoon was in grunt heaven.

The grunts had no other place to go, or anyone else to talk with.

Regardless of how bad the day had been or who was carried out on the chopper, when they came back they could only wash off the blood at the pump and shed their sopping cammies. They had only one another. Nighttime inside Fires was no place for the loner, the introvert, or anyone who wanted peace and quiet. There may have been different tastes in music, but not on the nights I was at Fires. Somehow they stored enough battery life for a few scratchy speakers hooked to iPods with heavy metal sounds that no one over twenty-five can comprehend.

During the 2004 battle for Fallujah, the Marines harassed the insurgents by rigging up giant loudspeakers that blared out soothing tunes like "Hells Bells" from AC/DC: *I'm rolling thunder, pouring rain. I'm coming on like a hurricane. My lightning's flashing across the sky. You're only young, but you're goin' to die. Won't take no prisoners, won't spare no lives."*

Third Platoon embraced that sentiment. They had cut loose from society—no girls, sex, beer, bars, cars, McDonald's, families, holidays, sports, TV, college, or job—nothing beyond laughing at night and killing in the morning. The worst punishment in the platoon was psychological banishment—the feeling that the others didn't think highly of you. Garcia kept his hands off how things were settled inside the squads. If a squad leader gave extra duty to someone, that was squad business. If things got too bad, Staff Sergeant Cartier would handle it.

On November 9, Lt. Robert Kelly of Lima Company was killed by an IED a mile south of Fires. He had enlisted in 2003 and was on his third combat tour. When his father, Marine Lt. Gen. John Kelly, heard the news, he said, "We have a saying in the Marine Corps and that is 'no better friend, no worse enemy, than a U.S. Marine.' We always hope for the first, friendship, but are certainly more than ready for the second. If it's death they want, it's death they will get, and the Marines will continue showing them the way to hell if that's what will make them happy."

A text of the general's remarks was circulated throughout 3/5.

"Every squad received a copy of General Kelly's speech," Sergeant Thoman said. "It had a huge effect. We weren't leaving Sangin until we repaid the hurt."

Sergeant Deykeroff saw it the same way.

"By this stage," Dy said, "we were all in the fight. We were taking the area back and hurting those who had hurt our brothers. We wanted payback."

On November 10, the 235th birthday of the Corps, 3/5 lost another Marine. LCpl. James Stack, twenty, of Chicago, was shot in the head and killed. He left behind a wife and one-year-old daughter. Stack had written to his father that "one minute you would be having a good time with your friends and joking around, and the next day they were gone." He was a national champion air pistol shooter in the 2008 Junior Olympics. "I can shoot better than they can," Stack wrote, "don't worry about me. I'm coming home."

In one month, 3/5 had suffered fifteen dead, forty amputations, and over seventy others wounded. In London, the *Sunday Times* published a story entitled "U.S. Humbled in Bloody Sangin." The casualty rate was unparalleled in the Afghan war, and it would continue to be.

Back in the States, there was shock among the families of the battalion and the general public. Every night, Secretary of Defense Robert Gates signed condolence letter after letter. He didn't put his sense of loss on display, but the evening TV news captured his somber expression. A decent, caring man, the attrition of 3/5 affected him deeply. Perhaps the daily toll was too heavy for slight, elusive gains that might prove temporary. In eastern Afghanistan, U.S. Army forces had pulled out of the Korengal Valley after taking heavy losses. Gates suggested pulling the Marines out of Sangin.

The Commandant of the Marine Corps, Gen. James Amos, adamantly refused.

"We don't do business that way," he told NPR. "You would have broken the spirit of that battalion."

Secretary Gates deferred to the Marines. Reflecting on that decision, he later wrote, "I thought to myself . . . that pulling them out would possibly have been one of my worst mistakes as secretary of defense. These Marines had been hit hard, very hard. But despite their terrible losses, they were very proud they had succeeded where so many others had failed. And justifiably so."

The Marine high command, however, did not dispute the costs.

"I don't think there's ever been a battalion in the Marine Corps at any time," Maj. Gen. Richard Mills, the Marine commander in Afghanistan, said, "in World War II, the Korean conflict, Vietnam, that has pulled a tougher mission than what 3/5 has right now."

Third Platoon knew they had a tough mission. They had no illusions about their chances. One drizzly day when the fifty-one Marines were all inside the wire at Fires—the snipers, squads, and mortar crews—they all took a few hours to respond to a detailed questionnaire I gave them (Appendix D).

One question asked what each would choose "if you had it to do over again." Almost all responded, "I'd be right here." Most wished those back home could understand how hard they were trying. For their sacrifices, they desired a higher recognition than those in the rear. This has been the sentiment of all foot soldiers since Alexander the Great.

A majority believed the Pashtuns were untrustworthy, either because they were aligned with the Taliban or because they were intimidated by them. When a Marine patrol approached, the women and children ran away if there were Taliban fighters nearby. The villagers knew the Marines would respond with heavy fire. For the Marines, the hasty evacuation by families was a reliable early warning system that ambush was imminent. At the same time, the fields nearer to Fires grew heavily populated once the Taliban pulled back. Cows, sheep, and donkeys were everywhere. The Marines could walk in the hoofprints of the animals, safe from IEDs, until they were beyond sight of the sentry towers.

Third Platoon was finding about one IED a day and averaging four firefights a week. With no intelligence offered by the farmers, their demands for payment for war damages went unheeded. The Marines directed complainants to the district governor's office and walked on. As they went from compound to compound, they occasionally met families genuinely glad to see them, while other farmers scowled and turned their backs.

As for the enemy, 3rd Platoon believed the Taliban were better fighters than the Afghan soldiers, but not by a wide margin. They didn't view the Taliban as terrorists like Al Qaeda, dedicated to attacking America. They knew Afghans were fighting to determine the future of Afghanistan, not the United States. In like fashion, the Marines related their daily struggles at Fires to the cause of defending America.

"I know that body counts are not a measure of what we want these days," Major General Mills said. "But I can tell you that with the heavy casualties that they [3/5] have suffered, they have inflicted ten times that amount on the enemy."

In the theoretical world of benevolent counterinsurgency, the general wasn't supposed to talk that bluntly. The metaphysical mission was to persuade the Pashtun tribes, rather than to kill the enemy. As the top commander through mid-2010, General McChrystal had laid down a strict rule.

He wrote, "I wanted to take away any incentives that might drive commanders and their men to see killing insurgents as the primary goal."

McChrystal had previously commanded the Special Operations Forces that focused on killing. As the overall commander in Afghanistan, McChrystal divided tasks. The SOF—7 percent of the force—were dedicated killing teams, while the conventional forces—93 percent of the force—were to avoid killing.

"Military history must never stray from the tragic story of killing," wrote the eminent historian Victor Davis Hanson. "To speak of war in any other fashion brings with it a sort of immorality. Euphemism in battle narrative or the omission of graphic killing altogether is a near criminal offense of the military historian."

In Afghanistan, that omission from the battle narrative became a direct order.

"I directed all units to cease reporting . . . insurgents killed," General McChrystal wrote.

Small teams of Special Operations Forces were praised for killing Taliban leaders, while conventional forces were treated differently. McChrystal even supported a proposal to award medals for "courageous restraint" to grunts who did not return fire in populated areas.

David Petraeus took over in the summer of 2010. He diligently kept in touch with many unofficial sources and received a torrent of complaints about onerous restrictions. His solution was to quietly pass the word that the chain of command below the top had interpreted McChrystal's Tactical Directive too literally. Thus he avoided rebuking McChrystal by revoking his directive, while signaling that he wasn't going to be a hardass about enforcing it.

The platoon was fortunate in having firm commanders. Colonel Kennedy and Lieutenant Colonel Morris supported the platoon. Lieutenant Garcia received no cautionary "guidance" from above. It remained the judgment call of those on the patrol when to shoot and when to refrain. The squad leaders were mature; all had combat experience. All also had a wife and children waiting back home. They weren't cowboys, but they didn't want to place the pieces of their Marines in body bags.

Day 33. 198,000 Steps

On patrol in sector Q1C, 1st Squad hacked through heavy vines for two hours to approach a mosque from a safe direction. Inside the small building, the Afghan soldiers found two shovel heads, three illumination flares, six mortar rounds, two Icom battery chargers, one kilo of opium tar, a small bag of blue powder, electric wires, cleaning gear for an AK, and vials of animal medicine. While they were searching, a man drove up on a motorcycle, watched them for a few minutes, and drove away. As they were leaving an hour later, he drove up again. When the askaris yelled at him to come over, he hastily drove away.

A Marine shot at him and he leaped off his bike, disappearing into the undergrowth. The patrol pursued, bursting into a nearby compound and finding blood splatters. The owner dragged out a slaughtered sheep. He said he locked his gate at sunset and minded his own business. He added that since he was poor, the Marines should give him money.

Whatever the man knew, he wasn't divulging. The Marines weren't detectives and the translator, Rocky, had no interrogation training. Insisting he was lying, the askaris wanted to beat him until he talked. The Marines vetoed that, but saw no sense in dragging him back with them, since the district governor was sure to release him. Lacking any better option, the Marines left the compound. This was typical. Unless they had absolute physical evidence, the Marines did not make an arrest.

Day 34. 204,000 Steps

On November 15, LCpl. Clay Cook of 1st Squad shot a man talking on an Icom. Some farmers brought his body to Fires. Since he wasn't from the area, they wanted the askaris to bury him. The askaris jeered and yelled at them to leave. The farmers walked a short distance back down the road, dug a grave, dumped in the body, stuck a piece of cloth atop a pole, and went back to their fields.

Day 36. 216,000 Steps

Thoman was leading 3rd Squad through the P8S sector, HiMars, where Marine artillery had wrecked several compounds. A few families were scraping by, too poor or outcast to leave the ruins. When a poor farmer held out his hand, Thoman took out a piece of waterproof paper and scribbled a note saying damages should be paid. The interpreter, Stevie, told the farmer to take it to the district governor.

At another farm, women and children huddled in a corner. Their father had been killed; they had been bombed a week ago and were afraid the Marines had come to kill them. Thoman signed another chit, requesting payment for fourteen pomegranate trees. Next to the children, the Marines found two car batteries with wires attached, wrapped in plastic. They threw them into the canal, but did not take back the chit.

The Marines knew they were dealing with a miserable situation. One entry in the platoon log for mid-November read, "At bldg 23, family came out. Took pictures of man, of house, his kids and elderly woman. Claimed to be his mother who[se] husband had been killed several months ago. Elderly woman acted unhappy with our presence. All lns [local nationals] saying they were afraid we would kill them. Also a woman at bldg 18 with no husband and young kids said she had to move there because her house had been bombed 10 days ago and the kid's father had been killed. She was their grand-mother."

The Marines were neither friendly nor hostile to the farmers. The grunts were focused on the fight and detached from the people. The poverty was stark and most farmers asked for something. The violence was also as pervasive as it was hidden. You could get blown up anywhere, but you couldn't blame the farmers for staying silent or fearing the Marines. The grunts gave candy to children, returned grins if farmers smiled, and walked past those who didn't.

Capt. Tim Nogalski, 3/5's intelligence officer, treated Afghan professions of loyalty with skepticism. Government officials, tribal sheiks, merchants, drug dealers, mullahs, Taliban, and farmers had four years to perfect their lines with the British before the Marines arrived. No promise, oath, or pledge of allegiance could be taken at face value.

"It's impossible to assess the number of enemy," Nogalski said. "The Taliban can't coordinate enough fighters to attack a single Marine platoon. But on the video screen, I watch whole neighborhoods evacuate enemy casualties and carry away the weapons. I can't differentiate the people from the Taliban."

The intelligence of real use to Nogalski were target packages compiled from informants and electronic intercepts. In the past month, Objective White had been killed. Objective Black was a psycho who had killed his own father. Objective Kassidy was a traitor inside the Alakozai tribe who was trying to assassinate the top sheiks. Objective Wondra was the shadow district chief who had captured three sheiks last summer. In return, the Alakozai had kidnapped Wondra and released him in return for their sheiks. The score was one enemy leader down, and three to go (unless others replaced them).

Day 38. 228,000 Steps

Lantznester, the SAW gunner, and LCpl. John Payne were covering the rear of a patrol, watching an old man who had walked outside his compound wall, followed by several boys. After the Marines filed by, he gestured to the boys, who scampered out into the field, yelling back and forth and looking at the ground. When one boy shouted and pointed at the scuff marks left where the Marines had passed over an irrigation ditch, the old man grabbed a shovel. From several hundred meters away, Lantznester watched him through his telescopic sight.

"Sergeant Dy," he called over his mike, "that farmer looks shady. He's digging an IED hole on our back trail."

"Light him up."

Several Marines opened fire. The man collapsed and the boys ran inside the compound wall. The patrol continued on.

"Our counterinsurgency training in the States was good," Lantznester said. "We were taught to help the people. But it didn't work out at Fires. The farmers didn't like us foreigners. Our terp, Stevie, was great. He'd kick the Afghan soldiers in the ass when they needed it. He warned us when atmospherics in the fields were turning bad and he'd argue with the farmers."

Every American platoon had a Stevie, an Afghan youth with quick intelligence and determination who taught himself English watching TV soaps, signed on with a contractor, and was sent to the grunts, the bottom of the translator totem pole. After a few months or years eating, sleeping, fighting, and straining to improve his pidgin English, Stevie employed *fuck* as adjective, verb, and noun with the same facility as any grunt. The Stevies became Americans. They thought like the grunts, swaggered like them, looked askance at Afghans, and desperately hoped to earn a Green Card. Without Stevie, 3rd Platoon was deaf and dumb. With Stevie, well, at least somebody yelled back over the captured Icoms at the Taliban.

Day 39. 234,000 Steps

At mid-morning on November 20, 3rd Squad was patrolling in Sector P8Q, always dangerous. The point man, LCpl. Carlos Garcia, stepped on a pressure plate that shredded both his legs. Ignoring the danger, LCpl. Kyle Doyle and others ran forward to strap on tourniquets. Doyle, twenty-one, from California, had joined the Marines after reading that they were a brotherhood. Now his close comrade had been struck down.

"Carlos was praying as we were running with him," Doyle said. "Time was going slow and fast for me."

The immensely popular engineer was carried back to Fires and medevaced as a double amputee.

Second Squad returned to P8Q and found another IED. The squad also destroyed a cache of ammonium nitrate. A man riding by on a moped paused to shoot at the patrol, and then drove off. The squad found a second IED, with wires to a battery. Getting another hit on the Vallon, the Marines probed with their knives, digging up the head of a dog with a metal collar.

Banshee 3, a sniper keeping overwatch with the squad, saw a man with an Icom pop his head out of a compound. A few minutes later, he reappeared with a shovel, dug cursorily for a few seconds, looked at the Marines, and ducked back inside. After he repeated this twice, Banshee 3 put a round into his chest. Before leaving P8Q, 2d Squad uncovered and destroyed a third IED.

Several hundred meters to the west, Lance Corporal Gorcie, walking point with 3rd Squad, stepped on an IED and was evacuated.

Day 40. 240,000 Steps

The next day, 1st Squad attempted to conduct a census. The war in Afghanistan would have ended in a few months had the Taliban worn uniforms. Instead, by posing as civilians they walked right by American soldiers. Biometric tracking and databases were standard in the States; anytime a car is stopped, the police run an immediate check. The Chicago police carry handheld devices that send finger-prints over the airwaves and get a response in minutes.

To do the same in Sangin, 3rd Platoon was given a brick-sized computer called HIDE. The idea was to enter the names, photos, eye iris, thumbprint, location, tribe, and family members living in every compound. While the concept made sense, the HIDE was clunky and poorly designed, requiring twenty minutes to enter too much data about each person. The Marines considered biometric patrols worthless, because HIDE never provided them with a positive hit. Worse, spending an hour at one compound gave the Taliban time to set up an ambush.

Sure enough, after 1st Squad lingered at a compound, they received harassing fire from a tree line to the east. A fire mission was called in. In an adjacent field, three small children were standing rigidly next to two adults. Suddenly a man ran out from the trees, ducked behind the kids, and backed across the field, keeping the children between him and the Marines, who canceled the fire mission.

Through their high-power scopes, Banshee—the snipers—had watched similar scenes. When a man walked among those working in the fields but stopped to shake hands or exchange greetings, the snipers knew he was not a local. If he became uneasy, he moved closer to the farming families. Browning saw one man balance a child on the handlebars and another on the backseat as he drove away on his motorcycle.

First Squad continued northeast, passing through the P8S sector where sheep the size of ponies were grazing. In P8S there were compounds with steel doors on sliding tracks and black-and-white TVs in the living rooms. The Taliban shadow district governor lived in a house in P8S, decorated with bright Persian rugs on wooden rather than dirt floors. But he was never home when the Marines came calling.

Day 41. 246,000 Steps

First Squad "got PID on 2 MAMs with ICOM," meaning positive identification of two military-age males. Both men were killed. They were wearing green chest rigs containing AK-47 magazines. It took twenty minutes to sweep a clear lane 300 meters to the bodies. During that time, someone had made off with the Icom and the rifles, leaving behind only a radio antenna. The Taliban had scant equipment, and they hoarded every scrap.

The squad found nothing of value on the bodies. That was typical. Garcia sometimes noticed a new stick figure scratched on the snipers' wall, but the patrol had not reported searching a body as required by the rules. He didn't bring it up. He let the squad leaders decide when to risk the IED threat by going forward to search a body, and when to move on.

Later that day, Garcia was accompanying 3rd Squad north of Fires when they were pinned down by accurate fire. Garcia called a mortar mission and the 60mm shells hit the compound after two quick adjustments. The Marines blew a hole in the compound wall and Cpl. Kameron Delany pitched a grenade into each room before entering. But the enemy had already fled.

Corporal Delany, twenty, from Texas, had been promoted early for his aggressiveness. He consistently took chances at point. He modestly allowed that the state of Texas was the most patriotic, free-spirited, brave, wholesome, individualistic, God-fearing, and God-blessed state, to say nothing of the Dallas Cowboys, otherwise known as America's Team. He planned to return to his humble state and join the police department.

"I respect life," he said. "But somebody has to do the ass kicking."

It took repeated patrolling to find an ass to kick. The Taliban used compounds as protected firing positions. Fifteen minutes usually went by before a squad had identified which compounds the shooters were in. It took another fifteen minutes or more to set up a base of return fire and send an enveloping team behind a point man with a Vallon. Before the Marines were in a position to assault, the Taliban ran out the rear. Most compounds had an outside ditch used as a latrine that ran down to a canal. The ditches and irrigation streams allowed the Taliban to avoid enfilade fire as they escaped. Their sneakers would stink, but they were still walking upright.

Third Platoon continued to rely upon close air support for cover. Each squad informed Inkerman of its intended route, and in the ops center Spokes Beardsley put a tic on his photomap as the squad called in each checkpoint. First Squad was midway across sector P8T when it was pinned down by fire from Compound 38. The Taliban were shooting through murder holes and the return fire of the squad bounced harmlessly off the thick walls.

Beardsley called for the two F-18s he was tracking on the daily air chart. The lead pilot, Capt. Scott "Lumpy" Foster from Marine Squadron 232, scanned sector P8T with his video pod.

"Driftwood, this is Maker. I see no movement below me. Nothing."

Lumpy asked his wing mate, Canadian Capt. Chris "Chester" Horch, to take a look. Horch agreed. It looked normal to him. The Taliban and 1st Squad were both under overhead cover.

On the ground, Sgt. Joe "Mad Dog" Myers, twenty-four, from Ohio, was the forward observer with the squad. However, the final decision for an aircraft to fire was reserved for Beardsley. An avid reader and gifted storyteller, Myers had joined the Marines in 2000 after reading books like E. B. Sledge's *With the Old Breed*. Sangin was his last tour before getting out and going to college.

Myers radioed the compound number (#38) and GPS grid location of the target to Spokes, who was watching the video from the F-18 pods on a small screen called a Rover. He gave directions to each pilot until the pod on each aircraft was aligned on compound #38. Lumpy then rolled in first with a 500-pound bomb, crushing the compound. Twenty seconds later, Chester followed with another bomb that burst in the air—the now standard shake-and-bake tactic. Enemy firing ceased. Myers notified Beardsley, who thanked the pilots, who flew back to Kandahar airbase while 1st Squad walked back to Fires.

Beardsley had linked the air to the ground with a precision unmatched in history, a combination of amazing technologies—video cameras, digital downlinks, exact telemetry—and common procedures developed over decades between Marines in the air and on the ground.

Back at the hospital, LCpl. Jeff Sibley, the sniper, had recovered from his bullet wound. Once he had mended, he felt embarrassed being in the same ward with Sergeant Humphries, another member of 3/5, who had suffered an amputated leg.

"This Afghan," Sibley said, "we had shot a few weeks earlier was also on the ward. He should have been in prison."

Although desperate to return to Fires, Sibley wasn't allowed on board a helicopter because he didn't have a helmet and flak jacket. When a clerk in the supply building refused to give him the gear, Sibley demanded to see the senior NCO.

"You a HOG?" asked the master gunnery sergeant in charge.

Upon graduating from sniper school, a Marine is presented a bullet on a thin chain. He is officially a HOG, Hunter of Gunmen. When Sibley nodded yes, the master gunnery sergeant turned to his staff.

"Give this lance corporal," he said, "whatever he wants."

Sibley flew into Fires with a box stuffed with knives, gloves, boots, and Mitch helmets—the small, black helmets worn by Special Operations commandos.

"I brought back Christmas early," Sibley said.

Chapter 6

THANKSGIVING

"I do, therefore, invite my fellow-citizens . . . to set apart a Day of Thanksgiving and Praise to our beneficent Father. . . . To these bounties, which are of so extraordinary a nature that they cannot fail to penetrate and soften the heart habitually insensible to the everwatchful providence of Almighty God."
—PRESIDENT ABRAHAM LINCOLN, 1863

Day 43. 258,000 Steps

A mullah came to Inkerman on the 24th of November, complaining that the doorway to his one-room mosque in sector P8Q was booby-trapped. Lt. Tom Schueman gathered a handful of Marines from 1st Platoon to investigate. Because the company had lost thirty-five killed or wounded in seven weeks, there weren't enough grunts for such unscheduled patrols. So Gunny Carlisle and Sgt. Jason Peto from the headquarters section volunteered to assist as two riflemen. Carlisle was a force of nature, overburdened with muscles and testosterone and unaffected by his senior rank. There was no chore he would not undertake.

Once at the mosque, an engineer disarmed an 82mm mortar shell lying in the doorway. In case more IEDs were found, 1st Squad came forward from Fires with extra demolitions. Schueman climbed on top of a roof to look out for trouble. As the squad approached, two men on a motorcycle scooted out of a compound to his right. One was shouting into an Icom and Schueman shot him at a hundred meters. When the driver accelerated, the wounded man fell off. He lay still for a few seconds, then pushed himself up and staggered into an adjacent compound.

Gunny Carlisle, who had seen the man go down, shouted up to Schueman.

"Hey, we'll cut across the field and pick up the blood trail."

Carlisle and Peto set out and minutes later Schueman saw them enter a compound Marines had previously used as an overnight outpost.

"There's IEDs here," Carlisle radioed minutes later.

Schueman sent over the engineer, LCpl. Arden Buenagua, who had disarmed the mortar shell in the mosque. He knelt down near Carlisle and was working on the IED when it detonated, killing him instantly.

Buenagua had written on his Facebook page, "I like meeting people that are interested in things that I'm into and strange cats that are entertaining. I make friends pretty easily since I just start talking to people." His mother said he joined the Marines "to get some direction in his life. Arden became a young Marine. The way he talked, the way he acts. . . . A total transformation of my son."

Garcia grabbed 2d Squad and rushed out from Fires, bringing a body bag. As they neared the mosque, the Taliban opened fire. Hearing the shooting, Carlisle and Peto entered a room to provide covering fire from a window. Peto tripped a second IED, receiving wounds that would prove fatal. He was on his third combat tour and had been previously wounded by an IED in Ramadi. His father, two brothers, and an uncle had served in the Corps. He left behind his wife, Tiffany, of Vancouver, Washington.

"I saw Peto's boot fly into the air," LCpl. Kyle Doyle said. "It seemed to freeze up there. It took me two weeks to get over it. If you looked at a picture of me in high school and who I am now, it's two different people."

The blast hurled LCpl. Jeffrey Rushton, twenty-eight, into the courtyard. He had joined the Marines when he was twenty-four, determined to fight terrorists, then go back to his wife waiting in San Diego and attend college.

Gunny Carlisle, the pillar of Kilo Company, also went down, his upper thigh and half of his buttocks ripped off. Third Squad's corpsman, Manuel Gonzales, was peppered with shrapnel. One killed and three wounded in a blink. While the wounded were stabilized, Marines fired light rockets, called LAAWs, at the far tree line and Corporal Laird brought up his team of snipers. Once they began to place rounds knee-high along the tree line, the Taliban pulled back and the medevac chopper came in.

Abbate ran out to where Gunny Carlisle lay facedown. Taking one knee, he shot at the tree line, shouting, "You hurt my gunny! No one messes with my gunny!"

When the firing died down and the helos swooped in, Abbate and Laird picked up Buenagua's destroyed body. They tried to keep him in one piece as they folded him into the black body bag. Abbate took the lead with the legs in the front of the bag, while the torso rested on Laird's shoulder. By the time they placed the body on the helicopter, Laird's face and lips were drenched with Buenagua's blood. Laird reached down to Gunny Carlisle, who was lying on his side in his sopping bandages.

"We're gonna kill them all!" Laird shouted. "Every last Taliban!"

After evacuating the dead and wounded it was late afternoon before a gear check was conducted. Peto's rifle could not be found. A rifle with its telescopic sight in enemy hands was a serious matter. Garcia took responsibility; it was his duty as senior man to ensure accountability. The failure signaled a bleak future career. Far worse, a Marine on patrol might be hit from long range.

Returning to search for the rifle in the dark would be perilous. A chest-deep canal lay between Fires and the compound. In late November, the ditches had an icy sheen. During the day's fight, five IEDs had been found or had exploded. Probably a half dozen more lay in wait. As the shivering Marines stomped around in the dark looking for the rifle, how many legs would be lost? One? Two? Five?

Garcia asked for volunteers.

"It's on us, sir," Sergeant Deykeroff said. "Second Squad will go back with you."

Garcia knew they were resigned to losing at least one man. He called on Abbate.

"Sergeant, if a few snipers come," Garcia said, "it will settle everyone down."

"Lieutenant, it's suicide to go out there in the dark," Abbate said. "I'm not sending any of my Marines to get blown up. I'm sorry, but we're not going."

Garcia called back to company, saying he was leaving the wire with a squad. Captain Johnson made no effort to hide his frustration about the missing rifle. But he wasn't foolish.

"Negative," Johnson said. "We'll keep watch with the G-Boss. Stay at your pos. Find the damn rifle in the morning."

The G-Boss was a powerful telescope perched on top of a fifty-foot pole. An operator back at company headquarters could see if men were prowling around at night. Still, Garcia slept fitfully, worried that the Taliban may already have found the rifle.

Day 44. 264,000 Steps

Before dawn on Thanksgiving Day, 2d Squad was already moving north, wading across the icy canal and fanning out around the compound. After a short search, Peto's rifle was found on top of a roof, where the IED blast had flung it. The Marines were shaking with cold, but a pissed-off Garcia decided to pick a fight before returning to Fires. He directed several mortar illumination shells to be fired off to the east into the P8T sector, a reliable hotbed of enemy activity. Sure enough, when the shells burst overhead, men ran crouched over among several compounds about 300 meters away. A flurry of bullets was exchanged. It was uncertain whether any Taliban had been hit, but Garcia felt better for ruining their breakfast.

The patrol returned to Fires, stripped off their sopping clothes, and slipped into their "happy suits"—comfortable cold weather trousers and jackets, white wool socks, and flip-flops. Around nine in the morning, they sat down to eat their Thanksgiving meal (ham). Over the radio, they heard a patrol from 2d Platoon had left from Transformer, the outpost on Route 611 one mile north of Inkerman.

Outpost Transformer consisted of a compound with a string of barbed wire on top of the outer wall, surrounded by scattered compounds and huge open farm fields. In early October, Sgt. Ryan Sotelo, a college graduate who'd been with 3/5 Battalion for three years, had moved his reinforced squad into Transformer. From the start, mistrust ran high between the Marines and the Afghan army squad also sent there. The askaris stayed inside their own area behind Hesco barriers and refused to search compounds on patrol. Once, when Sotelo asked the Afghan sergeant to look inside one building, the sergeant threw his weapon on the ground and stalked back unarmed to Transformer.

In late October, a corncob was pitched over the compound wall with a note for Rock, the squad interpreter. It read, "Abdul [Rock's real name], we know where your parents live in Kabul. Leave this post, or we will cut off your head with a shoemaker's wire." The only person who knew Rock's name was a district elder paid by the Marines for using his farm at Patrol Base Fires. Rock held no grudge.

"Sangin has simple-minded people," Rock told Sotelo. "You cannot win them over. All they care about is their next meal."

As if to mock the Marines, the Taliban had even set up a tax collection checkpoint on Route 611, midway between Inkerman and Transformer. In response, Johnson sent Lt. William Donnelly and 2d Platoon to join Sotelo at Transformer. The plan was to send out patrols to push back the enemy, but it was like living in a fishbowl. Next door to Transformer was a motorcycle repair shop where dickers reported the size and movement of patrols leaving the base. Every patrol might as well have had sirens and flashing lights.

And when the corn stalks were cut down after the first frost in early November, the Taliban had taken up positions along tree lines to the west across the Golf Course, 400 meters of flat mud field with not a speck of cover—no walls, no rock piles, no irrigation ditches. No place to hide.

Every day, the Taliban shot at the post, but the Marines couldn't unravel the pattern. They seemed to be fighting ghosts. Rock explained that these were local Taliban, farmers who walked into the fields with shovels and hoes, uncovered caches of AKs and PKMs, shot at Transformer, put back the weapons, picked up their shovels, and walked past the outpost on their way home.

Captain Johnson urged Donnelly to get after them.

So before dawn on Thanksgiving, a patrol at Transformer assembled in the cold dark for a gear check and final brief. Donnelly took Sotelo aside for a sanity check.

"We're good to go," Sotelo said. "But if we lose a Marine, Thanksgiving will never be the same for that family."

"I don't like it any better than you do," Donnelly said. "Let's get going."

At dawn, eighteen apprehensive Marines left the wire. As the squad leader, Sotelo was in tactical charge. Donnelly was farther back in line. The target was a Taliban leader—Kataghi—who lived somewhere near Compound 117 in sector P8R, also called Kotozay. In Ranger file, the patrol moved across the Golf Course, sprinkling white baby powder to mark the safe lane. Reaching the far side, the patrol walked past two men sitting by a fire, watching them.

So much, Sotelo thought, *for surprise.*

When they reached Compound 117, it was deserted, with crude drawings on the walls of helicopters being shot down. An Afghan soldier who had volunteered for the patrol shook his head and pointed to a compound on the far side of a wide field. With a fire team, Sotelo crossed the field and entered a house that had insulation in the walls, a washer-dryer, a cabinet with delicate china teacups, and purple drapes.

"Jackpot," Sotelo radioed to Donnelly, who was back in the file. "This has to be where Kataghi lives."

Sotelo walked outside as Donnelly walked across the field. Hearing *pop, pop, pop* from a tree line 150 meters to the west, Sotelo whirled and opened fire. Out of the corner of his eye, he saw Donnelly and a few Marines go flat to return fire. LCpl. Diego Rodriguez saw a shadow in the tree line and cut loose a long burst from his 240 machine gun. Sotelo oriented his fire team toward the threat and yelled across to Donnelly, who was lying in the field.

"Come on!" Sotelo yelled. "Gotcha covered."

The Marines behind Donnelly had fallen back. Donnelly didn't move. Even as Sotelo ran across the field to his platoon commander, he knew. The body was too still. Other Marines ran forward and turned him over. Donnelly, with a tight grip on his weapon, was dead, shot in the forehead. Sotelo called it in.

"Two Actual is dead," he said.

Lt. William Donnelly, twenty-seven, had married in September and died in November.

"Lieutenant Donnelly was real personable," Sotelo said. "He'd shoot the shit with us squad leaders, give us money to buy rice and chickens in the market—a good guy."

His sister later said of his death, "I don't think he would have had it any other way."

The Marines dragged his body out of the line of fire. A PKM had them pinned near Compound 117. Two Taliban emerged from the orchard behind 117 and hopped over the wall. The Marines traded shots with them at fifteen feet, and the Taliban hopped back. Sotelo threw a grenade over the wall and turned back to Donnelly, covering the body with blankets. They left his helmet in place and stripped off his armor. Sotelo then broke into a nearby compound to provide a rally point for his scattered squad. To bring back the body, eight more Marines left Transformer, only to be pinned down short of the compound.

Now two squads from 2d Platoon were engaged on the far western side of the Golf Course, with no supporting fire to cover their return. The Taliban had cut them off, the outcome Sotelo had feared. There was no reaction force waiting on call.

Back at Fires, 3rd Platoon had been listening to the incessant shooting. Curious, Sergeant Dy was walking toward the radio room when Garcia ran out.

"We got a hero," he said. "Lieutenant Donnelly's dead. Old Breed 2/1 is pinned down. Get all three squads."

Abbate threw in the snipers, yelling, "All gunfighters needed!"

Within minutes, the whole platoon was assembled.

"Second Platoon's north of the Golf Course," Garcia said. "We'll move northeast, relieve the pressure on them, and then link up."

At about nine in the morning, 1st Squad led off, heading northeast on a straight line toward Sotelo's location 1,500 meters away. Within minutes, they were stopped by fire from a compound in sector Q1E.

"Driftwood 2," Esquibel radioed to the Kilo ops center, "I'm stuck at 545 792. There's a PKM in Compound 3."

Capt. Spokes Beardsley told 1st Squad to get their heads down. Ten minutes later, an F-18 dropped a 500-pound laser-guided bomb on the compound. When the dust cleared, 1st Squad continued on.

Second Squad set out next, after the bomb run. Sergeant Dy saw pyro flares popping in the distance. The pinned-down squad of 2d Platoon was signaling where they were.

It's on now, Dy thought. *Payback time.*

After ten minutes, the point man, Wagner, stopped at a low stone wall to allow 3rd Squad to catch up. Two PKMs and a few AKs were shooting. LCpl. Leonard Rausch, twenty, from Wisconsin, ran forward to bring his SAW, a weapon he loved, into action. He had been over this ground before and, not worried about an IED underfoot, moved too quickly and slipped in the knee-deep mud. Reaching out to help him, Cpl. Armando Espinoza took a bullet in the ankle and went down. It was the second time he had been wounded in ten days. Rausch threw a red smoke grenade to alert the others that he needed help.

While Wagner and Delany pulled Espinoza out of the beaten zone, Abbate stood upright in the field, scoping the tree line for targets and firing short bursts from his M4. Using his 203 grenade launcher, Sergeant Dy arced a dozen explosive shells into the tree line with no apparent effect. If anything, the enemy fire picked up. Dy brought up his whole squad to provide covering fire, while Abbate and Laird helped carry Espinoza to the safety of a ditch. Lieutenant Garcia called in the big guns. Soon, 155mm Excalibur shells were pulverizing the tree line to their north.

It was time to push on to link up with the Marines protecting Donnelly's body. Laird took a deep breath, reached down, and hoisted Espinoza onto his back in a fireman's carry. His rifle in his right hand and his left holding tight on to Espinoza's forearm, Laird trudged forward.

Between one and two hours had passed since the firing began. By noon, 2d and 3rd Platoons were spread out in a dozen positions. Everyone was trying to avoid the open fields. All the Marines were moving in slow motion, the knee-deep mud in the sopping fields clinging to their legs like cement.

There were no battle lines. The enemy was everywhere and nowhere. There were probably only a hundred hard-core, professional Taliban in the district, and a similar number of "small-t Taliban"— local youths who worked their fields and only occasionally fired their AKs.

Thanksgiving Day seemed to be the grand occasion, as word spread of one infidel American invader dead and others trapped in the Green Zone. Ordinary farmers were dropping their hoes and, minutes later, AK rounds were snapping at the Marines from odd directions. White flags of the Taliban popped up on a few compound walls and windows.

On a battlefield of twenty acres, about a dozen small bands of Marines and Taliban were maneuvering. One squad of 2d Platoon had kicked off the fight, followed by a second. Garcia had brought out three squads, plus the sniper section and machine gun teams. In total, six friendly elements were on the move. On the other side, there were at least that many gangs, with excited farmers taking orders from regular fighters.

Delany ripped through ten magazines during the fight, but saw only two men dressed in the black garb of the Taliban. This was typical of a firefight. Lying in the mud, peering through the smoke at dense vegetation, ears deafened by the explosions, a Marine rarely glimpses the enemy.

"There! There!" Dy yelled, pointing toward a cluster of men running alongside a tree line. "Light them up! Shoot! Shoot!"

Lantznester flopped down, jamming the bipod of his SAW into the mud and aligning a hazy sight picture. He pulled back on the trigger. Nothing. Not a single snap or click. Not one bullet fired. *What the hell? This never happened!*

He jerked out the ammo can, brushed off a chunk of mud, resettled the can, and wiggled around to recapture his sight picture.

"Don't fire! Don't fire! That's 2d Platoon!"

Lantznester let out his breath and lay for a moment with his cheek on top of his weapon.

Back at battalion headquarters, the call had gone out for air support as soon as Lieutenant Donnelly went down. It was a gray, overcast day, with good visibility near the ground and a high cloud ceiling that did not impede flying.

About 9 a.m., Spokes Beardsley was in the company ops center when over the radio he heard the voice of a friend, Capt. Casey "Porch" Blasingame.

"Driftwood 22, this is Shoot-out," Blasingame said. "What have you got?"

Blasingame, thirty, from Texas, was flying a Huey armed with ten rockets and a machine gunner on each side door. Trailing behind was a Cobra gunship flown by Capt. Joe "Muff" Dadiomoff, twenty-eight, from Virginia. The Cobra was carrying fourteen rockets and a 20mm heavy machine gun. Each pilot had flown more than sixty combat sorties, and both were qualified weapons instructors.

"Shoot-out, we have Marines and bad guys," Spokes said, "scattered all over the place 400 meters west of Transformer. Mad Dog's on the battlefield. I'm turning you over to him."

"This is Mad Dog," Sergeant Myers radioed to the pilots. "We're under fire from the north. Got the whole fucking platoon out here. Trying to reach 2d. They're off somewhere to the east. How about getting to work?"

When back at Fires, Myers entertained 3rd Platoon with a constant stream of tall tales and impossible boasts. When he was amped, he spewed out a torrent of information.

Circling overhead, Blasingame was working off the same map as the grunts. He needed to mark the friendly positions before making a gun run. He was looking down at several scattered clusters of Marines, with no idea where Myers was.

"Mad Dog, pop smoke."

A minute later, he saw one purple smoke, and then a second. There was a pause, then a third purple.

"Bitches are using our smoke!" Myers radioed. "That's not us!"

"Which one isn't you?"

On the ground, Garcia made an adjustment and two more smoke grenades blossomed.

"We now mark two yellow smokes," Blasingame said.

"Affirm! Affirm!" Myers replied. "Both are us."

The Huey made a low pass from east to west so that the machine gunner in the starboard door could rake the tree line. The Cobra followed a few meters behind on a straight line over the trees. Capt. Eric Ewing sat in the front seat operating the 20mm gun, while Dadiomoff in the rear seat did the flying. As the two gunships rolled out to the left, the hot empty shells rained down on the Marines.

"You're slamming them! Slamming!" Myers radioed. "Do it again!"

As the aircraft came around for a second pass, Garcia pulled together the platoon and moved east toward Donnelly's position. Again the pilots came in low, at about a hundred feet. This time, Dadiomoff saw tracers, muzzle flashes, and RPG smoke trails from the tree lines, as well as the flashes of his 20mm rounds striking the trees and the ground. He glimpsed a few Taliban in their standard black darting among the trees.

"All right!" he yelled.

The pilots couldn't believe their luck. It was suicide for a man to shoot an AK or a PKM against two behemoths manned by a half dozen gunners eagerly looking for a single tip-off. Usually the Taliban were too disciplined and sensible to expose their positions. Now even gunners with RPGs were shooting into the air. The pilots saw the black puffs of the explosions, throttled back to locate the dust clouds from the back-blasts, and fired.

"Their muzzle flashes looked like blinking Christmas lights," Blasingame said. "We had target after target. Dirt and mud were flying up in the field from all our impacts."

On the third pass, the pilots were orbiting in a tight wagon wheel, with Blasingame pivoting his Huey to bring his port door gun into action. As he swept by the nose of the Cobra, Dadiomoff yelled over the radio, "Hey, Porch! Don't shoot me!"

The tree line was now smoking and 3rd Platoon had pushed by. But when the helicopters pulled off to catch up with the platoon, some Taliban again opened fire. For a fourth time, the Cobra lined up behind the Huey and again they attacked, shredding the wood line. Then for good measure, the pilots pulled slightly back and hovered, hoping someone would be foolish enough to shoot again and give away his hiding place. The trees smoldered and smoke curled up, but there were no more telltale flashes.

On the ground, 1st Squad and Abbate's snipers had linked up with 2d Platoon and placed Lieutenant Donnelly's large body on a pole litter. Garcia came in from the west with the other Marines. Everyone spread out inside a cluster of compound walls. They could clearly see Outpost Transformer to the southeast. Between them and Transformer lay the Golf Course.

Behind them to the north was the tree line where Donnelly had been shot. To their left was a 200-meter tree line called Belleau Wood. It was habitually loaded with snipers and IEDs. On a wall at Transformer, Sgt. Joel Bailey from 2d Platoon was firing burst after burst from a .50 cal at Belleau Wood. Artillery located at the battalion headquarters in Sangin joined in.

Standing behind compound walls with the gunships hovering overhead, the Marines were safe and sheltered. The mission was to carry Donnelly across the Golf Course to Transformer. The firing had died down, but Garcia wasn't fooled. Gibberish was still coming over the Taliban Icoms. They were out there, and they could see the Golf Course as plainly as could the Marines. Once the Marines were in the open, the Taliban were positioned to spring an ambush from the north and east.

First Squad led off, followed by the litter party carrying Donnelly. As they headed east across the Golf Course, the only enemy seemed to be the mud that slowed every step. Overhead, Blasingame and Dadiomoff were holding station above Transformer, the noses of their aircraft pointed toward Belleau Wood. Dadiomoff estimated the Marines were about a quarter of the way across the Golf Course when Belleau Wood erupted with muzzle flashes and the dirt clouds from back-blasts. Six or eight rocket-propelled grenades streaked toward the Marines, who flopped down in the mud with bullets kicking up mud spurts around them. The Huey rolled in on Belleau Wood, with the Cobra right behind.

"When we stepped around the corner into that field," Sotelo said, "we entered the world's longest shooting gallery. Rounds were coming from Route 611, from the compounds, from the Green Zone behind us, from the tree line to our left. It seemed every farmer had grabbed an AK and opened up. Brass was falling on my head from the Huey shooting above me."

As the gunships ripped up the tree line on their left flank, the Marines in the field got up and broke into a clumsy run, boots sticking in the mud. Sgt. Ryan Krochmolny, the strongest man in the company, slung Espinoza over his shoulder and shuffled along. When he got bogged down, Laird again grabbed the hand hole of the pole-less litter and staggered toward Transformer.

Abbate, carrying one end of a pole supporting Donnelly's body, was firing his 9mm pistol at a compound.

"Abbate's like Achilles," Rausch said. "He's what you want to be, a badass. He talks and walks it. But this show was ridiculous."

Myers was carrying the other end of the litter, talking to the pilots like a manic basketball play-by-play announcer. When he got too wound up, Beardsley cut him off from the pilots. Staff Sgt. Nick Tock, considerably more low-key than Mad Dog, was also directing the pilots.

"Our strafing runs," Beardsley said, "were forty meters in front of the Marines."

The pilots flew east to west to rake Belleau Wood, then turned left to shoot up the northern tree line where Donnelly had been hit. Each round-trip from end to end took about two minutes.

"Casey and I could clearly see the Marines," Dadiomoff said. "We tallied to target, triggering down on the tree lines next to them."

On each pass, Dadiomoff and Blasingame alternated firing rockets, to avoid going Winchester and running out of ammo. The fierce heat of the explosions flamed the bushes and ignited the bark on the trees. By the fourth run, Belleau Wood was ablaze, red flames flickering above the battlefield.

The Afghan soldiers in the middle of the Marine Ranger file were laughing as they walked toward Transformer.

"They say they're happy," Stevie, the interpreter, yelled. "They are on the Marine side."

When 1st Squad was halfway across, 2d Squad broke from cover and attracted its own bee's nest of snapping bullets.

"It was chaos," Rausch said. "I'm suppressing with my SAW. We cut through this section of compounds and I peek out to see this open field of mud with no cover. And out we step."

Rausch saw a PKM and an AK lying in the mud. He didn't stop to pick them up.

"There were small groups of farmers watching from the edges of the field," Rausch said. "None seemed to have a weapon. Yet I was hearing *pop, pop, pop*—rounds going by like on the firing range. It was definitely weird. Do you shoot at a farmer?"

In the Cobra, Dadiomoff had a problem. He was out of 20mm and small rockets, leaving only Hellfire missiles, which took three or four minutes to align. His fuel gauge indicated twenty-six minutes of air time remained, and the refueling base was twenty-two minutes away. In the Huey, Blasingame had ammo for one more gun run.

"I'll loiter," Dadiomoff radioed to Blasingame. "You finish the run and we'll see if we can get home."

The Huey made a final, lone strafe along Belleau Wood's burning tree line. Below, every Marine was exhausted after slogging through the mud and shooting for hours. The pace slowed to a walk, with Sergeant Dy yelling to speed it up.

"Mud was kicking up," Dy said, "like someone was lighting off tiny firecrackers. I was thinking, we won't all make it across. Someone's gonna get hit."

Toward the front, Laird staggered along with Espinoza on his back. Occasionally, Laird put him down, sprayed the tree line with his M4, then picked him up again. He felt spasms in the small of his back, but what the hell.

As the RPGs exploded and gunships roared overhead, Espinoza, doped up with two hefty shots of morphine, kept muttering, "This is so moto! So moto!"

When Garcia started across with the rear guard, a few Marines up ahead had paused to catch their breath.

"You're not armor-plated!" Garcia yelled. "Move your asses!"

Once Garcia and his rear guard reached Transformer, a relieved Dadiomoff turned his Cobra east away from the Green Zone and flew across the rocky desert toward Forward Operating Base Edinburgh. Blasingame followed in the Huey. If the Cobra spiraled down out of fuel, the Huey would land and pick up the crew.

The Cobra reached base with less than six minutes flying time remaining. In three hours of nonstop combat, the Huey and Cobra had burned through 2,600 rounds of heavy munitions and twenty-one high-explosive rockets, aimed at targets visible from one hundred feet in the air.

After shutting down their helicopters, the helicopter crews went to the mess hall for the Thanksgiving meal. They pushed the food around their trays, their minds still back at Transformer.

"If I never flew another mission," Dadiomoff told me later, "I'd done what I signed up to do. The Marine air-ground team worked. Mad Dog, Spokes, Casey, our crews—together we saved grunts from dying out on that Golf Course. But we lost a Marine, a platoon commander, that day. It didn't feel good."

In the afternoon, a medevac chopper landed at Transformer and lifted out Donnelly's body and the wounded Espinoza. Abbate placed his snipers along the wall, scoping west. Belleau Wood continued to burn. Stevie, listening over a captured Icom, said that the Taliban were attending to their casualties. Through the G-Boss, Marines at company headquarters watched as women with wheelbarrows and men on motorcycles took away dead and wounded. After guzzling down water and loading up with ammunition, 3rd Platoon hit the road, heading back to Fires. No one shot at them.

"There were fifty of us in one long trail," Garcia said. "You don't fuck around when hell walks by."

Lt. Cameron West was gone, and now a second of Kilo's three platoon commanders had been struck down in the snap of a finger.

Based on radio intercepts, informers, and the rash of funerals, the Taliban had lost about twenty fighters. For the Taliban to challenge gunships was a mistake, although understandable. Shooting at so many Marines out in the open was a natural instinct. The Marines were focused on retrieving Lieutenant Donnelly's body. The Taliban knew where they were headed, and why.

Once the shooting began, it spread and escalated quickly. As the sound and bedlam increased, orders shouted over the Taliban Icom radio nets were drowned out. The Marine interpreters listening in back at Inkerman couldn't understand what was being shouted, and neither could the Taliban gangs.

With several Marine squads to shoot at, the gangs stayed too long. Once they started shooting up at the gunships, their muzzle flashes told the pilots where the targets were. In a gunfight, the human brain switches off. It feels terrific to blaze away. The Taliban paid for losing control and abandoning their customary caution. The crews of the Huey and Cobra helicopters received the Bell Helicopter Award for the Outstanding Air Engagement of the Year.

Thanksgiving 2010 marked a change in attitudes. The Marines were more angry than intimidated.

"We were so pissed off after Lieutenant Donnelly," Sergeant Dy said, "it didn't matter how hard the next fight was. Our attitude was— you kill one of us, we kill twenty of you."

Revenge has spurred redoubled efforts in every war. In Vietnam in 1966, Battalion 1/9 engaged a Viet Cong battalion personally known to Ho Chi Minh, North Vietnam's leader. Angered by the losses among his favorite guerrillas, Ho promised revenge, calling 1/9 *"dib bo che,"* "the walking dead." He vowed to set mines until every Marine was blown up.

Only a few miles farther south, in my village of Binh Nghia, we were regularly attacked by the one-armed commander of the P-31st local Viet Cong company. He was furious that we had the nerve to move into his territory.

In Sangin, a few weeks prior to the Thanksgiving battle, to the north of Kilo's area, the Marine Red Devils squadron had bombed twelve targets simultaneously. The Taliban leader in Sangin, and more than a dozen of his fighters, had been killed.

Now, after the Thanksgiving battle, the Marines and the Taliban in Sangin were determined to destroy each other.

Chapter 7

GONE

"You never know how much you need Jesus until Jesus is all you got, because you live day to day, not knowing if you're going to have your legs or life the next."
—MICHAEL WILLIAMSON, ARIZONA

Day 51. 306,000 Steps

A week after Thanksgiving, 1st Squad headed north toward sector P8Q. They had a lead on the facilitator who had emplaced the IEDs that killed Buenagua and Peto. When the squad reached the corner of two tree lines, the two-man sniper team dropped off and hid in the underbrush. Abbate was carrying the M40A5 sniper rifle and Laird the standard M4.

"I've played peekaboo," Abbate said, "with this guy on the last two patrols. I know he's around."

First Squad pushed on and was crossing into another tree line when LCpl. Juan Palma, who was at point, spotted two sets of clothes folded neatly under a bush. The Marines grinned and settled in to wait. After fifteen minutes, the patrol again pushed on. Abbate and Laird didn't move from their hide. A few minutes later, a man on a motorcycle putted up a nearby path and signaled to a man with a shovel. The IED would be waiting when the Marines came back.

Sniper conditions were perfect. Laird whispered the range—115 meters. On scope. On target. Fire. The round ripped through the man's face just below his nose. Instantaneous body collapse. Matt Abbate laughed and punched Jordan Laird in the ribs.

"That," Matt said, "was for Buenagua and Peto."

The snipers caught up to the squad at the edge of a field. The Marines hid in the shrubs to see what would happen next. After a few minutes, two farmers ambled along. Through his spotting scope, Laird saw a rifle barrel sticking out of the bottom of a man-dress. When Laird dropped him, the tree line to the front erupted with AK and PKM fire.

First Squad quickly gained fire superiority and maneuvered toward a compound, marked on the photomap as Building 64. The Marines saw the head of a man in his fifties bobbing up and down in the furrows of a field as he crawled away from the compound. They shot him and the firing continued. One man kept sticking out his head at the compound wall.

"I see one turkey necking," Abbate said, concentrating on his sight picture.

Back at Fires, 3rd Squad strapped on their gear and headed north to help. At company headquarters, Spokes Beardsley called in two F-18s that were flying in a nearby holding pattern.

"We didn't think we needed air support," Lantznester said, "but they pushed the birds to us, so we used them."

Once air was on station, the procedure called for a shake-and-bake mission—one bomb to shake the compound to its foundations, followed by a bomb that burst in the air to scythe down any squirters. It was the forty-third close air support mission for the platoon.

The Marines were lying on line in a flooded, furrowed field, about 200 meters from the compound.

"Heads down!" Laird yelled.

As the lead F-18 swept in to their front, Sibley saw the black puff of an air burst by a rocket-propelled grenade that had a one-in-a-million chance of hitting the jet. The aircraft dropped a 500-pound bomb with a delayed fuse that obliterated a section of the compound wall. Following procedure, there was a pause of thirty seconds. A column of dust now clearly marked the target. The second F-18 rolled in, dropping another 500-pound bomb that exploded in the air, loosing a thousand sizzling shards to scythe down any enemy running out of the rubble.

Abbate was lying prone near Laird. As the F-18 roared in, Laird tried to squeeze his body inside his helmet. He heard a chunk of metal hit the ground and skid by him at sonic speed. He grinned in relief.

"That was close!" he said, turning toward Abbate.

Matt was lying within arm's length, facedown. It took only a second for Laird to see the blood gushing from his neck. Maybe Matt had raised his head for a fraction of a second to get eyes on the insurgent, or maybe the shard had torn through the ground when his head was down.

Laird pushed Matt over onto his back and ripped out a thick bandage. Other Marines rushed over, fumbling for their bandages. While Laird called for a medevac, the corpsman, Stuart Fuke, pressed gauze deep into the wound.

"Get off me!" Abbate gurgled, flinging Fuke backward.

Blood again spurted out.

"Hold him down!"

Four Marines pinned down Matt's arms and legs. Fuke grabbed

handfuls of gauze and LCpl. Dylan Nordell packed them into his neck.

"I can't breathe!"

"You couldn't talk if you couldn't breathe, bro!"

The Marines held Abbate firmly, keeping pressure on his neck. Laird checked the time. Five minutes had gone by. Where was the rescue bird? Come on, come on.

"This sucks," Matt muttered. "I can't believe it. This sucks."

"You're gonna be okay," Laird kept repeating. "We got the bleeding stopped. You're gonna be okay."

"It burns," Matt gurgled, "like fire."

"A good burn, bro. It's that stuff in the bandage that stops the bleeding."

Another glance at the watch. Twenty minutes. Finally, rotors were heard.

Esquibel knew wounds. In the Fallujah battle in 2004, when two fellow snipers lay wounded, he helped to stanch their blood flows. Now the situation was the same.

"When you take him," he radioed to the inbound pilot, "tell your crewman to keep the compression bandage tight."

The chopper came in fast, settling in on the far side of the field. The desperate Marines placed Matt on a poleless litter, a piece of canvas with handles, and sloshed over. Halfway across, they slipped, and Matt fell into the mud. The British chopper crew ran up with a pole stretcher and Matt was quickly loaded on board, face-first. Laird and Nordell crawled halfway inside to hold the dressings.

"Get off the bird!" the flight medic yelled, pulling at Nordell.

"Put your fucking hands on the compress!"

The crew was accustomed to grunts trying to stay with their wounded.

"We got him! Back off!"

As the helo lifted off, the crew shifted Matt's body and the mass of gauze flopped open.

"Hold it tight!" Laird yelled into the thumping noise of the helo blades. "Tight! Tight!"

En route to the hospital, Matt Abbate died on board the helicopter.

The entry in the 3rd Platoon log was brief.

"At 1300, 3rd sqd departed to sector P8Q IOT support ist squad ambushed to the north from bldgs 63, 64 and 65. Airstrike ended enemy threat but also created a friendly casualty. HA 1894."

Third Platoon had lost the sergeant with the easy grin and wacky expressions. The Marine who helped everyone else, always leading from the front, was gone. Six inches of exposed flesh between Matt's helmet and his armored plate. One inch of sizzling metal. A hand not pressed tight as the helicopter lurched skyward. Amid battle's fury, who can judge the cause?

Grunts live with death; they give it and take it. But they don't cope with death any better than anyone else. When one is killed, his comrades feel numb. Death is a black hole, the absence of explanation.

"It is not the young man who misses the days he does not know," the Roman general Marcus Aurelius wrote. "It is the living who bear the pain of those missed days."

The world of an infantryman is unlike any other, and a grunt's motivation in battle is hard to judge from the outside looking in. The grunt makes instant choices in the heat of battle. He must keep his honor clean even when fighting an enemy who hides among civilians. He must resist the sin of wrath. Abbate had shown the right example.

"When we went out the next day," Sergeant Deykeroff said, "there was no calling in artillery or anything like that. No revenge. That's what Matt wanted. Just do your job."

A few weeks after his death, the sniper platoon attended a remembrance ceremony. The talk wasn't of the fighting, but of Matt's weird sayings and oddball antics. He was friendly toward everyone, and the snipers took turns telling funny stories.

The battlefield is a giant craps table. Every *crack!* on patrol is a white-hot slug of lead breaking the sound barrier as it misses you. Any grunt who is not a fatalist is foolish. Death is as random as it is unexplainable. If you're very skillful—like Matt—you might tilt the odds a little, but not much.

Chapter 8

ENEMY RESPITE

"We're scared. [But] we still fight for those who can't fight."

—BRETT STIEVE, WISCONSIN

Sgt. John D. Browning, twenty-six, replaced Abbate as the leader of the ten-man sniper section. Although J.D. had grown up hunting and shooting on a ranch in Georgia, he considered sniper school to be the hardest training he'd received. He had to navigate by compass in the mountains for days on end, hit targets half a mile away, and accomplish missions behind simulated enemy lines. At the end of eleven weeks, only thirteen of thirty in his class graduated. Since then, he had served two tours in Iraq and been wounded once.

Browning admired the tenacity of the Taliban. One time, he was walking in a shallow ditch to avoid revealing his position when a Talib popped up on a wall only a few feet away, firing a PKM machine gun from his hip Rambo-style. Browning called him "real ballsy."

Fortunately for J.D., the machine gunner was the worst shot in Sangin. Not a single bullet hit home.

When Browning first arrived in Sangin, a British soldier had warned him, "You'll never get two hundred meters outside the wire." By the time he took over in December, J.D. was confident there was no mission he couldn't accomplish with a four-man sniper team. J.D. had read the book *Outliers,* which described how experts practice for 10,000 hours. J.D. had fired more than 100,000 bullets.

On December 4, 1st Squad was pinned down in sector V3J by PKM machine gun fire, and Mad Dog Myers had called back to Fires for mortar support. Back at Inkerman, the watch officer in the ops center listening to Mad Dog's emphatic radio transmission declared a TIC. Troops in Contact meant that a unit was in trouble and needed help, a condition that permitted the use of air and artillery. Spokes Beardsley authorized an air strike of four 500-pound bombs. The PKM ceased fire and 1st Squad returned to Fires.

To Captain Johnson's exasperation, 3rd Platoon had developed a perverse sense of pride. They never called in a TIC. Instead, they called for their own 60mm mortars, leaving it up to the company to decide if heavier support was needed.

Outside 3rd Platoon, the toll on the battalion was continuing. On December 5, Pfc. Colton Rusk, twenty, of Orange Grove, Texas, was shot and killed. He had been voted "senior class favorite" in high school. His parents adopted his military working dog, a black Labrador named Eli.

On December 6, Cpl. Derek Wyatt was killed, and the next day his wife, Kait, delivered their son, Michael.

The 800 grunts in the 3rd Battalion, 5th Marines had been together for eighteen months. Every man knew at least 200 others by their first names. A day after a death in one company, the other companies heard about it from someone who knew the deceased. That closeness spread stress in a way we grunts hadn't experienced in Vietnam.

One night out in the rice paddies back in 1966, my rifle company was hit by mortars as we crouched in our holes inside a grove of palm trees. It was pitch black except for the flashes of the exploding shells. One Marine, badly wounded, was screaming for his mother, his raw terror shivering to listen to. Others tried to comfort him, but he died shrieking. At dawn, his body was carried out in a poncho liner. He was one of five replacements flown in an hour before the mortars hit. We didn't even know his name.

The opposite was true in Afghanistan. When a grunt was killed, everyone in the company knew him personally. In 3/5, it was especially tough because the deaths were coming only a few days apart. On average, a battalion in Afghanistan lost one man a month; 3/5 had lost twenty in two months.

It was excruciating for the families back home. No one was emotionally prepared for the onslaught. At Camp Pendleton in California, the wives knew each other. The same stream of emails and cell phone messages that nurtured close bonds also heightened anxiety and made sleep impossible. Standard procedure was not to release names of the fallen until the next of kin had been notified. But in the digital and cell phone age, news of an IED strike carried back to the States as swiftly as the sound of the explosion. *Who was it this time?*

Gen. Jim Amos, the Commandant of the Marine Corps, met at Camp Pendleton with the families of 3/5. As an aviator for thirty years, Amos knew the shock that followed each plane crash. As a wing commander in Iraq, he had written letters to bereaved families. Now as the Commandant, he was meeting with the families of a battalion that had been battered, and would continue to take losses.

Amos was by nature an empathetic man, a listener with an understanding manner. When he met with the families, they hit him with a hundred questions: Why weren't we warned Sangin was a hellhole? We didn't sign up for this! What are we accomplishing? Why aren't the Afghans fighting? Why can't another battalion take some of the strain?

Amos was not willing to pull 3/5 out of Sangin. That would have been defeat, encouraging the Taliban to defend with equal ferocity elsewhere. To quote Napoleon, "The moral is to the physical as three to one." 3/5 was staying put to slug it out.

Of course, that brought discomfit to the families. The stress-filled meeting stretched on, hour after hour, with no resolution possible. Marines fought until they won. Their mascot was a bulldog. Winning was the core value of the institution.

General Amos was in a rough spot. It would be idiotic to express that battle cry to anxiety-ridden families. Nor could tender words assuage legitimate fear. The Marines of 3/5 would continue to fight and to die, and their families would continue to worry.

Day 56. 336,000 Steps

Garcia sent 2d Squad into P8Q, while he brought in 1st Squad from the north, trying to catch the enemy between them. As they waded across the wide canal at the entrance to P8Q, Sergeant Dy's squad drew PKM and RPG fire. The Marines dove for cover and Dy radioed the coordinates of five shooting positions located in the rubble of bombed-out buildings called "Bad-Guy Central."

Dy saw a man about 150 meters away duck out of one compound and run hunched over to a nearby rubble heap. Dy waited until the man lay down and then lofted a 40mm grenade onto the heap. The Marines laughed and followed up by shooting an AT4 rocket at the same spot.

First Squad had moved in from the north. While the smoke from the rocket was still hanging in the air, Mad Dog Myers came running down the canal bank, waving his radio handset.

"Dy! Get down!" he yelled. "Danger close!"

"What!?" Dy yelled back, deafened by the gunfire.

"Just get down!"

Myers grabbed Deykeroff, pulling him down while frantically waving at the other Marines to do the same. Seconds later, a salvo of hundred-pound Hellfire missiles chewed up the rubble pile. When his ears stopped ringing, Dy looked up to see a giant, gray four-engine aircraft thundering by.

Beardsley flew KC-130s, the workhorse of transportation aircraft. The KC-130 community had converted a few of the aircraft into the world's largest gunships. Weighing 160,000 pounds and over one hundred feet in length, "Harvest Hawk" bristled with missiles and telescopes. Using his pilot contacts, Beardsley had asked the Hawk to do a fly-by. When Mad Dog had heard the shooting from 2d Squad, he had persuaded Garcia to allow him to call in a Hellfire shot. Myers and Spokes Beardsley, back at Inkerman, were immensely pleased with themselves. Sergeant Dy couldn't believe the size of Harvest Hawk; it looked like a Martian spaceship.

After the firing stopped, Hawk spotted men carrying away three bodies. Uncertain whether they were Taliban or sympathetic farmers, Hawk let them live.

Three miles to the south, the battalion lost another Marine. An IED tore into Cpl. Christopher Montgomery, tearing off his legs and left hand and lancing his stomach with shrapnel. Before succumbing in the hospital, he told his mother, "God has a plan for me. I don't know what it is yet, but there's a plan, and whatever it is, I will fulfill it."

———

Back at Fires, there was a change in squad leaders during the first week in December. Sergeant Thoman was promoted to staff sergeant and moved to Transformer to take over as the platoon sergeant. Sgt. Philip McCulloch took over 3rd Squad. It was his second chance to show he had the right stuff. From Galveston, Texas, he had a rough upbringing and tended to be too hard on his men. Before the company had deployed to Afghanistan, he had been transferred from 3rd Platoon and assigned to company headquarters.

A month earlier, Mac had been riding in a Humvee that was hit by two rocket-propelled grenades. The first exploded, thrusting the truck sideways. The second grenade pierced partway through the armor and stopped next to Mac's face, failing to detonate. After a few days in the hospital, he convinced the doctors to let him return to the company. Now he was back with 3rd Platoon, anxious to prove his worth.

On December 8, he led 3rd Squad on a routine patrol. A kilometer north of Fires, a few Taliban shot at them. The patrol gave chase. A few more Taliban joined in, shooting from the west. The Marines hit one, but when they bounded forward, the gang to the north let loose a fusillade of bullets. The squad kept coming, hitting a second man before the others reached a far tree line. Now two kilometers from base, Mac called for mortar support and pushed after the gang, slowed by carrying their fallen comrade.

The running gunfight continued northeast for another kilometer. A third Taliban went down. Spokes Beardsley provided a section of two Cobras. When the gunships hit a few Taliban, a second section of helicopters flew over and joined in. Another Taliban went down. Harvest Hawk lumbered loudly onto station. As it flew over the battle area, one Taliban panicked and broke from cover. The Hawk belched and a forty-five-pound missile called a Griffin blew the man apart.

Geometry dictates firefights. The mortars and air permitted McCulloch to attack from 90 degrees. On this day, the Taliban gangs were strangely slow to grasp that. By continuing to shoot at the few Marines they could see, they were setting themselves up for repeated pounding from the air. Third Squad had counted seven Taliban bodies in the six-hour firefight and retrieved several weapons. But they were four kilometers northwest from Fires. If they took one casualty, it would take hours of fighting to get them out.

"You've had your fun," Garcia said. "Get your squad back here."

By the end of the first week in December, interpreters listening to the enemy Icoms heard the word "Marine" mixed in with Pashto. In radio messages back to Pakistan, the Sangin fighters used sentences like "Marines run toward bullets," or "Marines have more bullets than we have," or "Why don't you come over here and shoot at them!"

Third Platoon kept up the pressure. On December 9, 3rd Squad detained a man with a wad of Pakistani money and an Icom. Unable to understand what he was saying, the squad released him. Third pushed on and found two IEDs. When two men ran away, heading down a ditch, they shot them. Stashed nearby in a cornfield, the squad found Icom parts, a shoulder-fired antitank tube, and several rounds.

On December 10, 1st and 3rd Squads were clearing compounds when they were hit by a hailstorm of bullets from a tree line. Esquibel called in the 60mm mortars. Then he and McCulloch sneaked along a compound wall to flank the enemy, who escaped out the back.

At the same time, Lance Corporal Palma, miffed at being left behind, grabbed a second Vallon from an engineer too hesitant to advance. Palma swept clear a path off to the flank, so that the machine guns could lay down a base of fire without endangering McCulloch. Lance Corporal Xiong brought forward a 60mm mortar team by following the trail of bottle caps dropped by Palma. The mortars put a quick end to the fight.

The engagement illustrated how the platoon had matured. The squad leaders worked out their own coordination in the midst of the battle. They had opposite personalities. McCulloch was exuberant; Esquibel was reticent. Esquibel was aggressive and measured; Mac was aggressive and unrestrained. To Esquibel, it was positioning his Marines to avoid harm, and then killing. To Mac, it was killing, and then positioning his Marines to avoid harm. Yin and yang.

That afternoon, company headquarters told all squads to return to base due to a "sensitive situation." Secretary of Defense Gates was visiting the Marines in Helmand. The last thing the senior staff needed was for 3rd Platoon to be engaged in a major firefight.

"I will go back convinced that our strategy is working," Secretary Gates told the press at Marine headquarters. "Frankly, progress—even just in the last few months—has exceeded my expectations."

In fact, there were two strategies, and Gates, a career bureaucrat, either straddled both or was too confused to distinguish the fundamental differences between them. The Marines were driving the Taliban out of Helmand. They were intent upon killing the enemy. Yet Gates had termed them "parochial" because they resisted being placed under the direct command of the military headquarters in Kabul (McChrystal).

"Earn the support of the people and the war is won," McChrystal, the top commander, wrote. "Strive to focus 95% of our energy on the 95% of the population that deserves and needs our support. Doing so will isolate the insurgents. Take action against the 5%—the insurgents—as necessary or when the right opportunities present themselves. Do not let them distract you from your primary tasks."

Far from distracting, the Marines were focused on killing the Taliban. Clearly, there was a disconnect here.

In March 2009, Obama had approved what Gates termed "a fully resourced counterinsurgency campaign . . . breathtaking in its ambition." To undertake this "breathtaking" endeavor, Gates had appointed General McChrystal.

The general had previously commanded the 7,000 Special Operations Forces that specialized in nighttime raids to kill the enemy. But with the fervor of the true believer in the nation building Gates opposed, McChrystal demanded that the 100,000 conventional coalition troops focus not upon killing the enemy, but upon protecting and persuading the people to support the Karzai government.

The strategy was based on an impossible theory; indeed, Gates called it a "fantasy." Pakistan provided the Taliban with aid and a 2,600-kilometer sanctuary. Karzai had provided wretched leadership, giving the ten million members of Pashtun tribes no reason to risk standing against the ruthless and unpopular Taliban. On average, an American patrol passed through any given hamlet about once a week, while the Taliban came and went as they pleased. To provide real protection to the 5,000 Pashtun villages would require 200,000 Americans and twice as many helicopters. The resources were not adequate for the strategy, and Karzai opposed it.

According to COIN doctrine, the *main* American objective was to provide security for the tribes, thereby gaining their support. The *secondary* effort was "neutralizing the bad actors . . . in a discriminate manner." This was gibberish. Only by killing "the bad actors" could security be provided. And even when the Taliban were killed by 5 percent of the military effort, the tribes were not persuaded to support the Americans. Survey after survey confirmed widespread Pashtun resentment of our troops.

When Secretary of Defense Gates said in Helmand, "our strategy is working," it was impossible to know to which strategy he was referring—destroying the Taliban or persuading the tribes to reject the Taliban.

On the 14th of December, Captain Johnson ordered 3rd Platoon to cease patrolling and return to base. Back at district headquarters, the farmers were complaining bitterly about the platoon. With the constant fighting, they couldn't till their fields and it was time to plant the poppy. The Marines should patrol only every other day, they demanded—or, better yet, not patrol at all. Leave the district. We don't want your "protection."

Shortly after arriving, Lieutenant Colonel Morris had set up a council of elders to advise him and the district chief. The council included representatives from two major tribal confederations—the Panjpai, with a heavy Taliban influence, and the more moderate Zirak, whose strongest tribe was the Alakozai. Since the council included drug lords, even one called "Mr. Poppy," and Taliban sympathizers, Morris was skeptical of its benefit. Of thirty-one members, fifteen were suspected of criminal or insurgent behavior. But at least it was an outreach tool.

Lt. Karl Kadon, the battalion civil affairs officer, was just as skeptical. He was spending $250,000 a month on projects, many aimed to help the poorest subtribes. He had no illusions about buying loyalty. In four months, the villagers had whispered the locations of only four small arms caches, compared to twenty-six discovered by combined Afghan-Marine patrols.

Kadon was vexed by the exorbitant costs Afghan contractors charged for simple jobs. It cost a million dollars to blacktop one kilometer of flat road, and a quarter of a million per kilometer for gravel. Like any powerful sheik, Kadon set aside a few days each week to dispense cash for war damages and to mollify petitioners selected by the district chief. Sitting behind his desk, the lieutenant worked quickly, reviewing each case, and asking basic questions that often stumped the claimant.

"What is your name?" Kadon asked one farmer.

"Faisal Juzalay."

"The name on your card is Gazalan."

"He's my brother. What difference does it make? You pay me $500. My brother had two goats and two rooms blown up."

Kadon knew the tribes wanted the foreigners' money, while reciprocating with nothing.

"Your rich brother gives each goat a private room? Go away. Come back with a better story."

Skepticism about Pashtun honesty pervaded the ranks.

"Legitimacy in Sangin," Lt. Col. Steve Grass, Kennedy's deputy, said, "is the tribal acceptance of orders from whichever group can kill its enemies and reward its friends. About half of Sangin is on the side of the Taliban. The other half is waiting to see what happens."

In the face of an illiteracy rate of 80 percent, erecting a durable structure of government in Sangin was like building sand castles at low tide. Before the Marines, the British had to deal with a district governor who couldn't read or write. Such officials faked it by signing documents they couldn't read, later denying their own signatures. Resolution would be reached, only to be disputed the next day. This led to constant reappraisals, with bargaining based upon the comparative strengths of the negotiators at each round. As if this weren't exasperating enough, the true tribal leaders had long ago fled or reached a secret agreement with the local Taliban.

Afghan agreements with British or Marine commanders were temporary truces. No deal was considered binding a day or a week later. The residents of Sangin understood that the government had no enduring foundation. Here this year, gone the next. They considered no commitment sacred, sensibly aligning with whoever demonstrated power in their neighborhood or farming sector. Tribal and parochial politics, beyond the ken of Westerners, were as ethereal and complicated as a spiderweb. Want loyalty? Buy a dog.

"There was a pledge from the elders," Maj. Gen. Richard Mills said, "that fighting would cease by insurgents against coalition forces and foreign fighters [Pakistanis] would be expelled from the area." In return, the Americans would cease patrolling, release a murderous bomb maker, provide money, and allow the tribe to patrol its own area.

In mid-December, Kennedy and Morris decided to test the cease-fire proposal. Maybe some fence-sitters would side with those Alakozai sheiks who resented the local Taliban leaders. Maybe they'd actually kill some of the pricks. Of the six district governors in Kennedy's area, one was disreputable and three added no value. Sangin had one of the two decent governors. A cease-fire would raise his stature with the tribes. And it would show good faith with the British, who were keen on the idea.

Day 64. 384,000 Steps

On December 15, Kennedy agreed to a cease-fire limited to Kilo Company's area. The Alakozai would have a few weeks to prove themselves. With patrolling suspended, Morris shifted 3rd Platoon three kilometers south to clear a sector called Patrol Base America. Third Platoon was pleased it had gained the reputation of being a go-to unit. Browning's sniper section and the reservists, however, were not pleased that they had to remain behind to defend PB Fires.

Six hundred meters southeast of 3/5 battalion headquarters at FOB Jackson, the zone called PB America consisted of two square kilometers of tree lines, tangled underbrush, and deep canals. Marines on the staff at Jackson warned 3rd Platoon that PB America's terrain was treacherous.

The dividing line between the Marines and the Taliban inside PB America was a road called Carrot. An hour after arriving on December 16, Garcia initiated a reconnaissance across Carrot. First Squad began by launching a seventy-foot detonation cord. When the cord exploded, it set off a few IEDs and opened a safe lane. The explosion also startled some Taliban waiting in ambush.

When they opened fire too early, 1st Squad pitched out a few smoke grenades. Grabbing a Vallon, Palma rushed to the point position and led the squad forward. Seeing this, McCulloch swung 3rd Squad around the southern flank, while Garcia called in a mortar strike. The Taliban, squeezed between the two squads, pulled out.

The next day, 3rd Platoon again crossed Carrot, with India Company providing a forward observer team. The team picked out two Taliban spotters in a far tree line and called in artillery and F-18 gun runs. Under cover of the strafing, Sergeant Dy led 2d Squad into the smoldering underbrush. They found one body with a battery pack and an AK with a grenade launcher attached to the barrel. Searching farther into the bush, Dy stumbled onto a concealed canal. In the shallow water, a body was bobbing up and down, an AK barrel pointed skyward. When Dy dead-checked the body, Garcia yelled at him.

"Don't waste rounds," Garcia shouted. "He's a stiff. He's not breathing water."

Dy waded in to retrieve the AK. But instead of the sweet-sick stink of death, he smelled fresh fruit. The backpack of the corpse was stuffed with oranges crushed to mush by 30mm slugs. Under his man-dress, the dead man was carrying an Icom radio and a flashlight with a red lens for night work.

Second Squad pushed ahead to a mosque that was searched by a few Afghan soldiers. Waiting outside, the impatient Marines poked around and uncovered a cache containing an RPG, two rockets, IED materials, and several hundred AK rounds. When Delany, the Texas-bred-and-loving engineer, blew the cache, the detonation set fire to some corn stalks. Ignoring the flames, Delany was casually walking back to the squad when an IED cooked off. As he scampered safely away, the Marines broke out laughing.

Garcia shook his head.

"You go home in a body bag," he shouted, "and I get an investigation. Stop fucking around."

In high spirits, the platoon moved into an abandoned compound and raised the American flag. LCpl. John Payne, twenty-one, also from Texas, decided to pose with an AK while sitting on a donkey. The donkey responded by drop-kicking him into a wall. Payne planned to be a history teacher. At the least, the donkey would figure into a geography lesson.

On December 17, Battalion 3/5 suffered its twenty-first killed in action. LCpl. Jose Maldonado, twenty, of Mathis, Texas, had been a star football and baseball player in high school. More than anything, Jose had wanted to fight for his country.

"I'm honored to say we didn't lose him to a gang fight," his cousin said. "We didn't lose him to an overdose. We lost him in an honorable way, defending his country."

Day 72. 432,000 Steps

Two days before Christmas, 3rd Squad came across a group of men and boys idling by the side of a trail. This wasn't unusual. The men worked less than the women and often sat around, chatting with each other. This group had several batteries and cell phones. Sergeant McCulloch pitched the batteries into a canal, used the HIDE handheld computer to take their pictures and names, and signaled to the engineer, LCpl. Colbey Yazzie, to move out.

Yaz was a thickset, twenty-one-year-old Navajo with a bright smile, a diffident manner, and iron will. His father had served in the Army, and Yaz planned to return to the reservation in Nevada. He said he wanted to work in a mine with his uncle, but no one in 3rd Platoon saw that happening. Yaz liked San Diego and Laguna Beach too much.

LCpl. Arden Buenagua, killed by an IED on patrol with Lieutenant Schumacher a month earlier, had been Yaz's best friend. Yet day after day, Yaz took point, refusing to flinch at the death waiting under his feet. Third Platoon had a mystical faith in Yaz, who could smell IEDs.

As Yaz was moving northeast on the path, he "got a bad feeling." He probed the ground with his knife and uncovered a thick lamp wire. Following the wire for several feet, he found it was attached to two IEDs—thirty pounds of explosives packed in a Crock-Pot and ten pounds in a plastic jug. Two separate pressure plates were waiting to rip apart the Marines.

"My buddy Arden Buenagua deserves the credit," Yazzie told me. "He found ten IEDs in our first two weeks in country. He taught me what I know."

Later that day, a sniper from India Company, patrolling with 3rd Platoon, stepped on a pressure plate, losing his foot.

A few tree lines away and an hour later, 2d Squad shot a teenager. The distraught mother ran up, screaming, "Why did you kill my boy?" In response, Sergeant Dy held up the son's AK, gave her some money, and moved on.

Back in the States on Christmas Eve, LCpl. Kenny Corzine, twenty-three, of Bethalto, llinois, died of wounds suffered in an IED blast earlier in the month.

"We are all family," his pastor, Phil Schneider, said. "This is our son, our brother, our friend. His sacrifice was not in vain. His sacrifice has strengthened our community, our nation and our pride."

On Christmas Day, Cpl. Jeff Sibley, back at Fires after recovering from his gunshot wound, hitched a ride to company headquarters at Inkerman. He had a long talk with his wife, who was about to give birth to their daughter, Aubrey.

"Sergeant Dy had been born on Christmas," Sibley said. "He told me to make June 25 Aubrey's half birthday, so she'd get presents like other kids. I thought that was cool, because I'd be home by June."

I can't get my mind around living in two worlds. Back in Vietnam, when Marines went into the bush, that's all there was. We lived on the other side of the moon. One day in 1967 in my old village of Binh Nghia, when the squad was under the command of Sgt. Vinnie Mc-Gowan, the four-star admiral in charge of the entire Pacific theater dropped in by helicopter. Vinnie's team had been pressed hard and had fought well. With the cool of a West Sider from New York City, he showed the admiral his tiny fort, answered a few questions, saluted at the end of the ten-minute fly-by, and forgot about it.

Not so fast. An old-school gentleman, the admiral handwrote a note to Vinnie's parents, praising their brave son. You can imagine the rest. Mrs. McGowan, having not heard in weeks from dear Vinnie, dropped the official envelope on the floor and called Mr. Mc-Gowan. Also expecting the worst, he raced home, read the admiral's praise and wrote Sergeant McGowan a blistering response. For the next six months, every member of Vinnie's team wrote their wives or parents at least once a week.

Out in the bush, one-way communications to home is hard enough. How grunts handle Skype calls, hearing about the Oscars or overdue bills or homework, well, God bless them. As an old grunt, that is beyond my ken.

Also on Christmas Day, Rausch, who threw the red smoke to help a wounded comrade on Thanksgiving Day, happened to be at battalion headquarters when General Amos flew in.

"You've been in a hell of a fight," the Commandant said. "The least I can do is come out here."

The next day, Rausch returned to 3rd Platoon, proudly showing off a medallion the Commandant had given him. The rumor was if you slapped down that coin inside a bar in the States, someone was sure to buy you a drink. Rausch, twenty, would have to wait a year before testing the rumor, if he got home.

In a Christmas letter to the families of 3/5, Lieutenant Colonel Morris wrote, "The bottom line is that we are hurting the enemy and concurrently doing everything we can to help the Afghan people choose to support their national government over the Taliban."

The Marines were dying in the fields of Sangin. But there was no indication the people of Sangin would ever support their government in opposition to the Taliban.

On December 28, 3/5 lost another Marine, Cpl. Tevan Nguyen, twenty-one, of Hutto, Texas. He left behind a three-month-old son.

"He didn't drink, he never smoked and he believed in prayer," his cousin said. "He always made you smile."

Chapter 9

MIDWAY TO HOME

"The flag reminds us of the sacrifices made by so many."
—CHATCHAI XIONG, MINNESOTA

B y January, the two-week-old cease-fire in Kilo's area was breaking down. The unwritten agreement between the governor of Helmand and the Alakozai tribe proved too good to be true. Rather than leave the area, the Taliban had brought in reinforcements.

"We've reassured them [the Alakozai tribe]," Mills said, "that we're going to be here for them, that we're not going to abandon them."

However, the Marines were certain to abandon them. President Obama had already informed his commanders of the time limit. Before sending in the Marines, President Obama met with his top commanders. According to journalist and historian Jonathan Alter, Obama asked General Petraeus, "I want you to be honest with me. You can do this in eighteen months?"

At the time, Petraeus was in charge of the Central Command, the Middle East theater that included Afghanistan.

"Sir, I'm confident we can train and hand over to the ANA [Afghan National Army] in that time frame," Petraeus replied.

"If you can't do the things you say you can in eighteen months," Obama said, "then no one is going to suggest we stay, right?"

"Yes sir, in agreement," Petraeus said.

As of January 2011, those eighteen months had expired, and Petraeus had replaced McChrystal as the commander in Afghanistan. Both remained ardent advocates of the COIN strategy of nation building. But by 2011, President Obama had lost faith in the strategy. He ordered the slow but complete withdrawal of American forces. The Marines at Sangin might be the last in the queue to leave, but leave they would.

The Afghan forces were spotty at best. The Afghan army commander in Sangin, Captain Ahmed, was solid. He exhorted his men to fight. But the Afghan soldiers were few and dispirited. The police were worse. They never ventured out of the district square and had not made a single arrest since 3/5 had arrived. The National Directorate for Security agents were better, but not by much. On paper, the NDS was supposed be a combination of the FBI, Texas Rangers, and state troopers—tough, dedicated guys. During December alone, 3/5 had detained fourteen suspects, including two caught with IEDs. Two were sent to the provincial jail. The NDS quietly released the other twelve.

During the Christmas cease-fire, the local Taliban had remained unified and obedient to their seniors in Pakistan. Browning's sniper section, scoping the fields around Fires, reported that some farmers weren't responding to greetings and waves from passing Taliban. But the farmers hadn't gestured for them to leave. Rather than allowing the Alakozai to expel the insurgents, the cease-fire had enabled the enemy to regroup and bring fresh supplies into Kilo Company's area.

On New Year's Day, Colonel Kennedy ended the Christmas cease-fire. When I asked him about it, Kennedy shrugged. Despite nice words and solemn promises, he hadn't seen any change on the ground. So it was back to war.

The confidence of the local Taliban had been shaken. They had been pummeled in the Thanksgiving fight. Since then and despite the Tactical Directive, 3rd Platoon had become more self-assured in calling for air. Spokes Beardsley consistently came through, and Mad Dog Myers had an easy, if high-decibel relationship with the gunship pilots.

The local Taliban had complained to their high command in Pakistan: "Why don't you come over here to fight them!" The battalion staff referred to these as small-t Taliban, meaning locals and part-timers who rushed back into the fields to harvest poppy, with the drug dealers paying $10 a day. The Taliban was an amoeba drawn from a hundred Pashtun subtribes with dozens of different motivations. Afghan loyalties ran from the family to the clan to the tribe. In Sangin and a hundred other districts, the part-time wannabes took orders from the "made-men" within the local Mafia-like franchise that reported to the top council or shura, ninety miles away in Quetta, Pakistan.

The top boss there, Mullah Zakir, had been released from Guantánamo prison in 2007. During the 2010 cease-fire, Zakir responded to the pleas from Sangin by sending two or three dozen big-T hardened fighters from Pakistan. This followed the sensible procedure explained nearly two centuries earlier by Clausewitz in his classic book, *On War.*

"A commander can more easily shape," Clausewitz wrote, "and direct the popular insurrection by supporting the insurgents with small units of the regular army. Without these regular troops to provide encouragement, the local inhabitants will usually lack the confidence and initiative to take to arms."

Third Platoon sensed an immediate difference in enemy tactics. It was standard for the Marines, once they took fire from one direction, to flank that position. Now, whenever they flanked, they took fire from another angle. Instead of one PKM machine gun supported by two to four AKs, there were two PKMs, each covering the most predictable route toward the other. And with the ammunition resupply from Pakistan, Garcia couldn't rely on the Taliban pulling back after the initial exchange of fire.

The Taliban gangs, with the fighters from Pakistan sprinkled among them, began shooting at odd times and odd places. If someone supplies the bullets, enthusiastic teenagers stake out home turf by firing their rifles. Even when ordered not to do so, they can't resist pulling the trigger just to hear the noise and feel the recoil. It makes no difference whether you're in Vietnam in 1966, or Iraq in 2005, or Afghanistan in 2011; the local insurgents will always take potshots at a passing patrol. It seems silly, a testosterone thing, but it happens worldwide.

Halfway through its seven-month tour, the 800-man battalion had taken over 200 casualties. Over 500 IEDs had been found, and about another one hundred had exploded.

Of the 136 Marines in Kilo Company, nine had been killed and forty-five wounded. Even with some replacements, the company was down to ninety-six men, a reduction of 30 percent. Another dozen were banged up but refused medical aid above the company level. Like football players, they rejected by silence the very concept of traumatic brain injury. IED explosions were something you shook off. You saw that big white light, your peripheral vision had jagged zigzags, a fast movement caused a flick of pain around your forehead, and then after a week or so, you were back to normal. You were dinged, but all grunts are dinged. No problem for twenty or forty years, or maybe never. Back to work.

Every platoon in 3/5 was waging a straight war of attrition, exchanging American for Afghan lives. If the Marines killed enough Taliban, the Afghan army might—*might*—have the self-confidence to take over. The hope—*hope*—was that Afghan officials would then gain the support of the people, who would turn against the Taliban, many of whom belonged to their own families.

Strategy is the application of resources to achieve a goal. Attrition wasn't a true strategy, because its success depended upon Afghan actions that the Americans did not control. The Americans could not select, promote, or even tell Afghan officials what to do.

The grunts in 3rd Platoon were pushing the edge of the risk envelope. In ten weeks, one in three in the platoon had been killed, lost a limb, or evacuated with gunshot or shrapnel wounds. In eighty-two days, they had found seventy-five IEDs and engaged the enemy about forty times. Altogether, the platoon members had seen about 150 Taliban and killed a few dozen, in addition to sniper kills of over thirty. Even allowing for double-counting, this is heavy stuff. You leave the wire, you get shot at, you see a spurt of flame, you shoot back, you hear a *crump!* and screaming, you taste that sandpaper grit on your teeth . . . you're in it.

In Sangin, don't bat an eye walking past women and kids hacking at mud clods like it's the Middle Ages. Watch the tree lines, and pour out hell at the first tiny sliver of red flame. Listen to Garcia, Esquibel, Deykeroff, and McCulloch. When the dirt spurts up in front of your eyes, don't flinch. You're a grunt. Don't ask questions about the idiotic mission. Your job is to pull the trigger, keep your humanity, avoid Leavenworth, and support your insane buddies.

Conflicting Visions

The counterinsurgency doctrines in Afghanistan and Vietnam were polar opposites in emphasis.

In Vietnam, focus was upon defeating the enemy. After the war, in 1980, the Marines published a field manual that emphasized this: *"Concentrate on destruction or neutralization of the enemy force, not on terrain."* That objective carried over into Helmand.

"We need to challenge the enemy where he thinks he has strength," four-star Marine Gen. James Conway said. "There's no place in a zone where we're not going to go."

However, in 2006 there was a new COIN doctrine, agreed to by the Marines, that focused on winning the support of the population rather than challenging the enemy. The new idea was to persuade the people to reject the Taliban and actively work alongside the officials from Kabul.

In 1980, the focus was upon destroying the insurgents in order to protect the population. In 2006, the focus was upon stealing the affections of the population away from the insurgents.

"We're here for seven months. We can't do that counterinsurgency stuff of 'clear, hold, and build.' We can show that we go where we want, and the Taliban can't stop us," said Capt. Nick Johnson. "At shuras, the elders ask us to stop patrolling. Who's telling the elders to say that? My answer to the insurgents is—we'll never stop coming."

The gap between what the grunts were doing and what the 2006 theory was espousing was not resolved. A commander manages what he measures. If killing the enemy was not to be measured, then in order to "manage"—that is, to *win* a war—the commander would measure . . . what?

When the Japanese army seized Southeast Asia, including Singapore, Thailand, and Burma in 1941, British Field Marshal William

Slim invigorated a beaten British corps and eventually crushed the Japanese. In his memoir, *Defeat into Victory,* he explained his command philosophy.

"Commanders in the field," he wrote, "must be clearly and definitively told what is the object they are locally to attain."

From the top, no clear and definitive objective was ever issued about Sangin. Secretary Gates believed in "rooting the Taliban out of their strongholds." He was quite specific that this meant challenging and killing the enemy.

But for unexplained reasons, Gates appointed two commanders in a row who strongly disagreed. General McChrystal sternly ordered that only 5 percent of the military effort be focused against the Taliban. General Petraeus held a nuanced, Delphic view of the Taliban. His strategic approach had to be carefully read and parsed several times to extract meaning.

"If you don't want to have to kill or capture every bad guy in the country," he explained in an interview, "you have to reintegrate those who are willing to be reconciled and become part of the solution instead of a continued part of the problem.... [Conduct] a comprehensive civil/military counterinsurgency campaign.... Areas of progress, we've got to link those together, extend them, and then build on it because, of course, security progress is the foundation for everything else, for the governance progress, the economic progress, rule-of-law progress and so forth."

This "comprehensive campaign" had to be conducted at a breathtaking (Gates's adjective) pace, because Obama had already decided to bring our troops home. Petraeus wanted battalions like 3/5 to clear one area and then extend outward like an oil spot. The scope of the task was stunning: sixty coalition battalions had to clear five thousand villages and then persuade Pashtuns living in those villages, which were scattered amid mountains and deserts adjacent to Pakistan's vast sanctuary. Petraeus was out of time and troops. Yet with inadequate resources and without Karzai as a reliable partner, he persisted with nation building.

The Marines were employing the hard tactics Secretary Gates urged to achieve the soft strategic goals Petraeus espoused. As the secretary of defense envisioned, 3/5 would batter the Taliban. Then, as General Petraeus envisioned, the Marines would remain for years in Sangin to help with economics, governance, and the rest of nation building. Plus, they would expand the oil spot another twenty miles north, opening up Route 611 to achieve the seven-year goal of installing a third turbine to the Kajacki Dam.

Left unresolved was whether the population was the means of winning the war (Petraeus) or the prize for winning the war (Gates). Third Platoon was at the tip of the spear for both strategies, fighting in a soggy wasteland occupied by monsters who set in mines to rip off limbs without debating strategic theories.

"These farmers don't have the backbone," Mad Dog Myers said, "to stand up for their families. The Afghan soldiers won't fight. Know what rules out here? The aimed fire of us grunts."

But was the goal to defeat the enemy on the field of battle?

"Troops risking their lives," Secretary Gates wrote, "need to be told that their goal is to defeat those trying to kill them."

Not so fast. General Petraeus held a different view.

"We're making progress," he said, "and progress is winning, if you will, but it takes the accumulation of a lot of progress ultimately, needless to say, to win overall, and that's going to be a long-term proposition. . . . I'm always leery of using terms like 'winning' because it seems to imply that, you know, you just find the right hill out there somewhere, you take it, you plant the flag, and you go home to a victory parade. I don't think that's going to be the case here."

Secretary Gates believed the troops deserved to be told that the goal was to defeat the Taliban. The military high command, however, could not decide whether the Taliban were a mortal enemy that had to be destroyed like Al Qaeda, or a localized opponent with legitimate grievances against the Karzai cabal. Thus, there would be no winning or defeating of the enemy. All 3rd Platoon could do was slug it out, day after day.

Day 82. 492,000 Steps

On the 2d of January, 2011, 2d Squad surprised two men emplacing an IED on a canal bank 150 meters outside the wire. Tim Wagner, twenty, from Nebraska, killed them both. Farther on, Kameron Delany, the Texan who liked walking point, surprised another gang and killed five, an unheard-of number.

"We got lucky," Sergeant Dy said. "They didn't know we were back."

On a subsequent patrol, 2d Squad killed a motorcyclist talking on an Icom and found six IEDs. The batteries were buried among tree roots to make detection harder. The sensitivity bars on the Vallon jumped around, but the metallic source couldn't be located without chopping through the heavy roots. The engineers marked off the danger zones. In a few cases, the Marines had to take a running leap to clear the suspected IED lane.

Palma's risk taking caught up to him. He and Hess, the engineer, were at point when a low-order detonation lifted them thirty inches off the ground. Palma got up with a badly bruised left ankle, but refused to be medevaced. For the rest of the patrol, he continued with his practice of hacking holes through roofs rather than entering compounds through doors.

For Hess, the effect of the explosion was worse. It was the fourth time he had detonated an IED and his nerves were shot. Garcia decided that was his last patrol. Hess had done more than his share.

———

Third Squad, on the first patrol back into the P8Q sector, came under machine gun fire. McCulloch called 60mm mortar shells down on a compound. Once the Marines reached the building, they found PKM casings scattered everywhere, but the machine gun crew was long gone. The conclusion was obvious: during the cease-fire, along with being amply resupplied, the Taliban had regained their eagerness to engage. In response, the squads competed with each other, lobbying Garcia to send them to the north and east, where the opportunities to shoot were highest.

"Suppose you picked the top guys from my high school," Jeffrey Rushton, who had joined when he was twenty-four, said, "and gave them world-class military training. Even so, there's no way they'd fight as good as us. It's not just training, it's a feeling we have of how to work together."

The outpost's isolation strengthened those bonds. The fire pits and man-caves were their social centers. There was no administration, no daily emails from families, no first sergeant with a list of chores. Their entertainment was each other. Unlike in the rear, they didn't live two polarizing lives, with ten hours at work followed by two hours visiting home with the click of a mouse.

Some grunts did fall short of expectations. Before deploying, Captain Johnson had dropped from the company twenty out of 144 Marines. After a few months in Sangin, Lt. Tom Schueman, the 1st Platoon commander, concluded that four of his forty men were not pulling their weight. But he kept them in the platoon.

Likewise, Garcia had four marginal performers. Two replacements who arrived in late December were too out of shape to stay alert on patrol, so they were assigned to the sentry towers on base. A third Marine too often flinched under fire, and a fourth tolerated being shot at without returning fire.

"I didn't want to send a problem child to anyone else," Garcia said. "I found a spot for everyone."

While 3rd Platoon had been at Patrol Base America, the dozen Afghan soldiers left behind at Fires had become accustomed to doing things their own way.

"There was no unit cohesion," Staff Sergeant Arney, their adviser, said. "I worked with two sets of Afghan officers in three months. When an officer isn't present, nothing happens. Soldiers come and go as they please."

Terry Walker, the Marine chief trainer in Afghanistan, had a more nuanced view.

"To understand the Afghan system," Walker said, "follow the money. Sangin is a shitty place. No way to make a profit. So it's an advantage not to have soldiers physically present. You want ghost names on a payroll list. If 20 percent physical bodies are missing, that's 20 percent free money for someone. Hell, I'm surprised anyone's out at Fires."

While 3rd Platoon was gone, the Afghan soldiers had taken the firewood from squad fire pits and cut a hole in the wire to buy food from the locals. Upon returning, the platoon restrung the barbed wire. Things came to a head when McCulloch asked for a few Afghan soldiers to accompany his patrol. The procedure had been automatic for months.

Not this time. The askaris gestured for Mac to leave without them. No one ever accused Mac of being diplomatic. When he started yelling and cursing, his squad rushed over to form a semicircle around him. Both sides were armed. The call went out for Lieutenant Garcia.

With his wrestler's skills and arms as big as a man's legs, he was the toughest man in the platoon as well as the leader. As he ran toward the Afghan fire pit, by habit he was carrying his M4. The Afghan corporal who was the ringleader saw him coming, ducked inside, and came out with a PKM. Without thinking, Garcia reached out and slapped the machine gun to the ground.

For a moment, no one moved. A dozen armed men shuffled around, not saying a word. Eventually a few Afghan soldiers sullenly joined the patrol. Bad karma, never resolved while 3rd Platoon held PB Fires.

"My bad," Garcia said later. "I should have seen it coming and defused the situation."

The problem went deeper than unit discipline. The askaris weren't trusted. Since the murders at 3/5 headquarters, two more Marines had been gunned down north of 3/5's area. The motivations for these killings were murky, a perverse mixture of injured personal pride, Islamist ideology, and tribal culture.

With lack of trust on both sides, the performance of the Afghan soldiers at Fires did not improve despite patrolling with the platoon. In his unruliness, unpredictability, and toughness, the Afghan soldier reflected his society—fragmented, tribal, and troubled.

Day 89. 534,000 Steps

On January 9, a Marine sniper dropped a man at 820 meters and 2d Squad surprised a man digging in an IED. After he escaped into the reeds, Delany followed the IED wire back to a hootch, heaved in a stun grenade, rushed in, dragged out the man.

"We shoved this dude in front of us," Lantznester said, "thinking he'll be the first to get blown up. I'm at the back of the patrol, where I got careless and trip. I heard this *pop!* and the ground rocked under me. I tried to run. I was having a heart attack. The explosion knocked me to the ground but the big package in the jug didn't explode. It was just a low-order detonation. All I had was a sprained ankle and Sergeant Dy yelling at me to catch up."

After his lucky escape, Lantznester decided to pray regularly. He was sharing a man-cave with Wagner and LCpl. David Hickle. When they went to bed each night, they listened to Tracy Lawrence sing "If I Don't Make It Back," a somber, disturbing choice.

Wagner began, "Boys, if I don't make it back . . ."

"Have a beer for me," Hickle responded, "don't waste no tears on me."

Third Platoon considered themselves blessed because they could sleep at night. The Marine reservists stood the night watches in the cold sentry towers, allowing the grunts to rest.

After the Civil War, Gen. Ulysses S. Grant wrote, "I do not believe the officers of the regiment ever discovered that I had never studied the tactics that I used." Similarly, 3rd Platoon made up its own fighting tactics.

Coaches for professional football teams spend thousands of hours preparing for a three-hour game. Every one-hour firefight or patrol into sector P8Q was obviously far more deadly than a football match. Yet the generals and senior staffs, who shuffled data back and forth like self-licking ice cream cones, offered no new concepts or tactics for those doing the fighting. Garcia was the coach.

"No one above battalion came up with anything new for us," Garcia said. "We didn't receive advice on tactics. It was killing every day. No Afghan informant helped us. Intelligence didn't drive ops; ops drove ops."

Captain Johnson put a huge photomap on the wall of the ops center, with a pin designating every IED found and tree line where fire was taken. Garcia, Schueman, and the others gathered weekly with Johnson to figure out the enemy patterns.

The Pentagon had spent $22 billion to counter the IED, mostly to purchase a fleet of excellent bomb-resistant vehicles. The equipment on foot patrols in Sangin, where the threat was highest, was primitive. Third Platoon discovered most IEDs by eyesight, with the Walmart-style metal detector occasionally providing confirmation. Intelligence resulting in the arrests of the IED makers was close to nonexistent, due to the wall of tribal silence that protected the Taliban network.

At the village level, Afghanistan wasn't much different from Vietnam. Some villages liked you, others hated you, and all knew you were temporary. Because you were the outsider, no one publicly gave you information. You survived by being the better fighter. Third Platoon repeated what worked, and no one from company level up to the Pentagon came up with a better idea.

The secretary of defense and four-star generals visited Sangin. Given their public statements later, it was questionable whether they grasped the claw-and-tooth nature of the fight. Their statements were vague and upbeat. But in all fairness, how can seniors grasp what is going on? Supposing every layer in the chain of command is too optimistic by only 5 percent. When the estimate finally reaches the top, it will be 50 percent in error.

In Vietnam, I was surprised when an Israeli brigadier general with an eye patch embedded in the bush for a week with a platoon nearby to us. We were fighting every night, and Moshe Dayan left understanding our battle. There was no lack of courage in American generals. Many would like to repeat what Dayan did.

In today's military, however, decorum among generals demands deference. In 2003, Maj. Gen. Ray "E-Tool" Smith, a highly admired warfighter, joined me in Iraq to write about the war. Several active-duty generals tried to throw Smith out of theater. Why? Because he was too expert. It seemed improper for him to write about another general's strategy. Similarly, an active-duty general embedding with a platoon would be seen as meddlesome or distrustful of his own chain of command.

This posed yet another dilemma never resolved. While it was unrealistic for a four-star to embed with a platoon, a sentient grasp of the combat and the mood of the troops was essential to command. Shakespeare had portrayed Henry V as wrapped in disguise visiting with his archers on the eve of the Battle of Agincourt.

A gulf persisted between the bruising reality of the battle and a mental model that led generals to believe, for instance, that Sangin "will nurture women leaders." The 1980 Marine counterinsurgency manual stated, "Attack the enemy relentlessly. Saturation patrolling to locate and fix insurgent forces followed by offensive operations to destroy them is the essence of tactical operations." The manual called for the constant deployment of squad-size patrols "over a selected area so that insurgents cannot move without being detected." That was exactly what 3rd Platoon was doing: attack, attack, attack.

General Petraeus explained that the expansion of counterinsurgency into nation building constituted "the graduate level of warfare." Gone was the clear order to "attack the enemy relentlessly." In its place, the grunts were given multiple tasks. They were advisers, constables, project managers, dispute adjudicators, and community organizers.

There was no military precedent for these ambitious tasks. Most twentieth-century counterinsurgency efforts by the West had consisted of the imposition of colonial power. In the 1950s and 1960s, the British in Kenya and Malaya and the French in Algeria and Indochina had ruled as the political lords. They selected the local leaders and told them what to do. This kind of colonial command was not an option in the twenty-first century.

Nor did America's role in Vietnam provide a more instructive model. There, the Viet Cong insurgency was quelled by a web of informants, relentless killing, and imprisonment, and the Viet Cong's own disastrous decision to leave the countryside to attack the cities in conventional formations in February of 1968.

In Vietnam, the Combined Action Platoons with American squads living in the villages succeeded because the people wanted them there. Conversely in Sangin, there was not one village where the residents would accept Americans. Even the Alakozai tribe that professed to hate the Taliban wanted the Marines removed from the district. Most of the farmers wanted nothing to do with Marine patrols, with their fearsome firepower. Higher headquarters might claim the intent was to "protect the population." In truth, the grunts were out there fighting alone without a population *willing* to be protected.

Third Platoon with a few token askaris were searching compounds, the exact behavior that the president of Afghanistan, Hamid Karzai, was condemning. But if they didn't search, the Taliban would have safe havens. Third Platoon set the record for the number of air strikes, the exact behavior General McChrystal had issued his Tactical Directive to prevent. In ten weeks, 3/5 had called in 177 artillery and air strikes, including twenty-four Hellfire missiles and forty-four 500-pound bombs. Without such heavy indirect fire, 3rd Platoon would have had to withdraw from Sangin.

The vast majority of compounds contained no civilians. The logbooks of 3rd Platoon and Kilo Company contain scattered references to civilian casualties among hundreds of entries. Undoubtedly more civilians were killed and compounds destroyed, but not in massive numbers. A farmer did not keep his family in a compound in areas where the Taliban at any moment could rush in, knock murder holes in the wall, and shoot at Marines, drawing a torrent of direct and indirect fire.

Conversely, 3rd Platoon had no social or amicable contact with the people. In response to my survey, three of its members said they believed the Afghan people are "worth fighting for," nineteen believed they couldn't be trusted and aligned with the Taliban, and thirty believed they were "OK, but intimidated by Taliban."

The doctrine of counterinsurgency as friendly persuasion was imposed from the top down. The top commanders in Afghanistan, together with the chairman of the Joint Chiefs, were its advocates and enforcers. They gave the orders. They weren't the coaches. They were the referees, ensuring our side played by their rules, while the other side made up its own rules.

Third Platoon, engaged in a straight-up slugfest, was fortunate. Colonel Kennedy, the regimental commander, had suffered losses trying to enact one-sided COIN in Ramadi, Iraq. On one visit to Inkerman, Colonel Kennedy was in the ops center when a video feed showed two Taliban crossing a footbridge. The watch officer was debating whether to call for artillery. Kennedy told him to make the call; if anyone objected, he'd handle it.

He had only one rule—clear, firm, and concise.

"Finish every firefight," Kennedy said, "standing on the ground where the enemy opened fire."

By the end of December, the snipers with 3rd Platoon had recorded forty kills and spent hundreds of hours glassing the fields and compounds.

"Going into January, our tactics didn't change much," Browning said. "We tried building the standard sniper hides, shifting our position at dusk, and dropping off ambush teams, but you can't really hide when every man, woman, child, and dog is watching you. What worked best was staying with the squads."

The Taliban were staying farther away from the Marine patrols, taking shots from 300 to 400 meters. The snipers had developed a sense for what were called "patterns of life"—things like when the villagers awakened, their morning ablutions, who worked in the fields, who attended evening prayer, and which families visited each other.

Eventually, the snipers could pick out which farmers were Taliban, even when they weren't openly carrying weapons. Most of the fighters were between twenty and thirty years old, clean, well groomed, with laces in their Skechers. They walked erect, with the casual arrogance typical of power among young men. Many seemed pudgy, because they were wearing magazine chest rigs beneath their man-dresses. The local Taliban didn't open fire when civilians were around; those from Pakistan didn't seem to care. Both groups used women and children as shields when they moved across the open. They knew the American snipers were out there somewhere.

In Helmand, every U.S. operations center down to company level was equipped with video screens attached to the fifty-foot G-Boss telescopes or, even better, tethered blimps floating at 5,000 feet, too high up to be shot down. Both systems had cameras that monitored in startling detail a circumference of two miles. An Icom could be seen in a man's hand, or a rifle barrel protruding from a pants leg. Dubbed the "Godcam," aerial surveillance made it impossible for enemy fighters to dart undetected across fields during firefights.

"The biggest difference since we got here in October," Capt. Tim Nogalski, the battalion intelligence officer, told me in January, "is that every company is getting technical tip-offs."

Still, the grunts at Fires gave the telescopes mixed reviews. They resented operators back at company using the cameras to spy on their outpost and to comment on tactics during patrols.

"Even when a squad leader," Garcia said, "puts a fire team in the wrong place, it pisses him off when the ops center calls to help him out."

Discounting this normal infantry bitching, the technologies were amazing. If the Taliban talked on phones, big ears were listening. If they moved, Godcam was watching.

When I dropped by the 3/5 operations center in January, a corporal was monitoring video of the market 300 meters outside the gates. On a huge, color flat screen, he zoomed in on two men sitting on a motorcycle. Dozens of men were walking by, browsing from shop to shop. Each passerby veered a few feet around the two men, without exchanging greetings. The two looked alert, not nervous, accepting the deference as their due.

"They're dirty," the corporal said.

As he kept track with the camera, the two puttered up to a rickety door on a mud building. A man came out, glanced around, and handed them a bulging sack. The corporal stayed focused as they drove up another crowded street. When they stopped for a few seconds at a dingy door, an arm thrust out a pickax. The two puttered away with the sack and the pick.

"Here we go!" the corporal shouted, as a dozen Marines stopped what they had been doing to watch the show. "I got Hawk on station!"

Five thousand feet above, Harvest Hawk was chugging in from the southeast, out of hearing range.

It was odd, watching two men committing unintentional suicide. They drove to a low dip in the road, as the bright aluminum camera peered down at its prey. One doomed Taliban hacked energetically at the hard-packed dirt road, while the other placed on a blanket each chunk chopped loose by the pick. They then pulled a jug from the sack and began to attach wires to it.

In the quiet ops center, we heard the voice of the pilot in Harvest Hawk.

"I have visual. Bombs away."

Bombs away? Like grunts, pilots change gears but not attitudes.

Hawk let loose a Hellfire. Inside the ops center, we heard clearly the loud *bang!* of the missile. Outside on the road, so did the two targets. Inside three seconds, they had hopped on their cycle and were gone. The missile had a twenty-second time of flight; they were ten seconds and 200 meters down the road before the explosion.

The corporal stayed focused on the pair as they raced up a hill and around a few blocks, before stopping in front of a large house. The rider banged on the gate, and when it opened they pushed inside. Within thirty seconds, they were pushed out. The owner of the house was no fool.

They hopped on their cycle and sped out of town toward the Green Zone. The camera patiently followed as Hawk circled. Once they hit an open stretch of road, the AC-130 fired a second Hellfire. The video screen showed a big black puff. Once the slight wind blew away the dust, the twisted cycle and two bodies lying in the road could be seen.

"That's a shack!" the Hawk pilot yelled over the radio.

No one in the battalion ops center suggested sending out a team to search the site. Not worth the risk. Let the townspeople bury them.

On a macro level, the killing was a demonstration of resources versus sympathy. The Americans had the wealth to apply millions of dollars of high tech to kill two men. More millions had been spent in Sangin for generators, schools, clinics, and roads. Yet the motorcyclist bombers had nonchalantly driven through the crowded market, unafraid of betrayal by those the coalition had aided for years.

By January, the shooting quieted down around Inkerman. One day, Corporal Laird joined a routine patrol with Lieutenant Schueman and 1st Platoon. When nothing happened for a few hours, they took a snack break on a grassy knoll above a few compounds. After eating a candy bar, Laird lay down with his cheek on his rifle butt. Idly looking through his scope, he saw a small opening in a compound wall 300 meters away. Crouched there was a man talking on an Icom, guarded by a second man holding an RPG launcher. As Laird put his finger on the trigger, the RPG gunner walked across the opening. When the radioman followed, Laird hit him twice in the chest and watched as the man stumbled and disappeared from his sight picture. The next day, the corporal manning the G-Boss telescope at Inkerman reported a well-attended funeral near the compound.

"Before we got here," Schueman said, "we listened to lectures about counterinsurgency, drinking tea, meeting with key leaders. That was all bull. No matter what we do here, the people believe we'll leave and the Taliban will come back and kill them. Whenever the shooting dies down, I know it'll pick up again."

Up at Transformer, the fighting had slackened after the death of Lieutenant Donnelly. Many local fighters had died in that fight and the outpost sitting on Route 611 didn't threaten the interior Taliban routes to the Sangin market. By mid-December, the Marines had secured the mile of hardtop road between Inkerman to Transformer. Supply vehicles no longer had to take the circuitous six-hour trip through the desert. With 611 open for traffic, the trip took six minutes.

"For us up at Transformer," Sergeant Sotelo said, "things improved by Christmas. Over a hundred refugees moved in around our outpost. We bought our food in the market. Kids accepted candy from us, instead of running away. They were flying kites that the Talibs had forbidden. Women walked out of compounds with their faces uncovered."

In mid-January, though, Sotelo was walking by an alley where children were playing when a burst of bullets sent him flat. Not seeing the shooter, he held his fire while the kids sought shelter. Then he angrily demanded that the villagers tell him what the hell was going on.

What were they doing? Those were their own kids out in the street. The Marines were spending $20 a day in the market. Why were they being so stupid?

Four fighters from Pakistan sneaked in a few hours ago, the villagers said, and threatened to kill anyone who informed on them. After that, the outpost took harassing fire, regardless of whether civilians were present. An enemy sniper took up a roost in Belleau Wood. Every afternoon, when the sun behind him was shining like a spotlight on Transformer, he took one or two shots at the sentry towers. It was only a matter of time until he killed a Marine.

A sniper team moved up from Fires and spent their first day rigging a dummy that was propped up on the wall, with the helmet, head, and shoulders showing. LCpl. Willie Deel crawled out on the sandbags, checking to see if the dummy could be seen from Belleau Wood.

"Deel, that's not smart," Corporal Laird said.

His warning was followed by the *smack!* of a bullet hitting a sandbag. Deel leaped back amid unkind comments about who was the dummy.

When the enemy sniper proved too crafty to kill, Captain Johnson sent up a 105mm recoilless rifle that fired a twenty-pound explosive shell. The sniper was sticking to his afternoon schedule. After a few days, the recoilless rifle crew had narrowed down the location of his lair. When he again sniped, the response was a half dozen shells aimed directly at the firing point. The sniping ceased.

A grunt accepts the danger as he does the mud, cold, heat, sweat, stink, and exhaustion; it's his environment. He copes with his own sense of humor.

"I got shot in the helmet," Cpl. Kevin Smith, a sniper, said. "I'm walking across a roof and *whang!* I'm sitting down, holding my helmet with a dent from a bullet. When I get back on my feet, my bud-dies refuse to stand next to me. I'm bad luck. My friends!"

Smith had a friend, Cpl. Jordan Gerber, who had a false front tooth. Before going on patrol, he would place his tooth inside his hollow butt stock. One day, when he was under fire, the stock popped open and out spilled the tooth. The Marines pawed through the dirt with bullets zipping by until they found it. A few weeks later, the same thing happened again. This time, the Marines didn't stick around to look for it.

Back home, there were tears and anxious phone calls. Jane Conwell Morris, the wife of the commanding officer, was getting a hundred emails each day, fielding the anger and anxieties of 800 families. One wife was convinced she heard her doorbell ring every night, with someone waiting to announce her husband's death.

"The families, especially the spouses, really almost lost their minds," Lieutenant Colonel Morris said.

In the age of Twitter, what happened on the battlefield instantly affected the home front. And what happened at home instantly reached the troops.

After being blown up in October, Lt. Cameron West had been evacuated to Bethesda Naval Hospital. For the first week, he had scarcely slept, fighting for breath as his sucking chest wounds healed. His mother, a nurse, and his father visited him each day. Both praised the medical care he was receiving.

Still, it was rough going. For weeks, bacteria gnawed at his right stump, requiring a painful daily wash-out to peel away the infected flesh from what was left of his limb. He lost two more inches off his leg and developed six infections causing blood clots that threatened to stop his heart.

"I had it easy," Cam said, "compared to the others. I saw guys from

3/5 with worse amputations than my leg and hand. Even my eye was getting a little better. Doc Long was paralyzed from the waist down. I was angry because I felt helpless. I wasn't in the fight."

In January, missing one leg, one hand, and one eye, Cam was transferred to Balboa Naval Hospital in San Diego, seventy miles south of the Marine base at Camp Pendleton. By now, he was friendly with a dozen other amputees and a hundred other injured from 3/5. They were assigned to what is called the Wounded Warrior Regiment to bolster each other's spirit. Cam was their leader.

So Jane Morris asked Cam to attend a packed meeting of 3/5 families and represent those in the fight 6,000 miles away. Before doing so, Cam reached back to Captain Johnson and his old platoon out at Fires. He was enormously popular, and 3rd Platoon told him their side of the story. When he stood to speak at the meeting, he was nervous but prepared. Speaking firmly to distraught wives and mothers was not a task for the faint of heart.

"Everyone in this room is scared and concerned," he said. "But I hear it from my brothers out there too. They need your support, not your complaints or tears, not from mothers, sisters, wives or girlfriends. Sure, you all have hard days—kids acting up, bills to be paid, things going wrong. Don't talk about that. Don't send whining emails or post idiotic comments on Facebook. For the rest of his tour— fourteen weeks—don't say one negative thing to your Marine. He has enough on his plate. You should be worrying about him; he shouldn't be worrying about you. He needs you. Keep saying, I love you, I miss you, I pray for you."

Chapter 10

THE ROUTINE

"There's no end to the bloodshed."

—VICTOR VALDEZ, TEXAS

I
n early 2011, I again flew to Helmand Province and met with Col. Paul Kennedy. In 2004, I had embedded with his battalion in Iraq. When I met Paul at his regimental headquarters south of Sangin, he was as terse as ever.

"You'd be bored and ignorant up here at regiment," he said. "I'll drop you off where the fighting is."

Day 91. 546,000 Steps

I arrived at Patrol Base Fires in time to join the morning patrol.

By way of greeting, Vic Garcia handed me two straps.

"You know the drill," he said. "One's for you. If you have to use the other one on someone else, twist the knob until he yells. And stay inside the bottle caps. We don't want to have to carry you back."

Like the horse stirrup or the bicycle, the modern tourniquet is so simple that it took centuries to invent. Cinch up the strap, twist the fist-wide knob tight, and the blood stops gushing out. A half century ago, my platoon in Vietnam had used narrow elastic tubing that sliced into the flesh without fully stanching the bleeding. In Vietnam, one in four of our wounded died, mainly from loss of blood. In Afghanistan, one in seven died, but the number of amputations skyrocketed.

The fifteen Marines in 3rd Squad wore armored vests sprinkled with dried mud, tan camouflage uniforms hard to detect from a distance, and weathered, unsmiling faces. A few wrapped tourniquets around their thighs; most stuffed them in their med kits. I unwrapped and stowed a tourniquet in each breast pocket.

Garcia didn't talk, keeping his distance as the Marines fell into a loose line. I noticed the tattered photomap attached to his left hand like a wedding band—the lifeline for calling in fires. At night, he probably used it as a pillow. On patrol, you'd have to cut off his fingers to pry it loose.

The patrol was heading north to sector P8Q. The mission was to walk for a couple of miles, avoiding mines while waiting to be shot at, hoping in return to light up the shooter. We passed by the mortar tubes aligned toward their barber-pole-aiming stakes, left the wire in silence, forded an icy stream, and plodded along in sloshing boots. Every patrol got wet, muddy, and miserable at the start, so there wouldn't be any hesitation later. The winter-dead landscape looked like a sepia portrait of Oklahoma farms during the Great Depression. Everything was a lifeless shade of brown—the fields, the furrows, the trees, and the walls of the compounds, some clustered together, others standing off alone.

The patrol wasn't in a hurry. Up at point, Yazzie, the twenty-one-year-old engineer, walked slowly, sweeping his Vallon back and forth with his eyes on the LED magnetometer needle on the handle of the metal detector. He focused on the dirt inside the length of his shadow, rarely glancing up, while his partner, LCpl. Kyle Doyle, watched out for snipers and dropped the caps of water bottles.

We walked with the war's paradox under our feet—fresh poppy plants. Looking as innocent as lettuce heads, the mind slayers were springing to life in every field. Back in the States, we were fighting an ever-losing war on drugs. Here in a faraway country, we were fighting a war on terror that required toleration of the very heroin we waged war against at home. Afghanistan's export of drugs created more human casualties than did the fighting. But to eradicate the poppy was the surest way to drive the farmers into the ranks of the Taliban.

The farmers had planted them in long, straight lines and we bruised few as we followed our own straight line, guided by the water bottle caps. Behind Doyle came the two-man machine gun crew. Sergeant McCulloch, twenty-four, followed the machine gunners. On a recent patrol, a bullet had nicked the inside of his thigh. Fearing that a second Purple Heart would mean a transfer to the rear, he bandaged the wound and refused to have it checked out at the battalion aid station. He walked with a limp, but so far had avoided infection.

The patrol walked in file with no concealment, preferring the open fields to the shrubbery alongside the irrigation ditches. Within eyesight of the platoon's fort, farm life was normal. Scrawny cows and sheep wandered freely, nibbling at stray patches of grass trampled as smooth as putting greens. Carrying thin switches, male shepherds, ages eight to forty, languidly followed their flocks. Wending north, the patrol walked where possible in the fresh hoofprints of the animals.

A thin man in a dirty brown man-dress and a shabby turban, followed by an old man and a few boys, scampered across a ditch to intercept the patrol. As the Marines walked past, he squatted down and extended a piece of paper, his mouth soundlessly agape, displaying enormous front teeth. McCulloch signaled with a clenched fist to halt.

"Turgiman," the turban man said, waving the card. "Turgiman."

The card was a standard form for listing war damage. If a Marine signed it, with an estimate of the damage, the farmer would collect money at district headquarters. Like most Marines, Mac had picked up a smattering of pidgin Pashto. He tried out simple words and gestures until he got the gist.

"Toothy here says we killed his cow," Mac said. "He wants two hundred bucks."

"Where's the cow?" Garcia asked.

"Says he buried it weeks ago."

Garcia dismissed the claim with a wave of his map.

"Dig it up," McCulloch said, handing the man back his chit, "and eat it."

The patrol zigzagged along, with the rear guard picking up the bottle caps. Each Marine had a sector to watch. One glance around, one glance down at the caps. Around, down, around, down, never straying out of line.

Near a footbridge across a canal, Yaz clenched his fist, knelt, and scratched at the dirt. He took out wire cutters, snipped a few wires, held up two small boards wrapped in tape, and threw them to me. Glued to the underside of each board was a strand of wire. When a foot pressed down on the boards, the two wires touched each other, completing an electrical circuit connecting a flashlight battery to a plastic jug filled with explosives. Yaz attached a small charge to the IED, blew it up, and the patrol continued.

About a mile from the fort, the Marines passed women and children running pell-mell from a compound. More than a dozen cut across a field in front of the patrol, casting frightened glances. Over the radio, "Rubber Duck"—the call sign for a radio intercept unit at Inkerman—warned that two Taliban gangs were getting ready to open fire. Off to the right, three men on motorbikes puttered along a dirt road, paralleling the patrol.

"Dickers," McCulloch said. "Cheeky bastards."

It reminded me of a John Wayne western, with Comanches on the ridgeline keeping pace with a line of troopers. The Marines seemed indifferent to their watchers.

"They're not idiots," Garcia said. "Exposed like that, we'd cut them down in a second. Any shooting will come from up ahead, after the people clear the area."

Gradually the patrol route diverged westward from the road and the cheeky bikers. Halfway across a field, in a furrow with no discernible difference from a hundred others, Yaz stopped. Head down in concentration, he swept the detector back and forth a few times and raised his right hand, signaling an IED.

That's what makes the IED so insidious. Most give off a low magnetic signature. But some are missed, no matter how careful the sweep man is. Plus, the Taliban are sloppy. Fearing overhead drones, they hastily dig in the explosives and scamper away. Marines take extra care at the obvious places, like a footbridge or a trail intersection. But a Marine, farmer, or cow can step on a pressure plate buried anywhere, with no rational reason why that spot was chosen.

"Some of my engineers freeze up over time," Garcia said to me. "They know every step could be their last. After a while, they move slower and slower. And some are like Yaz. They keep up a steady pace, patrol after patrol. He never slows down."

Yazzie trotted back to talk with Garcia and McCulloch. All agreed to get out of there.

"We'll mark this spot for a sweep by the engineers," Garcia said. "It's too unstable for us. The assholes have rigged traps all around here."

Assholes, pricks, stinkies, fuckers, muj . . . the troops had no pet name for the enemy. Any term of contempt would do. Rarely did they use the words Taliban or terrorists.

For another half hour, the patrol walked north, with Vic Garcia in the middle of the file, far enough behind the point not to be pinned down, far forward enough to call in fire. Third Platoon's patrol area encompassed six square kilometers, containing hundreds of compounds scattered across about 2,000 fields. Vic's treasured photomap, overlaid with waterproof acetate, showed every field and tree line, with each compound stamped with a bright yellow number.

Vic occasionally called out something like "Number 23 at our eleven o'clock." Various Marines would yell back, confirming they were looking at the same compound. If there was disagreement, the patrol took a knee while Vic double-checked and oriented everyone on the same hundred-meter grid. They knew the hot spots, the tree lines and compounds where they were most likely to take fire. If even one Marine disagreed or was uncertain about the number of a compound, the patrol halted while Garcia double-checked their location on his GPS. They weren't in a rush. They had no appointment to keep, and the last thing they wanted was to call for fire support while not certain where they were.

When we reached the northern edge of P8Q, Garcia called out to me. "This is Belleau Wood," he said, "where we fought on Thanksgiving."

I looked at the shattered trees to my front and vast expanse of weeds and dirt leading back to Outpost Transformer to my right. I imagined Matt Abbate shuffling under fire across that field in the glutinous mud, pistol in one hand and the other holding the litter containing Lieutenant Donnelly.

In his classic book *Battle Studies,* French Col. Ardant du Picq observed that even brave men eventually shirk under fire. To overcome this, he urged commanders to instill in their ranks an esprit de corps—a "spirit of the body" that infused the soldier with the heritage of his unit.

At Belleau Wood in 1918, the Marines had checked the German advance on Paris. The 3rd Platoon log entry for Thanksgiving 2011 included the words Belleau Wood. Whoever wrote the log had linked that battle to their fight nine decades later. A "spirit of the body."

Yaz moved at his meandering pace for another half hour before stopping at the edge of a burnt-out field. On the far side about 300 meters away stood two large compounds, their walls gouged by bullets. White Taliban flags, the size of hand towels, were sticking above the tops of compounds farther in the distance. While the machine gun and sniper teams set in their bipods, Garcia radioed his GPS location back to the mortar pits.

"A blind man can see us here," Garcia said. "We'll give the muj thirty mikes to decide if they want to come out and play."

The Marines settled in behind their rifles.

"The stinkies can't resist sneaking a peek," McCulloch said, watching the walls through his telescopic sight.

Ten or fifteen minutes passed. No farmers ventured into the fields. The Taliban flags fluttered in the slight breeze.

"I see one," McCulloch said. "Murder hole on the left wall at three o'clock. Turkey necking."

Someone was stealing quick glances out of the small hole poked through the wall. Mac steadied the telescopic M4 on his left knee, sling wrapped in shooter position. Without taking his eye from the scope, he tried to direct a Marine sniper onto the target. When that failed, he took the shot himself. He squeezed off one round from his small caliber 5.56mm rifle. The *pop!* sounded as harmless as a kid's firecracker.

"Get him?" Garcia asked casually.

Seven out of ten times, a Marine should hit a six-inch diameter hole at 200 meters.

"Don't know," Mac said. "I think I saw him flinch."

No return fire came from the compound.

"Want me to look?" Mac asked.

Garcia shook his head without bothering to speak. By this time in the deployment, the platoon was calling him "the Juggernaut." No one wanted to let him down or dared speak back to him. There was no way he was allowing a Marine to cross that open field to check it out. Maybe the man was dead, and maybe not. Either way, that was the end of it.

A few Marines munched on crackers. One or two sipped water from their CamelBaks. The written rules didn't allow shooting at a man peeking through a hole in a wall. The rules required a man to be pointing a rifle before he became a target. No one said *good shot,* or *you probably missed,* or *why'd you take that shot?* Third Platoon had modified the rules to take account of Sangin.

After a while, a man in a black turban and tan man-dress puttered by on his motorbike. He showed no fear when the Marines waved him over.

"Delta rasha!" Mac yelled. "Come here."

Mac grabbed the man's hands, muttering that they were too soft for farm work. The man reached into a handbag and handed over a clean document. McCulloch held it up to the sun and squinted, as if looking for a hidden hologram.

"Fuck, this is a message from Osama bin Laden. *Death to infidels* or some shit like that."

"Give him back his card," Vic said.

"Claims he's a mullah going to market," Mac said. "We let too many of these fuckers go."

"Tell company to follow him with the Boss scope," Vic said.

The man wended his bike across the fields toward the road. The ops center, watching him through the G-Boss telescope, radioed that he was driving north. The market was three miles to the south.

"See, he was lying," Mac said. "Checking out our strength."

After a while, Garcia decided to return to base.

"The muj don't like the setup," he said. "It's not in their favor."

Like football teams, small units display individual fighting styles. The Taliban reminded me of the rice paddies south of Da Nang in 1966. Back then, when we moved at night, lookouts in the hostile villagers clacked bamboo sticks to warn of our movement. That was definitely spooky. Similarly, in Sangin the warning net of handheld radios allowed small teams to slip ahead of the Marine patrols. When the patrol crossed an open field, the Taliban opened fire, hoping for a hit or a rash rush by the Marines across a minefield.

The Marines' counter was equally simple. One four-man fire team with a Vallon peeled off to flank the enemy, while another kept up a base of fire. If the Taliban remained in one position too long, the mortars would find them.

Yaz was leading the patrol across a field with scorched topsoil when he stopped a third time. Again he uncovered a pressure plate IED.

"I can't figure out the pattern," I said.

"There isn't any," McCulloch said. "The stinkies are fishing. Throwing bait in the water, hoping for a hit."

Tarawa, 1943. *(Sgt. Tom Lovell, USMC)*

3rd Platoon, Kilo Company. (*Lt. Victor Garcia*)

Col. Paul Kennedy. *(Bing West)*

Brig. Gen. Larry Nicholson. *(Bing West)*

3/5 in Fallujah. *(Bing West)*

3/5 note on Fallujah bridge. *(Bing West)*

Cpls. Jordan Laird
and Jacob Ruiz on the first patrol.
(Cpl. Jordan Laird)

Patrol Base Fires.
(Bing West)

Flood at Fires,
October 14, 2010.
(Sgt. Christopher Carlisle)

Tense before a patrol. *(Bing West)*

A farmer asking for aid.
(Bing West)

2nd Lt. Victor Garcia and Sgt.
Philip McCulloch.
(Bing West)

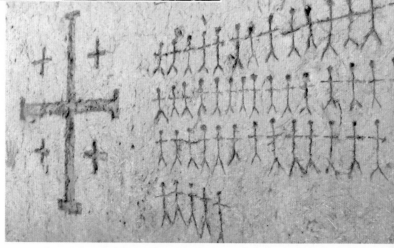

The sniper wall.
(Bing West)

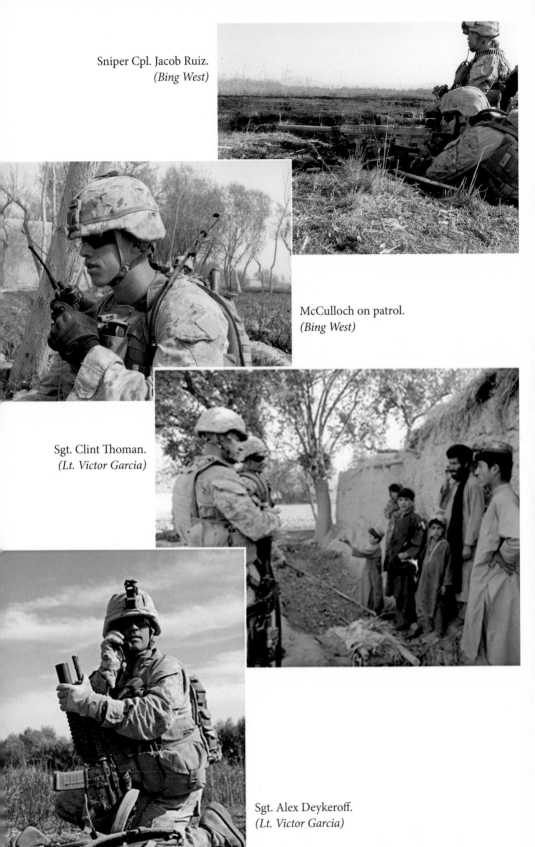

Sniper Cpl. Jacob Ruiz.
(Bing West)

McCulloch on patrol.
(Bing West)

Sgt. Clint Thoman.
(Lt. Victor Garcia)

Sgt. Alex Deykeroff.
(Lt. Victor Garcia)

LCpl. Arden Buenagua (KIA) and Gunnery Sgt. Christopher Carlisle. Note the murder hole. *(Sgt. Christopher Carlisle)*

Carlisle is hit.
(Sgt. Christopher Carlisle)

Medevac for Carlisle lands.
(Sgt. Christopher Carlisle)

Carlisle and Buenagua evac.
(Sgt. Christopher Carlisle)

Cpl. Armando Espinoza
is hit, Thanksgiving.
(Sgt. Christopher Carlisle)

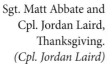

Sgt. Matt Abbate and
Cpl. Jordan Laird,
Thanksgiving.
(Cpl. Jordan Laird)

Marines thank F-18 squadron.
(Capt. Joe Dadiomoff)

Cobra and Huey,
Thanksgiving.
(Bing West)

The Green Zone. *(Bing West)*

Sgt. Joe "Mad Dog" Myers. *(Bing West)*

Taliban taunt with flags. *(Bing West)*

Machine gunners. *(Bing West)*

LCpl. Colbey Yazzie.
(Bing West)

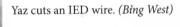

Yaz cuts an IED wire. *(Bing West)*

Yaz cuts away a pressure plate.
(Bing West)

Yaz detonates an IED.
(Bing West)

McCulloch with a pressure plate.
(Bing West)

A patrol leaving Fires.
(Bing West)

A Taliban outpost.
(Bing West)

Marines shooting, Sangin.
(Bing West)

3rd Platoon under fire.
(Bing West)

Breaching a Taliban fort.
(Bing West)

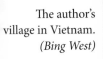

The author's
village in Vietnam.
(Bing West)

Poppy in Sangin village.
(Bing West)

1st Squad, 3rd Platoon, 2011.
(Bing West)

Combined Action Platoon, 1966. *(Bing West)*

Yazzie, Garcia, West, McCulloch.
(Bing West)

Three waifs in HiMars.
(Bing West)

A Sangin sunset.
(Bing West)

Approaching sector P8Q.
(Bing West)

Lts. Tom Schueman,
William Donnelly (KIA),
Cameron West (WIA),
Victor Garcia.
(Lt. Victor Garcia)

LCpl. Juan Dominguez's wedding.
(© Nelvin C. Cepeda/U-T San Diego/ZUMA Wire)

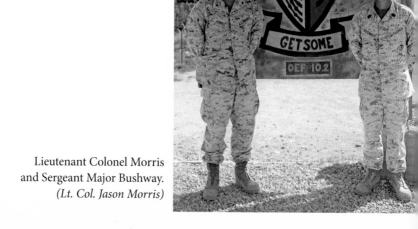

Lieutenant Colonel Morris
and Sergeant Major Bushway.
(Lt. Col. Jason Morris)

We were in the middle of nowhere. What were they fishing for—a Marine, a cow, a kid? There was no rhyme or reason to place a land mine in a field indistinguishable from a thousand others. Or maybe that was the cold ingenuity of it. After all, except for Yazzie's sixth sense, one of us would have stepped on it. Maybe that was worth someone else's cow or child.

A few minutes later, the patrol walked past a crumbled wall, startling two large, dark brown coyotes. Again Yaz knelt, disarmed a pressure plate, and blew up a jug of explosives.

Less than a minute later, the *crack!* from a high-powered sniper rifle from the left sent everyone to the ground. A PKM machine gun opened up with short bursts from the right, on the far side of the burnt-out field.

"They're pissed and tired of waiting," Garcia said. "Trying to sucker us across to where the IEDs are."

Garcia sent McCulloch around to the left to outflank the machine gun. Mac saw a man in a dark brown man-dress running away, leaving behind a jug of explosives and two pressure plates. He heard the bolt of a sniper rifle clack open and close, a sign the sniper was close ahead. But it took ten minutes for Yaz to sweep a path forward, ample time for the sniper and the machine gun crew to flee. Mac found a pile of spent cartridges behind a wall and retraced his steps back to Garcia.

On the way back to the fort, the patrol passed three waifs—the oldest about seven—standing in a row amid the rubble of their front door. The house stood next to a large field where, a few months ago, a Marine had stepped on a pressure plate. As soon as the explosion erupted, the Taliban opened fire. Amid the screams and frantic yells for a medevac, the Marines had called for covering fire. An artillery shell had crushed one end of the farmhouse.

Since then, rains had packed the debris into sodden heaps of bricks, clay, and broken concrete. This was the shattered hamlet the Marines called HiMars, after the rocket-assisted artillery shell that had destroyed it.

The father was hoeing nearby. He ignored the Marines' greetings. The clothes sagged upon the tiny frames of his undernourished kids. Unlike the children we had passed in intact compounds, none of these waifs darted forward with extended hands, shouting "Sharana! Sharana!" (Candy.) They were silent, their enormous eyes following each armored giant who walked by. The pace of the patrol quickened, no sorrow more doleful than a numbed and undernourished child.

Once within sight of the fort, the tension left the Marines. You could almost hear the collective exhale of breath. Home again, with no one down. They stood around, ejecting bullets from rifle chambers before entering friendly lines. One Marine wandered over to a bush to take a pee.

"Hey," he yelled, holding up a twisted black tube. "Boelk's 203."

Months earlier, LCpl. James Boelk had stepped on an IED a few feet outside the fort. His dented grenade launcher had lain in the underbrush since his death.

A half century earlier, I had served as a platoon commander. Had things changed much in fifty years? No pilot from 1965 could sit in the cockpit of a fighter aircraft in 2012 and feel comfortable. Infantry platoons had not experienced comparable technological advances. Since Vietnam, we had added night-vision devices, bulletproof armor, digital communications, overhead surveillance, and dining rooms in the rear. Everything else was pretty much the same—the organizational structure, the sound leadership, the patrol rhythms, and the rambunctious ferocity of the Marines.

Of all the differences I saw in fifty years on battlefields, the conservation of human life was the greatest. This applied to all combatants—European, American, and Afghan. In two world wars in the twentieth century, the West had engaged in industrial-scale slaughter affecting all combatants. In the twenty-first century, the West and its Islamist enemies had reverted to the tribal mentality of combat. Everyone knew each other in a tribe like the 3rd Platoon or the Taliban warrior band. No piece of ground or inanimate objective was worth dying for. Both sides took care of their own; both sides pulled back if outflanked or overmatched.

The Sangin Taliban were one tribal branch of the pan-Islamist terrorist movement dedicated to slaughtering others, provided there were scant losses to themselves. In Pakistan, the Taliban cultivated some suicide bombers. But none were sent to Sangin to wander zombielike into the rifle sights of a Marine. They called their fallen comrades "martyrs," but none rushed forward to die. When they sensed they had an edge, they pressed forward carefully, not presenting a target. They were like the Apaches in the 1870s, cruel, brave, and not foolish. They skulked around the ditches and undergrowth. They advocated rhetorical, not real sacrifice. The Taliban did not want to die.

The West was the same way. In World War II, terrain objectives were assaulted time and again until they were seized. The fatalistic notion about the brief, brutal life of a grunt persisted two decades later in the jungles of Vietnam. However, the swift invasion victories in Kuwait in 1991, in Afghanistan in 2001, and in Iraq in 2003 changed that mind-set. Technology and maneuver resulted in success with few losses.

In Afghanistan, the coalition fought, but carefully. It wasn't a kill-or-be-killed war. Instead the West, including the Marines, embraced the concept of killing, while running the least possible chance of being killed in return. The grunt was so weighted down with armor that he had little agility. In place of employing fire-and-maneuver in a fight, a platoon applied an overwhelming mass of bullets and explosives.

Day 92. 552,000 Steps

In the morning, the patrol went out again, pushing north two kilometers. In a grove of trees next to a gravel wash, the Marines stumbled across an old four-door Toyota. It bore a strong resemblance to a recent BOLO (be on the lookout) warning about a car being prepared for a suicide bomber.

The Marines marked the location and pushed on toward a cluster of compounds flying the white flags of the Taliban. Through the centuries, armies have held aloft their battle streamers. It's a way of saying, "Here we are, all ye foolish enough to give challenge." Back at Fires, the platoon had rigged a flagpole at the patrol base and flew the Stars and Stripes, with the maroon-and-gold Marine flag beneath.

Soon after we saw the Taliban flags, a machine gun burst kicked up a dust line to the right of Yaz. The Marines dropped prone and returned fire. The Taliban were split into three firing positions. The nearest was a tree line along a ditch 300 meters to the Marines' front. Tiny figures were darting back and forth, popping off a few shots from behind one tree trunk and then another.

About a dozen Marines were lying in a rough row in the soft grass along the bank of a canal. On the far side, across a large and very open field, was a tree line along another canal. On the far bank was an imposing compound flying the Taliban flag. Bullets were cracking overhead, coming from the tree line and holes in the compound wall. In the time it takes to read this sentence, I watched one man, about 200 meters away, dart out from behind one tree and duck safely behind another.

Lying near me was a first sergeant from battalion headquarters back at Jackson. Sometimes staff members joined a patrol. It helped them understand what was going on and, if there was a firefight, they were entitled to the coveted Combat Action Ribbon. The first sergeant had assumed the classic prone rifle position, sling wrapped around his left biceps, right cheek on the stock, finger on trigger, peering intensely through his three-power scope. *Crack!* One shot.

"Yes!" he yelled.

One kill for headquarters. Garcia glanced up and half smiled. The other Marines on the firing line showed no reaction.

"You too?" I asked Browning, who had just taken a shot.

"Mine's dead," Browning confirmed.

Every firefight is a cacophony. To an outsider, it seems bedlam. One persistent Taliban kept shooting from the right side of a large compound wall about 250 meters away. The Marines were responding with short bursts. The noise from an F-18 roaring by was deafening.

The object of all the shooting, in technical terms, is "to attain fire superiority." That means you smother the enemy with fire until he ducks and returns fire blindly or stops shooting. He is trying to do the same—perhaps you stop shooting to attend to someone wounded or you crouch down because you're scared. When you see someone not shooting, you kill him, because it's easy to do. Soldiers have the instincts of sharks. They pick off the weakest first.

The sergeants must control the rate of fire, so that the overly excited don't run out of ammo. After a dozen times, a squad or platoon develops an innate rhythm. Every action you take is automatic. Call it "learned instinct." The rhythm of battle is the same in Afghanistan as it was in Vietnam.

"The battle raged around us interminably," a Marine wrote about Vietnam. "One could not distinguish individual rifle shots; the roar of several dozen automatic weapons—both ours and theirs—

simultaneously firing on full automatic shut out all other sound. So too did the dozens of grenades exploding both farther down the hill and also amidst our positions. Nobody truly had any idea what was happening anywhere except around his own position."

The noise deafens you. Everyone is blazing away. You are in your own bubble, watching your fire team leader for a signal, and he is watching the squad leader, who is watching the platoon commander, who is talking on the radio with eyes fixed downrange.

"Myers," Garcia shouted, reaching his right arm out for the radio handset without turning around.

No response for a few seconds. Sergeant Myers was farther down the line, looking toward the compound.

"Goddamnit, Myers!" Garcia's voice was a whiplash. "When I want you, I want you here now! Stop fucking around!"

The line of Marines jumped as if jolted by an electric charge. It was the only time I heard Vic raise his voice during a skirmish. In all fairness, Myers was only three Marines away. It was not like he had wandered far off. He responded like a firecracker had exploded in his ass, leaping over Marines and thudding down next to his platoon commander.

"Driftwood 2-2, this is Mad Dog," Myers radioed. "How me, over?"

Driftwood—Spokes Beardsley back at Inkerman—told Myers that the F-18 pilot had eyes on two men on the roof of Building 38, listed on the maps as abandoned.

Myers turned to Garcia.

"Spokes says the planes are too low on fuel to stay on station. Shift to mortars?"

Garcia pointed to a spot on his map. Myers studied it, checked his GPS, and nodded.

"We're at 7950 8013—at the canal west of Compound 38," Mad

Dog shouted into his voice mike. "Hit the east side of 38 by the tree line. Give me one adjust."

Within two minutes, the black puff from a mortar shell drifted up, about twenty meters to the right of the compound. Myers radioed an adjustment and several rounds landed in the compound. The enemy firing ceased.

We were all lying on the canal bank. A few feet in front of us, water was flowing at a fast clip through a four-foot gap in a concrete sluice gate. It looked like you could leap across the gap, but each Marine was loaded down with ninety pounds of gear and ammo. McCulloch looked at Garcia.

"Good to go?"

"Work your way up the right side of the compound," Garcia said.

Yaz, Doyle, and Palma easily hopped across the sluice gate and moved by rushes toward the compound wall. Mac hung back waiting for Garcia, who had the jumping ability of a concrete block. For Vic, every irrigation ditch offered a challenge. Hopping over a puddle was an accomplishment.

He hesitated, took a three-step run, and launched 260 pounds of bulk and gear into space. It was like watching a bulldozer fly. Plunk. His right toe came down on the edge of the other side and he grasped an outstretched rifle stock. One small step for 3rd Platoon.

Two hundred meters ahead, Yaz slapped a C4 charge on the compound wall, blew a hole, and the Marines went in fast under the concealment of the smoke. The deserted compound had a sad, disheveled air. Inside one room, the ashes of a fire glowed next to a blackened teakettle and a bag with spilled rice. To keep out the chill, a blanket was draped over the doorway entrance. The three or four men who had slept on the hard earth had escaped out a narrow passageway in the back.

In the outside ditch lay the bodies of the men killed by the headquarters first sergeant and Browning. The other Taliban had pulled out, leaving no weapons behind. The patrol pushed on to the north-west, as the F-18 pilot had suggested before he left station.

Garcia was on the radio with 1st Squad, which was moving up on our left flank. The Taliban were hiding somewhere in the fields be-tween us and the squad. Searching Compound 40, the squad found a shooter's nest on the roof, littered with spent brass, a few shells still warm to the touch. Banshee 1, a Marine sniper, climbed onto the roof and glassed the fields through the telescope of his 7.62mm M12 sniper rifle. He slowly brought the reticle to rest and fired one bullet, striking a Taliban center mass at 440 meters.

"Hold your positions," Garcia radioed to his squad leaders. "We might get another squirter."

Nothing moved in the fields. The Marines waited fifteen minutes, pulled down a Taliban flag, and returned to base. Yazzie and Doyle had detected three IEDs, one of which would certainly have struck down Marines had Yaz not been there. The result was the patrol took no casualties on Day 92. They weren't cocky about it. They knew more losses were certain to come.

After the debrief, Browning walked behind the snipers' cave and carved one more stick figure in a mud wall. The rough outline of the cross of St. George was scratched next to the rows of stick figures.

At one point during the patrol, I was kneeling next to a sniper, Cpl. Jacob Ruiz, and his spotter, LCpl. Jeff Sibley. They were glassing a man talking on an Icom outside a compound several hundred meters away. Ruiz, a pleasant young man, dialed in a windage correction and took a shot, missing to the left. The three of us laughed as the man scurried inside the wall. I thought nothing more about it.

Later during the fight, BBC reporter Phil Wood and his television crew were at the rear of the column, unable to move forward to get combat footage. Ruiz was nearby, watching a spotter with an Icom.

"Got PID [Positive Identification]," said the sniper. "Cleared to engage."

As Ruiz lined up his shot, he allowed BBC to film it. The Marine Corps is proud of its sniper heritage. *Slate* magazine had posted a quote by Marine General James Mattis.

"We have an overweening sensitivity to the slaughtering of our enemies," Mattis said. "I've put medals on Marines who have killed guys at 700 yards. And I've come right out and said it: 'That was a beautiful shot.' You must reward the kind of behavior that you want."

Ruiz behaved as he had been trained. He had killed a man at 700 meters.

"We watched him talking on his radio," Ruiz said. "Then he went inside, and came back out trying to look inconspicuous."

When the video of his shot was shown on the BBC in London, it resulted in a military investigation. After seven weeks of nerve-racking testimony under oath, Ruiz was exonerated. Yet still, the order came down the chain of command not to shoot men talking on Icoms. Ruiz had acted properly as a Marine, but don't do it again. It was an odd way to reward the behavior the Marines wanted.

Farmers used cell phones rather than the short-range Icoms. In one fight while we were being hit with RPGs, I had heard a farmer in the house behind us shrieking over his cell phone. The Marines left him alone. When I asked why, a corporal laughed and said the odds were he was calling a neighbor, screaming, "How the hell can I get out of here?"

The high command later rescinded the order, leaving it up to those in the battle to decide what to do about a guy talking on an Icom during a firefight.

This isn't to excuse or make light of war's wrecking ball. The fighting in Sangin was always distressing and often tragic for the civilians. When the Taliban opened fire, Marines responded with five times more firepower. The BBC's Phil Wood interviewed on camera several angry elders after Ruiz took his shot and the firing had finally stopped.

"We don't want your help," one elder said. "We don't want your money. You shouldn't kill us and destroy our property."

The constant skirmishes destroyed compounds, livestock, and other property, and left in their wake civilian casualties, frenzied mothers, and terrified children. In every fight, 3rd Platoon tried to hang on to the enemy and not let targets fade away to shoot another day. Not a day went by without shots echoing across Sangin. Not one day.

Civilian casualties always are more than those of the fighters. On the first day of the 1944 landing at Normandy, French civilian casualties were estimated at 45,000, compared to 12,000 allied military casualties. In Sangin, the Pashtun tribes weren't willing to suffer casualties to throw out the Taliban. And although countrywide polls reflected a popular dislike of the Taliban, there was no draft, no tax, and no effort by the Kabul government to rally the people. President Karzai referred to the Taliban, responsible for 70 percent of civilian casualties, as his brothers, and reserved his bile for the American-led coalition that caused the other 30 percent. He incited resentment against the Americans whose presence prevented the Taliban from hanging him.

When I polled 3rd Platoon about what would happen when the Americans left, 43 percent believed the Taliban would be the stronger force, 20 percent believed the Afghan soldiers were stronger, and 37 percent believed both sides were about equal. In short, the platoon gave an advantage to the Taliban, but not a decisive one. Afghans would decide Afghanistan's fate.

Time and again, ambiguity persisted in distinguishing a cunning enemy from a hapless civilian.

First Squad, with Palma at point, was patrolling up in P8Q. Cpl. Kevin Henson scoped seven men in black walking quickly across a field 600 meters away, herding women and children. A few minutes later, Palma took fire. The Afghan soldiers on the patrol, responding quickly, started shooting at a second gang moving in on the flank. Garcia called in the 60mm mortars and the Taliban pulled back, leaving behind two bodies but no weapons.

When 1st Squad next returned, LCpl. Clay Cook dropped a dicker at 375 meters. On the man's body, the Marines found a wad of Pakistani rupees, a list of names, a Pakistani bank account number, the key to a Pakistani rent-a-car, and a petition to free the prisoners held in Kabul. A family who was watching the search of the corpse nervously asked Stevie, the interpreter: the Marines won't leave us, will they?

A few compounds away, three men and an elder were standing in the courtyard, gesturing at the frightened family. Insisting the men were Taliban posing as farmers, the Afghan soldiers asked Garcia to arrest them. Lacking any evidence, Garcia knew from experience that the district police would release them. So he gestured for the patrol to continue on.

Day 97. 582,000 Steps

Colonel Kennedy gathered a small task force and headed up Route 611. Accompanied by Afghan Brig. Gen. Zalmay Wesa and Lt. Col. Jason Morris, Kennedy intended to seize a fording point used by the Pakistani Taliban, about fifteen miles to the north. Along the way, Kennedy kept stopping to chat with villagers who had never seen an American. At about the fourth stop, he gave a short, smiling talk about how good life was going to be and moved to the back to let the elders talk among themselves. A man in a dirty man-dress walked up with a rock in his hand and hit Kennedy full in the face, stunning him and bashing in his nose. The man was shot before he could strike a second and possibly lethal blow.

The elders variously described the assailant as insane, a drug user, and "a person of no account." But what had the poor man heard every day among the villagers that provoked him to want to kill a complete stranger? Had a cunning enemy manipulated him, or did he reflect the simmering rage of the community?

Kipling's expression "East of the Sun, West of the Moon" seemed apt. In the middle of nowhere on the other side of the earth, an American colonel was bashed in the face by a villager who had never met him. Pressing gauze against his broken nose to lessen the bleeding, Kennedy proceeded north to the fording point, denying he had headaches.

When 3rd Platoon heard their colonel had been bludgeoned, they shrugged. It didn't surprise them. Nothing about Sangin surprised them.

Day 98. 588,000 Steps

On January 18, 3rd Squad was hit by machine gun fire, again up at P8Q. A Cobra and a Huey were on call, so McCulloch directed them to chew up the suspected tree line. P8Q was a shooting gallery. No farmers, no people. Both sides went there to fight.

One kilometer to the southwest, 2d Squad was busting up two small boats on the bank of the Helmand River. Seeing a battery, Cpl. Kacey Harmon stooped down and began tracing the wire back to find the jug of explosive.

As J. D. Browning backed away, another Marine muttered, "Shit, we're standing next to another one."

As the two gently backed away, Harmon tripped an explosive, throwing him in the air and fracturing his leg. Despite catching some shrapnel in the face, Delany tiptoed over to Harmon and pulled him out of the minefield. A sniper with a Mark 12 telescopic rifle took three shots at a man talking on an Icom. The man continued talking until a fourth bullet struck and killed him.

Later that day, in sector P8T, Palma was hacking a path through thick vines—standard 1st Squad take-the-toughest-way procedure. The squad was trying to sneak up on three Taliban that an F-18, call sign Maker 32, was tracking. The situation was a bizarre combination of seventeenth-century Indian tactics and twenty-first-century technology. To stalk a man who made $200 a year, the squad was listening over a $17,000 radio to directions from a pilot in a $40 million aircraft circling 10,000 feet above them. The hunt ended when Yazzie detected an IED. During the time it took him to disarm the pressure plate, the F-18 lost track of the prey.

The squad was carrying a new radio detection device, code name Wolfhound. Stevie, the interpreter, translated the enemy chatter he was picking up.

"My bag [of IEDs] is full. Where do you want me to go?"

"Dig it in anywhere. You are safe. No one is behind you."

"Be careful of 3rd Platoon. They are snipers."

Both sides developed standard tactical procedures. Now that the fighters from Pakistan had settled in, the Taliban usually fired from two or three directions so that the Marines could not freely maneuver. IEDs were buried at all likely crossing points between tree lines and canals. The enemy moved in gangs of three to six and shot from long distances, most gunfights lasted less than ten minutes, and at the sound of an approaching helicopter, the shooters ran safely away using the cover of irrigation ditches and tree lines.

The Taliban were good tacticians. They adapted quickly. The Sangin nizami, or commissioners, had readily accepted the Pakistani fighters and insisted on zakat, or training, for two weeks for each fighting band in the district. But after the Thanksgiving battle, the Taliban did not mass again.

It was a squad war. Each squad, reinforced with two engineers, a machine gun crew, and a few snipers, went out alone. Following the point man with the Vallon, the Marines walked at a snail's pace across the open fields. A mortar would wreak devastation among the exposed Marines. Fortunately, the Taliban did not purchase mortars in the Pakistani bazaars. The tubes and shells were too heavy to smuggle in.

Garcia gave no motivating speeches. He expected the squad leader to do his job, and the squad leader expected the same of his fire team leaders.

"Every squad here at Fires is tight," Rushton said to me. "We're brothers. It's like a marriage. You nag each other, saying stuff like, Don't chew that way. But if someone in your squad cries at night, you don't blab to another squad."

Over the next few days in mid-January, patrols destroyed three more IEDs, two found by Yazzie. While searching one compound, they found several schoolbooks. The owner explained that he secretly taught school. The patrol hurriedly left, hoping their visit hadn't set up the teacher for a Taliban inquisition.

First Squad was patrolling in Q1C when Sibley observed a man in a clean, light green man-dress walking nervously back and forth in a field. With Browning staying behind in a sniper hide to provide cover, the patrol headed toward the man, who ran away. Searching a nearby compound, the Marines found a rocket-propelled grenade. Two men in the compound next door said they had seen nothing.

Stevie, the translator, was convinced both were Taliban. But believing both would be released if he arrested them, Sergeant Mac simply shook his rifle at them and the patrol pushed on.

In P8Q, 3rd Squad found four IEDs, thirty pounds of explosives, and a bag of PKM brass. The empty shell casings in the bag weren't worth a dollar, but there was a market for items of even the tiniest value.

To vary the routine, 2d Squad set up a vehicle control point in Q1D, hoping to catch the Taliban moving supplies. While standing in overwatch, Yazzie uncovered a pressure plate attached to a jug of explosives. From his vantage point, he watched as one motorcycle after another approached the checkpoint, then abruptly turned off and bumped away across the fields. A frustrated 2d Squad soon shut down the checkpoint.

"The farmers weren't running away," Yazzie said. "They just didn't want to be hassled by our searches. With rain coming down every day, the Taliban weren't moving around as much. The atmospherics were actually good."

On January 20, Sgt. Jason Amores, twenty-nine, of Lehigh Acres, Florida, stepped on an IED and was killed. He left behind his wife, Jennifer; a son, Korbin, nine; and a daughter, Violet, three. He was the twenty-fifth member of 3/5 to die.

"I have no idea what will happen when we leave," Vic Garcia told me. "We don't have contact with the people. Our mission is to hunt down the enemy. I tell my platoon—all that counts is to be the best. I don't care what the task is. Be the best at doing it."

Chapter 11

END OF TOUR

"Recognition for the sacrifice for a cause that's not known to them."

—PORFIRIO ALVAREZ, CONNECTICUT

With February came weeks of freezing drizzle, interspersed with bursts of heavy rain. Garcia didn't slack off the pace. Months of patrolling and searching compounds had forced the Taliban to abandon any secure base. The enemy had to keep moving as long as 3rd Platoon kept on the pressure.

For America, World War II was the defining war of the twentieth century. Seventy years ago, a strict and total draft system was in place. Males of military age were expected—and ordered—to serve. For a brief half decade, America was one big, unified, and committed community. In 1943, the draft meant that ten million men stood an equal chance of being a grunt on the front lines. The vast majority considered it a duty and an honor to serve in uniform. We call them the Greatest Generation.

But by 2010, only two million men were eligible for military service. Of those who were qualified, one in a hundred volunteered for the military. The twenty-first-century grunt belonged to the One Percent Generation.

The members of 3rd Platoon expressed the mixture of pride and resentment typical of their tiny, and from their point of view, exclusive club. After their four-year hitch, most would return to civilian life with no pension and no enhanced job skills. Society accorded them no special recognition. No one in an airport could—or perhaps should—distinguish the grunt from the many more numerous troops who served honorably in the rear.

As LCpl. Adrian Barbiera expressed it: "We do all the shit that nobody else sees."

Day 119. 714,000 Steps

On February 8, 3rd Platoon joined with 2d Platoon at Transformer to search the sector of V3J where Lieutenant Donnelly had been killed. The Marines started at the north end of Belleau Wood. With the mangled tree line under several inches of water, the Marines methodically swept south. Searching for the waterlogged IEDs, the grunts covered less than a hundred meters per hour. Most IEDs were marked by a stack of rocks or a cloth tied to a branch. The Taliban employed obvious markings only in their own secure areas, where they expected to have advance warning. By day's end, they had found forty-eight IEDs. Not one Marine was injured. It was the platoon's most satisfying day in February.

During the last two weeks of the month, the platoon engaged in only one gunfight and found only five more IEDs. Due to the miserable conditions, February was the quietest period in their tour.

"The rains helped enormously," Garcia said. "That relieved our stress when we searched. The last weeks in February, we found fifteen IEDs set in without batteries. It was too wet to wire them up. We had no intel on the human networks, or who was putting them in. But they didn't work underwater."

The sodden conditions enabled the shivering Marines to poke around freely. Even IEDs taped in plastic were waterlogged. On four occasions, Marines avoided losing their legs when the ignition fuses set off only low-order detonations, resulting in twisted ankles and faces white with relief.

Third Platoon attributed the decrease in fighting to the miserable weather; the high command attributed success to the counterinsurgency strategy. In February, as 3rd Platoon was sopping wet and happy about IED malfunctions, General Petraeus foresaw strategic success.

"We have finally gotten the inputs right," he said, "for a comprehensive counterinsurgency strategy."

By February, however, President Obama had decided that U.S. troops would steadily withdraw. The inputs were leaving.

The Marine reports supported Petraeus's optimism. In public, Marine generals emphasized friendliness, school building, medical clinics, women's rights, and the rule of law. Such projects and virtues would win over the Pashtun tribes and many of the insurgents. Indeed, Maj. Gen. Richard Mills, the commander of the Marines in Helmand, claimed the Taliban "have lost the support of the people within the province."

How the Marine command reached that conclusion was perplexing, to say the least. According to a province-wide survey, 71 percent of the people believed the Taliban would return once the American forces left. Worse, a survey in January revealed that 99 percent of those polled in Sangin believed that Marines/NATO caused all civilian casualties and that working with any NATO force was wrong.

Although money was available to pay for tips, Garcia never spent a cent in Sangin. No farmer in his right mind openly collaborated with a foreigner who would be leaving. Marines working for the Human Exploitation Team (HET)—trained intelligence agents—sometimes accompanied 3rd Platoon on patrols to recruit farmers. Most of the information they gathered was unreliable.

Amo Shuaraz, an Afghan-American from Idaho, was an undercover HET agent. He wore a Marine uniform, spoke fluent Pashto, and spent three years in southern Afghanistan. Amo was unwilling to predict what would happen when the Marines left.

"I can talk to a farmer for an hour," he said, "and not know if he's Talib. The Talibs lie too good."

Day 143. 858,000 Steps

In early March, the sun and the enemy both came back out. The Taliban had dug new firing positions into the soft earth on the far side of a canal in P8Q. When 3rd Squad was fording the canal, the enemy opened up with PKM and AK fire. Mac called in the mortars, while Lance Corporal Doyle cut around to the west, forcing the Taliban to pull out. Reaching the Taliban trench line, he found only a bag of the PKM and AK brass. Third Squad spent half an hour shoveling dirt into the trench.

It was a *fuck you* gesture. Colonel Kennedy kept hammering home one line: "Finish every fight standing on the enemy's ground." To sweep up to the Taliban position might take Dy or Mac two hours—or Esquibel four hours—but the Taliban knew that sooner or later the grunts were coming.

On March 5, 2d Squad went up to the northern end of P8Q. Garcia wanted to check out a cluster of abandoned compounds the Taliban had previously used as a staging area. Once inside P8Q, Dy set up a strongpoint behind a low courtyard wall where his machine gun team had good cover and observation.

This is a good spot, Dy thought. *If we're shot at, we're ready.*

Sure enough, the Taliban obliged with a burst of fire that zipped high above the wall. The machine gun crew cheerfully unloaded against a far tree line. Dy decided to close on the enemy, with the machine gun providing covering fire. When he lobbed a 40mm shell from his grenade launcher into the tree line, it was answered by a burst of fire from a compound off to his right.

Standard situation, Dy thought, *the Talibs are falling back to their alternate positions.*

Through his scope, Dy could see murder holes in the compound wall and dust rising from two nearby piles of hay and timber. One Taliban leaped up, fired a burst from his AK, and then turned away to hop on his bike. Standing erect, it took him a few seconds to kick-start the motor. He went down in a fusillade of bullets.

As the enemy pulled back, dust gave away a fighting position in a pile of rubble about 300 meters distant. Lance Corporal Wagner extended the tube on an M72 light-armor rocket and waved at Sergeant Dy for permission to fire. At that range, there was one chance in a hundred of striking the small target. What the hell.

"Fuck it," Dy shouted, "shoot the rocket!"

Wagner had set the sight to its highest elevation. Knowing that wasn't enough, he pointed the launcher several more inches into the air and squeezed the rubber-encased igniter switch. The chunky slug of explosive lofted up in a low, slow arc. It ran out of energy just as it reached the target, exploding in a bright blink that left behind a smudge of black dust over the rubble. The squad let out a victory whoop as Dy smacked Wagner on the back of his Kevlar.

The Taliban gang again fell back, leaving behind the body of the unfortunate gunman. When Garcia called for a fire mission, the ops center asked for a sitrep.

"Six actual," Captain Johnson radioed to Garcia. "What's that racket we're hearing?"

"Well, it's 3-5," Garcia said, referring to the third month and fifth day. "So we're getting some."

"Garcia," Johnson replied, "that's lame."

After six months of fighting against 3rd Platoon, the Taliban had learned to keep two fields and one tree line or irrigation ditch between them and the Marines. Often they stayed two tree lines away, a distance of about 400 meters. They couldn't hit a Marine at that distance. Unless someone was blown up by an IED and the squad was focused on the medevac, the Taliban had no desire to close with the Marines. If they miscalculated their escape route, they were in mortal danger. One sniper, Cpl. Royce Hughie, recorded three kills in a single day.

Browning, as the commander of the sniper section, repeatedly reminded the grunts to shoot a few rounds daily to make sure the aim sight of every rifle was properly aligned, called Battlefield Zero, or BZ. The average grunt, though, lacked the snap shooting skill to hit a dodging man at 300 meters. That expertise required firing thousands of rounds, and the Marines didn't have the time or money for that investment.

By March, Browning's sniper section had accounted for fifty-one kills, each verified by the sniper and his spotter.

"Sometimes a guy would drop like a sack of potatoes," Sibley said. "Mostly they flinched and disappeared. I felt bad when we hit a guy in the gut and he staggered off. He might not die. Most wore black. A lot had on man-dresses."

Their battle space encompassed eight sectors on the photomap, containing 1,314 compounds. The Taliban could see each patrol coming, but couldn't stop it. Sooner or later—a day, week, a month—

every Taliban gang crossed paths with the Marines. Relentless patrolling exacts a psychological toll on even the stoutest guerrilla.

On March 7, Secretary of Defense Gates visited the Marines in a forlorn town called Now Zad. He wondered, as he later wrote, "whether it had been worth what it cost them."

The next day, he visited 3/5's ops center in Sangin.

"Since October," he said, "3/5 has suffered the heaviest losses of any battalion in this ten-year-long war. This district was one of the most dangerous not just in Afghanistan but in the whole world."

He congratulated the Marines for having "killed, captured or driven away most of the Taliban." His remarks focused on defeating the local enemy, not on protecting the population.

"I relish," he said, "your victories, take pride in your achievements, and take satisfaction as you strike fear into the heart of the Taliban."

He emphasized winning on the battlefield, saying, "alongside the legends of Guadalcanal, the Chosin Reservoir and Belleau Wood will forever be added in Marine Corps history the legend of Sangin."

Five days earlier at the White House, he had concluded that President Obama, as commander-in-chief, had given up on the mission.

"The president doesn't trust his commander [General Petraeus]," Gates later wrote in his memoir, "can't stand Karzai, doesn't believe in his own strategy, and doesn't consider the war to be his. For him, it's all about getting out."

And what was the position of the secretary of defense? He couldn't make up his mind, or take decisive action.

"I was torn," he wrote, "between my historical perspective, which screamed for caution, and what my commanders insisted was needed for accomplishing the mission they had been given by the president and by me."

Gates, too, had lost faith in the counterinsurgency mission. His objective was to build up the Afghan forces and "dramatically weaken the Taliban," "rooting the Taliban out of their strongholds." He wanted "a tighter focus geographically" and faulted the Marines for sending their troops to "sparsely populated areas, such as parts of Helmand." This was a fair point; Sangin was at the end of the earth. Why was 3rd Platoon even there?

Had Gates ordered the commanders to narrow down the mission to building up the Afghan forces and bashing the Taliban, then Colonel Kennedy, Lieutenant Garcia, and a hundred other combat commanders would have proposed new tactics, reducing the losses to IEDs, and striking at the Taliban when and where they least expected it.

The president and the secretary of defense lacked the forthrightness to tell the generals that ten years of war were enough. The failed strategy did not change.

Day 150. 900,000 Steps

In mid-March, I returned to 3rd Platoon. Same mission, same patrol routine.

"We have to walk farther to get into a fight," Vic Garcia said. "Let's go up to P8Q. That's our best chance of drawing fire."

This display of martial spirit—a desire to seek out the enemy— was quite different from what happened in Vietnam. Gen. Norman Schwarzkopf, the commander of the American victory in Kuwait in 1991, was a battalion commander in Vietnam in 1970. He wrote, "the troops had become so demoralized by the mines and booby traps that they'd lost their will to fight." He was referring to a battalion that suffered 203 casualties from mines, about the same number of wounded that 3/5 had taken.

By 2011, the American public had tired of our military commitment to Afghanistan. Forty-five percent of the public, including veterans, believed the wars in Iraq and Afghanistan had not been worth the cost. Yet far from being demoralized, 3rd Platoon was trying to pick a fight.

Before leaving on the patrol to P8Q, I went over to the sniper's area to check their wall. Since my visit in January, the tally of enemy stick figures had increased from about forty to over sixty. Taken together, the sniper section and the three infantry squads reported killing 271 of the enemy. That's probably high by at least a third; shooters always think they hit more targets than they actually do. But when the air and mortar strikes are added in, it's not unreasonable that 3rd Platoon did kill 200 enemy.

On a wall near the stick figures were stretched the pelts of ringtailed coyotes and a few bobcats. Browning—who also cleaned and cooked chickens and goats for the platoon—entertained himself by climbing into a sentry tower at night and using his thermal sight to shoot the coyotes. The reservists on guard duty appreciated the diversion.

Garcia gathered the platoon for a group photo. Since October, the platoon had averaged one casualty per week, and they had two more weeks to go before heading back to the States. With more casualties likely, few smiled for the camera.

"Seven months with no break," Browning said, "was too long. We were tired."

Outside the patrol base, shepherds were tending their sheep and cows. Once outside the wire, Yazzie took point. I calculated he was close to one million steps.

"Yaz," I said, "how do you do it day after day?"

"Habit, I guess," he said with a shy grin. "You get used to it."

"How many IEDs have you found?"

"I don't know, maybe a dozen."

"Oh, way, way more than that, dude," Mac said. "You're awesome, the best in the battalion."

With a shake of his head, Yaz rejoined Doyle at point. Doyle had joined the Marines to get away from his hometown of Modesto. Now he was looking forward to returning home and going to college.

"Yaz and me," he said, "have found thirty-eight IEDs. He won't tell you that. He's superstitious about numbers."

We headed northeast, cutting across fields filled with thousands of ankle-high green poppy plants. Afghanistan produced 80 percent of the opium for the global heroin market. A blight the previous year had driven up prices. The farmers in Sangin anticipated a price of $200 for a kilogram of raw opium. During the harvest season in April, the farmers sliced open the pods dangling from the purple poppy flowers. A few days of sunshine baked the gummy substance into a black teardrop that was nipped off and placed in a sack. It was like collecting the syrup from maple trees in Vermont.

A hectare—a field one hundred by one hundred meters—yielded forty pounds of wet, raw opium worth $3,600, four times more valuable than a hectare of wheat. Buyers came to Sangin from Kabul, Pakistan, and Iran. Most of the fields were owned by shadowy syndicates, and the tenant farmers received only 10 or 20 percent of the sales price.

At the grunt level in Sangin, opium and hashish were ignored, except when askaris went on patrol stoned.

"We have our hands full with the Taliban," Maj. Steve Wolf, the regimental intelligence officer, said. "The drug problem is the Afghan government's business. We don't have a U.S. eradication effort."

We also walked through several fields of cannabis. In the rich soil next to the Helmand River, the yield of 300 pounds per hectare was twice that of the fields in Morocco, Afghanistan's major competitor in the global market. A poor farmer, without a tractor or much fertilizer, could earn as much from cannabis as from poppy. He had to work harder, though, filtering and pulverizing the leaves and kneading the resin into clumps of hashish to be sold to bulk buyers or in the local markets.

It seemed every Afghan soldier had his own stash, and it was hard to pick out those who were high on patrol. And with unemployment hovering around 40 percent, addiction to hard drugs was growing. In recruiting local forces in Helmand, the Marines rejected 17 percent of applicants for failing tests for hard drugs.

Near a fording point across a stream about a kilometer north of Fires, Yaz found and cut a thick white electric wire. Buried somewhere close by was a jug of explosives. Small groups of men glared at us and returned no greeting. After marking the spot, Garcia gestured to Yaz to push ahead.

"They're jerking us around," Garcia said. "This place is rigged. No sense sticking around."

Farther out in the fields, farmers, women, and children were hastening to shelter, a signal that enemy lurked nearby. Staying in file, the Marines knelt and prepared to return fire. Covering Yazzie's back, Doyle glassed the empty fields to our front. Off to our east, four or five men were idling along on their motorcycles, watching us.

"Fuckers," Mac muttered.

Captain Johnson came up on the radio.

"We're watching those spotters on the Godcam," he said. "Make sure you ignore them. We're at the end of our tour. Don't risk Leavenworth."

In the fall, the platoon had averaged one fight a day. Now it had fallen down to three a week. That was progress, but it hadn't altered the basic dynamics of guerrilla war. Since my last visit, the Taliban had been insisting the farmers aid them for the sake of Islam. Women, not men, now called openly on the Icoms, knowing the Marines wouldn't shoot.

When a helicopter gunship buzzed over the motorcyclists, McCulloch grabbed the radio and testily told the pilot to leave.

"Mac thinks," Vic said to me, "that no one should interfere with his private war."

Garcia kept a quiet, detached manner. The squad leader ran the show. On one patrol, Vic was carrying the SAW—the machine gun with an astonishing rate of fire. When a fight broke out, Sergeant Dy yelled that he had placed the gun in the wrong place. Garcia quickly hopped up to follow Dy's directions.

After the Cobra gunship left, Mac led us toward P8Q, where more small groups of men glared at us and would return no greeting. The white flag of the Taliban fluttered over an abandoned farmhouse 300 meters west of Transformer. I glanced quizzically at Vic.

"They still give us the finger," he said. "That compound is laced with mines. The hell with it."

Mac stopped in the middle of an open field and we all lay down, the machine gun pointed northeast and snipers scoping the tree lines. Garcia radioed the mortar crew back at base to stand by. The snipers reported that an unarmed man was crawling on his hands and knees to get a closer look at us.

"He might be a spotter," Vic said, "or an idiot. Leave him alone."

After waiting half an hour with no action, we returned to base. Garcia was apologetic.

"I was sure some asshole would shoot at us," he said.

Day 158. 948,000 Steps

Second Squad was patrolling into P8Q when Sergeant Dy saw several men in front of a small mosque from which the Marines habitually took fire. *Shit,* Dy thought, *we're in for it now.* He waited anxiously while his machine gun team wiggled into position to provide the base of fire. A single PKM round zipped past the squad kneeling in single file.

After six months of having the enemy shoot and run away, something snapped inside Dy. He wasn't playing it safe this time. He turned to his squad.

"Let's go!"

Gambling the Taliban hadn't rigged IEDs where they gathered, Dy ran across the field toward the mosque. A dozen Marines followed, spread out in a long line. One Marine shot a LAAW (Light Anti-Armor Weapon) that exploded against a wall, sending up a cloud of smoke. As the Taliban ran out the back, the Marines reached the compound and pulled out grenades to clear the rooms.

At the rear of the file, Corpsman Stuart Fuke, twenty-two, stumbled and went down.

"I'm hit!"

Lantznester saw him fall, ran back, and cinched a tourniquet around Fuke's thigh. Amid the din of the shooting, the other Marines didn't hear their shouts for help. Lantz and Fuke were feeling very much alone. Fuke had volunteered to join the grunts because he enjoyed their sense of humor. But leaving Lantz and him out in the open by themselves was carrying a joke too far.

Eventually Dy realized they were missing and the squad ran back. The high-velocity bullet had entered Fuke's thigh and exited out his ass. It was a serious wound, but of course the Marines couldn't resist a few wisecracks. Thoroughly exasperated, Fuke grabbed the radio and called in his own evacuation.

The platoon's ability to call for mortars was restricted. A new battalion, taking over to the north, insisted upon prior approval of any request for fire near its sector. Third Platoon had only a few weeks to go before rotating back to the States.

"After Doc Fuke was shot in the butt," Sibley said, "Lieutenant Garcia could have packed it in. Instead, he kept pushing us out. Sergeant Dy and I talked about it. We admired how he handled those last weeks, when there were too many restrictions on how we could fight."

To help, Spokes Beardsley had the Harvest Hawk AC-130 fly over whenever it was in the vicinity. With a loiter time of seven hours and a noise like a washing machine loaded with marbles, the monstrous aircraft intimidated the Taliban. A common Icom intercept was "Don't do anything when the big gray plane is here."

A week later, the electronics intercept team at Inkerman reported increasing frustration on the part of the Taliban shura in Pakistan. In the judgment of the senior insurgent leadership, the Sangin local rebels had lost their nerve and weren't engaging the Marines. So the shura sent in a second batch of jihadists.

The mosque in P8Q was the reception center for foreign fighters. The Sangin elders, harboring no love for Pakistanis, suggested they wouldn't complain if the mosque went away. This was tricky stuff, since President Karzai ranted about any perceived American transgression. On March 25, Garcia set out with 1st Squad. Video from the blimp showed that after firing from the mosque, the shooters escaped down a tree line. This day, the Marines had permission to return fire with artillery.

Sure enough, about 300 meters south of the mosque, the patrol took fire. But due to spotty communications, the ops center at Inkerman canceled the fire mission. Frustrated, Esquibel and Palma moved forward to try some rifle shots.

"Hey, Sergeant," Cpl. Porfirio Alvarez, twenty-three, from Connecticut, radioed, "you're cutting across the field you've put off-limits."

Esquibel felt a tremendous push under his feet and realized he was floating in the air. For a split second, he thought he was dead. Then he landed in the mud. He lay still, afraid to look at his injuries and fearful of setting off a secondary.

"Sergeant Esquibel?" Palma was shouting. "Esquibel, where are you?"

It had been a low-order detonation. Esquibel saw the yellow jug split open next to him, packed with explosives. Palma stood on the bank and looked down.

"Don't touch off secondaries," Esquibel said. "Fuck. How much is left of me?"

Palma looked at the mud-splattered figure.

"Looks like only a leg is gone. You're okay."

Palma's sympathy wasn't particularly reassuring. As tourniquets were applied, Garcia hustled over. It appeared to him that Esquibel would lose his foot, but not his leg. The sergeant who had taken such special care of his men hadn't made it to the end of his last tour. As the helicopter approached, a Marine threw a smoke grenade to mark their position.

"I see no smoke," the pilot said. "I won't land until you pop that damn smoke."

The field was filled with bright green cannabis plants. Even the mist floating over the field was green.

"What knucklehead," Garcia yelled, "threw a green smoke grenade?"

Day 166. One Million Steps

The next day, March 27, Lantznester was talking with Yaz, who was taking point on another patrol. Yaz had woken up out of sorts, and heading back up to sector P8Q did not raise his spirits. Third Platoon was turning over Fires next week and he had passed the one hundred patrol mark. This stuff was getting old.

"I think someone's hunting me," Yaz said.

"Dude," Lantz said, "you'll be fine."

A few hours later, Yazzie cautiously approached the long tree line marking the entrance to sector P8Q. Yaz had disliked this route since January, when the monstrous slug from a Dishka, a Russian heavy machine gun, had just missed him. With Doyle keeping watch behind him, Yaz decided to lead McCulloch's squad through a field rather than along a hard-packed trail.

Seeing a wire protruding from the dirt, he signaled the squad to halt. He knelt down on his right leg, extended his right arm, and began to shove away the loose dirt, as he had done a hundred times before. The pressure plate was so sensitive that the weight of his hand closed the circuit between the two wires.

Wham! The force of the explosion flipped Yaz's body upside down in the air and he landed on his back, looking up at the sky. He lay still, hoping his back wasn't broken. But his right leg kept twisting and quivering.

"What the hell?" he screamed. "What the hell!"

Doyle was kneeling over him, his face inches away.

"Don't worry, bro," he said. "We got you."

Badly concussed, Doyle was wobbling, trying not to lose consciousness as he helped his friend.

"Straighten out my leg," Yaz said. "It's caught on something."

The corpsman was hitting him with morphine. The last thing he remembered was McCulloch patting him on the shoulder.

"It's okay. We fixed your leg. It's okay."

Yazzie's right leg, mangled beyond repair, was amputated a few hours later.

That same day on another patrol, Corpsman Redmond Ramos stepped on another pressure plate and lost his foot.

"That IED maker had been watching us," Yaz told me from his hospital room. "He saw I never used that trail. He was real smart."

In the Vietnam village where I served, the top fighter was Suong, the leader of the farmer militia. Suong had started fighting in 1964, and no Marine could match his tactical instincts. One night in1974, years after we had left, Suong opened a gate in his hamlet and was blown apart. After a thousand patrols, the odds had caught up with him.

Third Platoon went into Sangin with fifty-one Marines, and concluded the tour with twenty-seven casualties—two killed, nine amputations, and sixteen concussions, shrapnel, or gunshot wounds.

LCpl. Colbey Yazzie was the magician and platoon talisman, too skilled to be struck down. Amputated leg. Lt. Cameron West had spent his life in the outdoors, too smart to be fooled. Amputated leg. Sgt. Dominic Esquibel was a meticulous man, careful to a fault. Amputated foot. Sgt. Matt Abbate was the Achilles of the platoon, its finest warrior. Dead. Over the course of one million steps, the odds will always catch up.

Chapter 12

THE ENDLESS GRUNT

"Out here in combat, we're different from others."
—JUAN COVARRUBIUS, TEXAS

I n April of 2011, Battalion 3/5 left Sangin. A fresh platoon moved into Fires and spent a week conducting joint operations. On the first patrol, Vic Garcia brought Lt. Chuck Poulton, the new platoon commander, up to P8Q. When a gunfight broke out, Garcia called in Cobra gunships.

"That's how it is out here," Garcia said. "Use your supporting arms. Don't let them breathe."

It was a confusing command environment. When briefing reporters, the high command quietly took credit for urging Special Operations teams to kill more Taliban. But the conventional forces were more restricted.

"I put out a memo [in May of 2011]," Petraeus said, "re-familiarizing all forces with the Tactical Directive."

A year earlier, the Marines had sensed that Petraeus was not going to enforce the Tactical Directive strictly. Over the intervening months, he had gradually relied more on the Special Operations teams to attrite the Taliban. Fire restrictions on conventional forces who were viewed as community organizers again tightened.

Despite the Tactical Directive, Poulton, who had done a combat tour in Iraq, adopted Garcia's tactics. Every patrol moved by bounds in single file, watched over by a base of fire with a machine gun, 203s, and a forward observer. At first, action was slow. It was the poppy season, the fields were ablaze with purple blooms, and the Taliban were helping with the harvest on their farms.

A few months later, though, when the fields were thick with summer corn, the gunfights and IED explosions resumed. One day in June, the platoon found eight motorbikes hidden in a corn row. After the Marines waited in ambush for several hours, ten Afghans came by, carrying shovels and showing clean hands. Chemical swabs revealed gunpowder residue on all. The district governor, claiming a lack of evidence, released them.

The war ground on. Eventually, Poulton's platoon sergeant, all three squad leaders, and the company commander were wounded. His platoon suffered two Marines killed and thirty-two wounded.

Back in the States, Secretary of Defense Robert Gates concluded his four years of service in June of 2011. He told President Obama that the commanders in the field believed we were achieving success.

"The more time you spend in Afghanistan," he told Mr. Obama, "the closer to the front you get, the more optimistic people are."

Lieutenant Poulton was not one of those optimistic people.

"We took over Fires and held it," Poulton said. "We're Marines. I'm proud of what we did. But we didn't blame the people for our losses. We were leaving Afghanistan and the Taliban were staying."

His battalion—1/5—had uncovered 895 IEDs, considerably fewer than the 1,315 reported by 3/5.

"We made progress," the battalion commander, Lt. Col. Tom Savage, said. "Still, Marines are bad for the poppy business, bad for the Taliban, and bad for some tribes. Will Afghan soldiers from tribes in the north take on Sangin as their fight? That's the key question."

Patrol Base Fires was closed down. The Marines were thinning out their units, and the Afghan soldiers laughed at the suggestion that they remain alone in the middle of the Green Zone.

In September of 2011, the 1st Battalion of the 7th Marine Regiment (1/7) took over from 1/5. I returned to Sangin. With the American withdrawal well under way, 1/7 was holding Sangin with half the number of troops that 3/5 had deployed.

The morning after my return, I accompanied a dozen Marines from B Company, each carrying ninety pounds of armor and gear, as they slogged through stifling cornfields in ninety-five degree heat. We headed for sector Q5H, where Lieutenant Donnelly had been killed. No Afghan soldiers accompanied the Marines. They were staying inside their bases away from the Green Zone until the corn was harvested.

When a four-foot cobra slithered across our path, the Marines shrugged; a snake couldn't blow off their legs. The patrol emerged from the cornfield in front of a small madras, or Islamist school. A black-turbaned mullah quickly herded the schoolboys inside the courtyard, while a dozen farmers glared at us.

We walked on, eventually reaching a tiny outpost called Pabst Blue Ribbon. Inside PBR, a dozen Marines and local Afghan militia were relaxing, overseen by a sentry with a machine gun. Such was the distrust that all Afghans handed in their weapons before entering the post. With no interpreter, the Americans and Afghans could only nod at one another. Although every Marine post and patrol was "partnered," the Afghans were learning little they could apply on their own.

We pushed on. Staff Sgt. Edward Marini, the lead engineer, uncovered and blew up two wooden pressure plates attached to yellow plastic jugs filled with ammonium nitrate. In six months, Bravo Company had uncovered seventy-seven IEDs and taken ten wounded. This tally was far fewer than in the previous year, proof that the Marines had largely cleared Sangin of active enemy.

Once the two IEDs were detonated, the platoon commander, Lt. Kurt Hoening, faced a choice.

"We'll get into a fight in Q5H," he said to me. "That means we come back down this path at dusk, and there'll be fresh IEDs waiting for us. I'm not risking my men to get into a fight that has no meaning."

Hoening had not yet been in a firefight that qualified him to wear the prestigious Combat Action Ribbon that symbolized a combat veteran. He placed the safety of his men above his own career advancement.

Back at base, he asked me to say a few words to his Marines, who were questioning what they were accomplishing out there on their own.

I thanked the Marines. It was an honor to have taken my last combat patrol with the battalion I had joined fifty years earlier. They might question what they were doing at the end of the earth where the farmers and enemies looked the same, and often were the same.

In Vietnam, I had fought a similar confusing war. But people and nations don't long remember policies. Marines have fought in 160 campaigns. Even historians can't remember the policy reasons for many of them. Policy is not the point.

You volunteered for the Marine Corps not to make policy, but to guard our nation. Marines fight wherever our commander-in-chief orders us to go. Your grandchildren will one day ask, Did you fight in Afghanistan? You will proudly say yes. You've had an extraordinary adventure, not shared by your peers back home. Some of your brothers were killed or lost limbs. You all knew that was the cost before you volunteered. Your fallen brothers would volunteer again.

The task of the grunt is to defeat any foe on the battlefield. Put him six feet under. Guard our nation so fiercely that no one wants to fight America.

Everyone wants recognition for a hard job done well. In 2011, 3rd Platoon had borne the hardest of the fighting. Most of the platoon told me they wished the people back home could understand the toils of the grunt. It may be of some comfort to them to know that their most famous platoon mate—Cpl. E. B. Sledge—felt that exact same way in 1945.

"As I strolled the streets of Mobile, civilian life seemed so strange," Sledge wrote. "People rushed around in a hurry about seemingly insignificant things. Few seemed to realize how blessed they were to be free and untouched by the horrors of war. To them, a veteran was a veteran—all were the same, whether one man had survived the deadliest combat or another had pounded a typewriter while in uniform."

When he enrolled at Auburn University in 1946, a clerk in the Registrar's Office asked him if the Marines taught him anything useful. Sledge replied, "Lady, there was a *killing* war. The Marine Corps taught me how to kill Japs and try to survive. Now, if that don't fit into any academic course, I'm sorry. But some of us had to do the killing—and most of my buddies got killed or wounded."

Back in the States, Lieutenant Colonel Morris visited the families of the fallen in the summer of 2011.

"Some were very angry," he told NPR, "yelling, why the hell did I lose their sons for this? What do you say? That his son died doing what he wanted to be doing and that he had a positive impact on the people of Afghanistan."

The unit patch of the 3rd Battalion, 5th Marine Regiment is a red-and-yellow shield. In one quadrant is the fleur-de-lis symbol of knighthood, bestowed by France after 3/5 stopped the 1918 German advance on Paris through Belleau Wood. Another quadrant is decorated with a line of green bamboo shoots, symbolizing the jungles of Vietnam. Atop the shield is a banner inscribed with the name "Darkhorse," the radio call sign during the battle at the "Frozen Chosin" Reservoir in 1950. On the bottom of the shield is printed the battalion motto: "Get Some"—an infelicitous reminder that the task of the infantryman is to kill the enemy.

In the past decade, 3/5 had six recipients of the Navy Cross, our nation's second highest award for valor. This was the highest number in any Army or Marine battalion. In August of 2012, I attended the Navy Cross ceremony at Camp Pendleton, California, for Sgt. Matt Abbate. Most of Matt's sniper section and 3rd Platoon were there, together with a thousand others. The stories of Matt had entered Marine folklore. Like Corporal Sledge, he was now a member of the Old Breed whose story would be told in boot camp.

Lantznester said it best: "We are war's fiercest warriors, and the fallen live on through 3/5."

After the parade, many of us adjourned to a biker bar in San Clemente. A hundred Marines, the extended Abbate family, and a few startled bikers toasted Matt and told war stories. Gunny Carlisle showed gross pictures of what the IED had done to his rear end, Vic

Garcia actually grinned as he drank beer, and Cameron West showed how he could walk with his prosthetic leg.

At one point, a lance corporal, fortified by a few beers, indignantly asked Garcia why he had not promoted him to fire team leader.

"You didn't work as hard as the other guy," Garcia said.

"Yeah, but I was with the platoon at Fires," the lance corporal said.

"And you slacked off," Garcia said, "when we got back. What you did in Sangin doesn't hack it back here."

The war was over for 3rd Platoon.

Cam West went back to Georgia, where he rides horse and tends cattle on his ranch. Vic Garcia headed off to Army Ranger school. Tom Schueman transferred to a recon company. Spokes Beardsley, whose eighty-nine air strikes in seven months was the highest total in the war, took a civilian job as a pilot instructor. Mad Dog Myers returned to Ohio and graduated from the University of Toledo, with plans to become a federal marshal.

Sergeant Deykeroff decided to stay in, as did Sergeant Thoman, who felt relieved to be home, saddened by the losses but glad that the Taliban had been pushed back. It had, he believed, been "a good fight." Esquibel was evacuated via Bagram air base near Kabul. While there, Yazzie and Doc Ramos were carried in. Yazzie's face was wrapped in a mound of bandages, but eventually the cuts healed. The three encouraged each other until they were put on separate flights to Germany.

Sergeant McCulloch was awarded the Silver Star and became a drill instructor. But when his hot temper flared against a recruit, the Marine Corps demoted him to corporal. He drank too heavily, and broke up with his wife. A knife-wielding psychopath assaulted Mac in a bar in Galveston, almost killing him. It took a year for him to partially recover.

When 3/5 returned to California, the high command kept the battalion intact and under close observation for three months. Their mental ailments were no higher than those reported by the rear-echelon units. Yet 3/5 faced the hardest sustained fighting and took the highest casualties in the war.

"Out at Fires, I had one genuine case of PTSD," Garcia said. "That Marine had stepped on four IEDs. After we returned to the States, I heard of three others from my platoon."

Sgt. J. D. Browning left the sniper section with thirteen confirmed kills. On his next tour, he qualified for the Marine Corps national rifle team and traveled the country in shooting competitions. He accepted the dying and killing as what he had signed up for.

"PTSD? We all had post-traumatic stress after serving at Fires," he said. "That doesn't mean a disorder. I have nightmares. That's to be expected. But to draw pay for nightmares for the rest of my life? No, that's not to be expected."

Cpl. Jordan Laird, married for eight years and with two daughters and a baby boy (named after Matt Abbate), took a job on the oil fields of North Dakota. He had two crushed vertebrae from carrying Espinoza across the Golf Course during the Thanksgiving battle.

"Up to eighteen, our parents took care of us," he said. "Then we signed up, and the Corps took care of us. When we got out and split up, it took us a year to learn how to take care of ourselves. That caused stress. But it's normal. Third Platoon had a grunt mentality—get on with your life."

Imagine you belong to 3rd Platoon. For seven months, you kill men and watch your friends die. You try not to think about dying or losing your legs. You rarely reflect on anything. Life is basic. You have your platoon family, ample food, a comfortable rack, and your rifle. At twenty years old, you are the power in the land. You sense it wherever you walk. Farmers, elders, sheiks, Taliban, headquarters staff, senior officers, every Marine who doesn't go on patrol—all admire your stature. You are the lion tamer, the man on the high wire, the race car driver, the risk taker whose life and limbs are no safer than a coin flip.

Then your tour ends. You don't carry a rifle anymore. You are not the death dealer when you wake up in the morning. You are just a corporal inside the rigid peacetime Marine Corps, or a civilian selling cell phones. You're no different than a million others your own age. You are no longer a warrior king.

When that happens, there will be stress. For some, it will be memories from Sangin. For others, the stress comes from the abrupt loss of power and self-confidence that out at Fires had encased each grunt as solidly as his armored vest.

"A counselor said the VA will pay me," Lantznester said, "because I was in 3/5 and got shot at. No way. I pay for myself. Some Marines are really messed up by that war. But too many others are taking stuff just because it's offered."

Cpl. Matt Smith found that his family came through for him.

"Once we were back, I drank too much," he said. "Even when I was having fun, dark thoughts popped up. I'd have flashes of depression, but a Marine isn't supposed to show weakness. If you've got a problem, deal with it. My dad, though, knew. He helped me out of it."

For Cpl. Kevin Frame, it was as though he had dropped down the rabbit hole in *Alice in Wonderland*.

"I used to be really someone—a Marine fighting a war," he said. "Once back in civilian life, I was making minimum wage. Unless you've been through it, you can't relate to the shock of that."

Cpl. Logan Stark enrolled at Michigan State University and produced an excellent documentary video on 3/5's tour, entitled *For the 25.*

"We were bred to be these big, tough creatures," Stark said. "All of a sudden [back in civilian life] . . . well, stress just happened. I saw how my moods upset my mom, and so I took steps to change. The good part that will never go away is that we were brothers."

Cpl. Jeff Sibley left the service and joined the family construction company. For relaxation, he drove a racing car and hoped to raise enough money to fund a racing team.

"We accomplished a lot in Sangin," he said. "Once the Marines left, though, the Taliban came back. I don't think about it. I don't want our losses to be in vain."

Garcia was more detached.

"Our job," he said, "is not to question politics or the strategic outcome of our battles. Marines push the fight to the enemy, no matter the cost."

Garcia's low point as a leader had come in October when Cpl. Juan Dominguez lost both legs and his right arm. Dominguez emerged as the symbol of 3rd Platoon. He invited them all to his wedding in 2013, where he wore his dress blues and when one of his prosthetic legs fell off, he pushed it back on, took his wife's arm, and continued walking.

"I am not some poor schmuck who stepped on an IED and now everyone can feel sorry for him," he told Gretel Kovach of *The San Diego Union-Tribune.* "I am a musician and living my life to the fullest that I can, for the guys who didn't come back."

Yazzie returned to his parents' farm on the Navajo Reservation in northern Arizona. He bought a black GMC Sierra truck for his nine-hour treks to southern California and planned to go to college in the fall.

"The people of Sangin," he said, "didn't want to be helped. They'd prefer us not being there. Of course, I'd do it again. We were brothers at Fires."

Corporal Lantznester returned with a similar attitude.

"Looking back, it was terrifying," he said, "not knowing which step was your last. One day, Doc Fuke and I were talking when rounds hit above our heads. Someone was aiming to kill me. Not just anyone—me. After Sangin, I won't let anything stop me."

Chapter 13

WHO WILL FIGHT FOR US?

"What does Sangin mean? They sent us there to fight—so we fought."

—GEN. JOHN KELLY, U.S. MARINE CORPS

The members of 3rd Platoon possessed the warrior spirit expected of Marines. They did not focus 95 percent of their effort upon friendly persuasion. Indeed, their aggressive, almost obsessive focus upon destroying the enemy seemed to contradict the restrained strategy of the high command. Third Platoon was determined to win. To them, that meant walking across the poppy fields without stepping on a mine or being shot at. That was a limited but practical definition of winning.

Placed in counterinsurgency context, 3rd Platoon was in the "clearing" phase, with "holding" by Afghan forces and "building" by Afghan government employees to follow. Whether that process would be carried out was beyond the time frame and control of 3rd

Platoon. How Sangin evolved—whether it progressed or regressed—depended upon the interaction among the Taliban, the tribes, and the Afghan army after the Americans left. The American strategy of protecting the population with an ever-expanding oil spot had postponed but not canceled that time of reckoning, when the Afghans would fight and barter among themselves. One thing was certain: the ferocity and cohesion of 3rd Platoon, which was welded together like steel plates, sprung from factors not attributable to the uncertain strategy.

Sangin: The Setting

After 3/5 left in 2011, four more Marine battalions rotated through Sangin district. By late 2012, the Taliban had largely stopped shooting and planting mines. Beaten down, the Taliban had decided not to contest the American troops patrolling inside the district. By staying on the offensive for two years, the Marines had won the battle of attrition.

"Violence has subsided," according to a 2012 article in the *Marine Corps Times*, ". . . but the overall U.S. toll in Sangin is staggering. More than 50 Marines have been killed here in fewer than two years. At least 500 more have been severely wounded. In practical terms, a half of a battalion in amputees has been created here."

Was Sangin worth the cost? In 2011, 3rd Platoon did not believe they had won the trust or support of the villagers. Nor did the battalions that came after them. Although the Taliban ruled mostly by fear, they had put down deep roots that sprang back to life as the Marines pulled out.

By the fall of 2013, travel along Route 611 above Outpost Transformer was once again perilous.

"Sangin is like an open space for the Taliban," the district governor said in September of 2013. "Anyone can enter, and anyone can leave."

The Taliban were sneaking back in again, launching ambushes inside the very markets constructed by the British six years earlier to motivate the farmers to reject the Taliban. The Afghan battalion replacing the Marines received a cold reception from the farmers.

"It's difficult to find local people who are against the Taliban," an Afghan colonel told a *New York Times* reporter. "This place [Sangin] is like a prison."

Sergeant Deykeroff posted the article on his Facebook page, with a three-word comment: "same old Sangin." The reversion showed how deeply the tentacles of the Taliban extended. The farmers weren't innocents yearning for freedom from the Taliban. Growing opium corroded the collective soul of the community. Afghanistan had the highest percentage of drug addicts in the world. The individual farmer knew he was destroying the lives of others. He knew the names and families of the dazed, thin men wandering around his village. There were no starving farmers in the fertile Green Zone. The rich soil grew whatever was planted—corn, melons, sunflowers, wheat, tomatoes, pomegranates, marijuana, poppy.

The farmer pleaded that opium was Inshallah—God's will. The estate owners in Kabul, the Taliban, the buyers from Pakistan—they were responsible for what the poor farmer planted. In his view, the farmer could no more rebel against the Taliban than he could refuse to plant poppy. Besides, poppy paid four times more than wheat.

The Taliban were part of a soiled social fabric that extended from Karzai downward. Their control over Sangin, where no Afghan official arrested a Taliban, could not be changed by Americans. Commanders at the top claimed the population switched sides. After the Thanksgiving battle, though, 3rd Platoon knew that the farmers threw in with the winners. No matter how momentarily dominant, the Marines were forever transient outsiders. Only Afghans could repair the damage their complicity had wrought upon their own society.

A majority in 3rd Platoon believed Afghanistan would remain a mess when they left. They were correct. By the end of 2013, the Afghan army had handed several outposts in Sangin over to the Taliban.

"Local residents and officials described a bizarre scene in the Sangin bazaar," *The New York Times* reported in December of 2013. ". . . Around midday, the Afghan Army arrived in an armored convoy, bearing Taliban commanders known to the locals. The men walked through the stalls, introducing the men and sharing laughs, witnesses said."

By mid-2014, there were no British or Americans in Sangin. The Taliban had remained. No Afghan soldier ventured into the Green Zone.

"It's sad," Vic Garcia said, "really sad."

The battle for Sangin failed in its strategic objective. Hundreds of millions of dollars were spent and hundreds of lives lost in the district over twelve years. The objective was to open Route 611 from Sangin to the Kajacki Dam in order to install another turbine. That did not happen. In the end, the district receded and became a besieged outpost.

"We left Sangin with a sense of accomplishment," Sibley said. "Our losses weren't in vain. We made progress. Now [three years later] . . . I don't want to talk about it."

Tom Schueman, the 1st Platoon commander, summarized the conflicting feelings.

"There were some good people among the farmers," he said, "but not the Taliban. Looking back, I had the worst time, and the best. It was my greatest honor."

In January of 2014, Battalion 3/5 lost their twenty-sixth brother. In early 2011, an IED in Sangin had sheared off the legs of Cpl. Farrell

Gilliam, twenty-five, from Fresno, California. Farrell had wanted to be a Marine since he was in the fourth grade. For four more years, he fought off massive infections and underwent thirty operations. In 2014, he took his own life.

"The war doesn't stop just because they come home," his mother said. "The war is not over for them. It still rages on in their hearts and in their heads and physical bodies."

The Strategy

In 2001, we went to war to destroy Al Qaeda in Afghanistan. When the terrorists escaped into Pakistan, Mr. Bush massively enlarged and changed the mission.

"Write this down," he said. "Afghanistan and Iraq will lead that part of the world to democracy. They are going to be the catalyst to change the Middle East and the world."

The question was how to destroy Al Qaeda. The answer was to build two democracies in the Islamic, authoritarian Middle East. In Afghanistan, at a cost of 2,400 American dead and one trillion dollars, we did not succeed in destroying Al Qaeda, or defeating the Taliban, or creating a true democracy. Our basic mistake was handing over freedom as a gift and doing the fighting for others. Our intention was good; our wisdom was bad.

Our military commanders willingly agreed to expand their mission. The defining document was the 2006 field manual on counterinsurgency, which was widely praised by academics and the mainstream media for its emphasis upon constructing rather than destroying. "Soldiers and Marines," the manual instructed, are expected to be "nation-builders as well as warriors." Our most revered generals embraced the mission of changing the Afghan culture.

While running for president in 2008, Mr. Obama had insisted,

"Afghanistan is the war that must be won." But Mr. Obama and his White House staff did not trust our commanders. He felt they were trying to trap him into rubber-stamping their decisions. As commander in chief, he did not stand behind his troops. He made it clear his heart wasn't in the fight. By December of 2009, he had downgraded the mission from "defeating" to "diminishing" the Taliban.

"What was interesting was the metamorphosis," National Security Adviser James L. Jones said in December of 2009. "I dare say that none of us ended up where we started."

"Metamorphosis" was a pompous word for pulling out without accomplishing a specific goal. Mission clarity and confidence decayed. In 2010, Secretary of Defense Gates replaced the top commander in Kabul with General McChrystal, who ordered the troops to focus upon winning over the population rather then defeating the Taliban.

To reduce civilian casualties, he severely restricted coalition firepower. Although the Taliban inflicted six times more civilian fatalities, President Karzai escalated his rants about American-caused casualties and released those imprisoned for killing Americans. The Pashtun tribes never came over to our side. Rather than positively altering Afghan attitudes, McChrystal negatively affected the attitudes of his own troops.

McChrystal was replaced by General Petraeus. Distrusting our military, Obama had extracted from Petraeus his assurance that a surge of American troops would yield success within eighteen months—by about January of 2011. Obama put in 30,000 more troops, bringing the U.S. total to 100,000. According to Secretary Gates, both military and civilian officials agreed that this number provided "a fully resourced counterinsurgency strategy." Actually, twice that number was needed to control thousands of Pashtun villages in a mountainous country the size of Texas. Petraeus persisted with expanding the "oil spot" deployment of U.S. troops that risked clearing districts beyond the areas Afghan forces were willing to control once we left.

Sangin was the inevitable overreach of a strategy blindly willful and excessively ambitious. Operational success in Sangin required the installation of a turbine at the Kajacki Dam. That never had a chance of happening unless the Marines stayed. So why were they sent there, knowing the Afghan soldiers could not hold open the road to the dam?

The most elementary risk assessment would include four enormous obstacles to victory: an unreliable Afghan government; Pashtun tribes not amenable to persuasion; a vast country requiring hundreds of thousands of troops; and a secure sanctuary for the enemy.

There was an alternative to "full-fledged, fully resourced counter-insurgency." Early on, several experienced commanders had put forth credible proposals based on lessons from Vietnam. The basic concept was to place conventional small units under the leadership of Special Forces, creating task forces to work intensively with the Afghan forces, at a fraction of the size and cost of our standard force structure. As the Afghan military was trained, our military would get out, leaving Kabul politics to the State Department. That was the road not taken.

Instead, in 2009, Secretary of Defense Gates said, "We are in this thing to win." But by 2011, he had concluded that our troops could do only two things: kill the enemy and train Afghan soldiers. He concluded that nation building was unattainable. Yet he appointed commanders—McChrystal and Petraeus—who ardently believed it was attainable. The contradiction has not been explained. All three were honorable, dedicated men who tried to do too much.

As Gates desired, the Marines in Helmand did severely attrite the Taliban. Colonel Kennedy called his approach "Big Stick COIN," meaning his goal was to destroy the Taliban. This was what Gates wanted. But the secretary of defense also believed the Marines were fighting in the wrong places—like Sangin—and resisted being placed under the top command of McChrystal. Gates wondered if their sacrifices were in vain. But he never addressed his misgivings directly with the Marine generals.

Much worse, our high command dithered, unable to decide whether the Taliban was a distraction or a mortal enemy like Al Qaeda.

Marine General Kelly said, "our country today is in a life and death struggle against an evil enemy," engaged in "pursuit day and night into whatever miserable lair Al Qaeda, the Taliban, and their allies might slither into."

Kelly was clear: kill the bastards. McChrystal, who was his boss, held the opposite view.

"The conflict will be won," he wrote, "by persuading the population, not by destroying the enemy."

Which was it? Were we in a death struggle with the Taliban, or were they a legitimate force in Afghan politics, deserving to share in the political power? No nation should ever go to war without the will to defeat the enemy.

Our top command praised the warrior spirit of our Special Forces. The American public responded accordingly. Amazon sold 400 books about the SEALs—more books than there were SEALs in all of Afghanistan. Our commandos were lauded for attacking the Taliban.

General McChrystal ordered our conventional units to spend only 5 percent of their effort killing the enemy. This conveyed the message that the conventional grunt was second-rate, not expected to strike fear into his enemies. A warrior has to hold within himself the desire –the thirst—to kill his opponent. Lacking that, he is in the wrong job. A grunt must walk onto every battlefield to win.

"Troops risking their lives," Secretary Gates wrote, "need to be told that their goal is to 'defeat' those trying to kill them."

Defeating the Taliban was impossible because Pakistan provided them with aid and sanctuary. After Vietnam, our military vowed never again to fight a war while granting a sanctuary to the enemy. In thirteen years, fifteen different generals served as the top coalition commander in Afghanistan. Several dozen other generals served under their commands. Yet not one general resigned or spoke out. We beat on against the tide, set on automatic by a refusal to review basic assumptions.

Despite the fine-sounding rhetoric of the generals, 3rd Platoon and all the other grunts were engaged in a war of attrition. The hope was that our forces would kill so many Taliban that their ranks could not be fully replenished, allowing the Afghan army to hold the remnants at bay. In Sangin and elsewhere, our conventional troops were engaged in slow-pitch attrition, accepting losses to IEDs in order to occasionally kill Taliban who chose to initiate contact. At the same time, our Special Operations Forces practiced fast-pitch attrition by means of heliborne night raids that minimized IED casualties.

Both methods inflicted steady casualties upon the enemy. By 2014, our commanders were saying the Taliban strength had fallen, giving hope to the Afghan army. Such success was *in spite of,* rather than because of, the counterinsurgency strategy. War, by definition, is a process of attrition. When it becomes the strategic goal, commanders have lost their way. Attrition is the absence of strategy.

In place of an exit strategy, Mr. Obama simply exited without a strategy, by moving the goalposts. In 2001, the objective for the invasion was to prevent terrorists from using Afghanistan as a safe haven. In 2014, Obama did away with that objective. The new goal, he said, was to show "resolve that terrorists do not launch attacks against our country."

Because resolve can be demonstrated by a speech, the Taliban no longer had to be defeated in battle. In place of deeds, words sufficed.

He preemptively pledged in 2014 that all U.S. forces would leave Afghanistan before his term ended in 2016, regardless of what happened on the ground.

"This is how," Mr. Obama said, "wars end in the twenty-first century."

What a tangled web we weave when we deceive ourselves. The war didn't end because Mr. Obama quit. Al Qaeda and the Taliban remained on the battlefield, undefeated. When Secretary Gates left office, he hoped Afghanistan, no longer winnable, would not "be viewed as a strategic defeat for the United States, or as a failure with global consequences."

Such a disastrous defeat appears unlikely. Marines at the grunt level did not believe the Afghan army would hold on to the Green Zone, yet the generals reported progress. Both perspectives are probably correct: the Taliban will dominate in the Green Zone, but the Afghan army can hang on to district headquarters and the cities, if we provide funding and air support. For $5 billion to $10 billion a year, we can avoid a collapse like the one symbolized in the 1975 photo of despairing Vietnamese clutching at the last helicopter leaving the American embassy in Saigon.

In a subdued speech at West Point in May of 2014 aimed at explaining his foreign policy, Mr. Obama declared, "America's character . . . will always triumph."

Avoiding a humiliating defeat is not a triumph of the American character. Mr. Obama was an irresolute commander in chief. Pledging that all U.S. military forces will leave by 2016 was the act of a politician, not a statesman. Our generals tried to do too much, and our commander in chief settled for too little. After 2016, a duplicitous Pakistan will exert more influence in Kabul than will the United States. The Taliban, the drug syndicates, the Kabul kleptocracy, and the Pakistanis will cut murky deals. Afghanistan will gradually fade from the consciousness of the American public.

For what enduring gain did we expend so much blood and treasure? The test of success is whether you would fight the war over again with the same strategy. No military commander would repeat our Afghan strategy.

Combat Cohesion

While our generals pursued the quixotic strategy of a benevolent war, our grunts remained loyal, tough, and realistic. Third Platoon fought the hardest sustained campaign of the war. One million steps, with death or amputation awaiting each step. Despite knowing the strategy made little sense, they did not falter or pull back.

I knew Colonel Kennedy was up to something when he first dropped me off with 3rd Platoon. As an old grunt, I could see the steel in them. But where did their resolve—and that of other platoons like them—come from? Who fights for us, and why?

To begin with, combat effectiveness has little to do with morality. Third Platoon didn't fight well because they believed in democracy. The Spartans and Romans fought skillfully to enslave others. German soldiers fought well for Hitler.

Patriotism or nationalism, however, is a powerful motivator. Cpl. Jacob Ruiz had endured a lengthy investigation after BBC video showed him shooting a man. I asked him what message he wanted to convey about serving in Sangin. He had a right to be angry, so his answer surprised me.

Ruiz said, "We'll do anything asked of us."

Third Platoon understood that they weren't pursuing, to put it mildly, the benevolent strategy of the high command.

"This war's stupid," Mad Dog Myers said. "Well, so what? Our country's in it."

Their sacrifices achieved no permanent goal, and won no Afghan hearts or minds. Counterinsurgency theory was irrelevant to them.

"The mission was never about hearts and minds," Rausch, the Midwesterner with the Commandant's coin, said. "We were there to fight."

Other coalition platoons—American, British, Dutch—may have been more understanding of the population. But no platoon controlled more of the Green Zone. "War," to quote columnist Kathleen Parker, "demands victory rather than understanding." If you are not willing to fight, don't come to Sangin. They were going to own the land on which they walked. That meant killing the Taliban. That was their objective.

"For thousands of years," Jordan Laird said, "there's been a group of people that has been set apart. They're the warrior class."

Third Platoon fought inside the structure of the Marine Corps. They embraced its traditions of discipline and toughness. They all wanted to be Marines, some since grammar school. Each had chosen to fight before he met those who would fight alongside him. In the Marine Corps, they learned how to shoot, obey orders, plan, and adapt. Everyone had a job, and every job focused on destroying the enemy. They believed in their tribe, "the few, the proud."

On November 10, the Marine Corps celebrates its birthday with pomp-and-circumstance balls at 135 American embassies and in cities across America. At one ball, the CEO of a major corporation watched as corporals and their wives walked up to the head table to chat with the commanding general and link arms for a photo.

"This rarely happens in the corporate world," he said.

A good military leader forms close ties with his unit. Tradition, heritage, and camaraderie unite the ranks. Those factors apply across the board. In themselves, they don't explain 3rd Platoon's singular tenacity.

They weren't fighting for their squad buddies, hoping just to stay alive. If that were their objective, they would have stayed close to Fires. Instead, they pushed steadily farther out.

But they were calculating about each move. Supreme Court Justice Oliver Wendell Holmes fought in the Civil War. Reflecting on that titanic struggle, he wrote, "To fight a war you must believe in something and want something with all your might." That was certainly true in World War II of the Marines who assaulted islands like Iwo Jima.

But Afghanistan was a highly limited war with elusive and changing objectives. Third Platoon was cunning. Garcia took small bites, alternately encouraging and reining in the squad leaders. The squads were careful not to be cut off. The goal was to kill without swinging with all your might and risking being caught off-balance.

Each month, the Taliban became more wary. They knew 3rd Platoon wanted to put down one or two of them a day. They referred to the platoon by name. They hated the snipers. They asked their leaders in Quetta, Pakistan, for more fighters. But the results were the same: the Marine patrols kept coming.

Why did 3rd Platoon fight with such ferocity? Successful people claim they made their own luck. Unsuccessful people complain about bad luck. The truth lies in between. Chance played a role in shaping 3rd Platoon, because each traumatizing event was offset by a counteraction. The platoon's cohesion was reinforced whenever it most threatened to crumble.

In early October, when Lopez and Catherwood were killed, Abbate organized the shocked squad and charged through the minefield. When the Taliban flooded Fires, Kilo Company headquarters responded by carrying ammunition through fields of mud. Gunny Carlisle went from man to man, promising Fires would hold. Captain Johnson urged the numbed Marines to remember their forefathers in the frigid cold of Korea. The company's radio call signs were Sledgehammer and Old Breed, references to Corporal Sledge on the blood-soaked island of Peleliu.

"A set of ties," the historian Aaron O'Connell wrote, ". . . bound

Marines together in ways not experienced by members of the larger and more diversified services. It was not only to the members of their unit that Marines remained *Semper Fidelis*, 'always faithful.' It was to an idealized and timeless community of ancestors—the entire 'family' of the Corps."

The day after the flood at Fires in October, Boelk was killed and Lieutenant West was evacuated without his hand and leg. Morale was bleak. Garcia immediately took over, and his reputation bought him time with the platoon. They were willing to be led, if he stepped up. Instead of holing up at Fires, Garcia took the platoon on the offensive, showing that the Taliban couldn't emplace IEDs everywhere. When a fight did break out, he called back to company, and Spokes Beardsley delivered two F-18s, demonstrating the overwhelming firepower on call to help them.

The snipers became part of the platoon, bagging a kill a day on patrols with the squads. The kills made a huge difference. The IED is insidious because you cannot strike back. One-sided attrition drains the best units. In the legend of Beowulf, the man-eating monster Grendel lurks in the dark green forest. Similarly, the Green Zone had gained mythic stature as the lair of the ferocious Taliban. The snipers turned it into a hunting ground.

On the daily patrols, the Marines shared the risk equally; any one of them could lose his leg or life. Through the daily kills, they shared the satisfaction of revenge. There's no genteel way of putting it. They patrolled to kill, and they saw the results. Success provided the platoon with confidence.

They slept in caves cut off from the world. Their isolation made them more dangerous. They had only one another, and their only outlet was to kill the Taliban. Abbate's verve was infectious. "Hellasick" made a mockery of the Taliban. "Until that day" became the platoon greeting.

The Thanksgiving battle was pivotal. The platoon ran to the sound of the guns, with the squads covering one another. Each squad leader—Esquibel, Deykeroff, Thoman, McCulloch—was a combat veteran. Mad Dog yelled for the gunships, and the gunships chopped down Belleau Wood. From that day forward, 3rd Platoon felt superior to the Taliban. The snipers carved stick figures on the wall, while every member of the platoon kept his personal count.

At night around the fire pits, every member from an incoming patrol went over what he saw, what seemed normal and what seemed out of place. The platoon developed a shared awareness of the situation around them. When they talked, they were adding texture to a common mental map, with everyone contributing.

In the first weeks, they had taken heavy casualties because they had no pattern recognition of the danger zones and likely IED hiding places. They named key terrain features like the Golf Course and Belleau Wood. When they stepped off, they had a collective image of the route they were taking and where they were likely to encounter opposition.

The platoon had depth of leadership. Like wolves, they become accustomed to the routine of the hunt. When a leader goes down, another must step forward, be accepted, and be followed. Lieutenant West went down and Garcia took his place. Sergeant Abbate went down and Browning stepped forward. Third Platoon was never without an Alpha wolf, never retreated to skulk in their caves.

The pressure of his peers motivated each Marine in the platoon. Once Garcia showed them that IEDs couldn't be placed everywhere, the habit of aggressive patrolling solidified into a routine that no one questioned, because everyone bought into it. They believed their tribe could defeat any foe. Group spirit bound them together. During a fight, when Sergeant Dy riffed by shouting, "We'll do it live! Fuck it!," he was signaling confidence in the other squads. Move to contact, identify the fields of fire, improvise, respond ferociously, and move on.

Men like Garcia and Abbate were born with courage in their genes. But how was courage transferred from one man to the next? Looking back, had Abbate been killed in the early October battle, the platoon might have spiraled down. By the time of his death in December, however, a social compact gripped the platoon: win every skirmish.

With December came recognition. The platoon was proud it had been selected to move south during the cease-fire to clean out the sector called PB America. By that time, each squad had developed a tactical rhythm. Instead of being intimidated, the platoon looked forward to engaging the Taliban.

When they returned to Fires in January, the outpost's isolation increased their bonds. They had only each other. There was no administration, no daily emails from the families, no garrison tasks, no first sergeant with a list of chores. Unlike in the rear, they didn't live two polarizing lives; they were spared the space capsule called the Internet. They could not escape to home by clicking a mouse. Outpost Fires was their castle, and beyond the gates lived medieval tribes that spoke a foreign tongue.

The heavy rains of February gave the platoon a break by soaking the IEDs. On different occasions, four Marines avoided losing their legs when they set off low-order detonations.

In March, with the end of tour approaching, Garcia lived up to his nickname of Juggernaut by keeping the pressure on sectors like P8Q. The platoon yielded none of the ground that it had seized.

"It would have been easy to slack off," Sibley said. "But the lieutenant was the same hardass all the way to the end."

In summary, 3rd Platoon's cohesion was due to inspiration (Abbate), leadership (Garcia), firepower (Beardsley), aggressiveness (McCulloch), steadiness (Esquibel), and raw spirit (Myers). The mission centered on patrolling until shot at, and then returning fire until the firefight was won. The strategic rationales—building a nation, installing a turbine at the dam, winning over the Sangin tribes—were at best flimsy. The platoon went forth to fight and kill the Taliban.

The platoon bought into Garcia's rule: do your best. They didn't care where each had come from, or would go once back in the States. On their tiny island called Fires, they had only one another, and one million steps to walk.

"We fought," Yazzie said to me, "because we were so pissed off about everything."

Yaz always looked for the clearest explanation. As he drives his macho truck to Laguna Beach, he might laugh at Aristotle's take on the platoon's spirit. But I doubt that he will deny it.

"We become . . . brave," the philosopher wrote 2,300 years ago, "by doing brave acts."

Finish every fight standing on the enemy's ground.

Acknowledgments

Will Murphy, executive editor at Random House, combines two remarkable skills. First, he can sense the major themes of a book before the writer has uncovered them. Thus, Will is able to provide guidance that saves the author a huge amount of time and angst. Second, Will moves at rapid speed in the editing process, not hesitating to point out what is trite or poorly written. Mika Kasuga, as assistant editor, is super efficient. She follows through on every task, keeps every deadline, and keeps accurate track of a draft in its convoluted iterations as I daily or weekly change what I have previously submitted. Fred Chase edits sentences and paragraphs with a dexterity that captures the essence of a narrative's arc. London King is always full of good cheer and shrewd advice as she arranges interviews about the book. In sum, in the writing, editing, and publishing of book after book, it is a pleasure working with the Random House team.

Teresa and Mark Soto teamed with Patty Schumacher, mother of LCpl. Victor Dew (KIA), to edit an excellent compendium of articles about the fallen, entitled *The Story of the 3/5 Darkhorse Marine Battalion in Sangin, Afghanistan.* Similarly fine work about Helmand Province was done by Ed Marek on his website, Talking Proud. Special thanks to Jim Binion, Matt Abbate's stepdad, for his understanding and support.

Conversely, official sources proved disappointing. The command chronology of the battalion could not be found, and the military mapping bureaucracy stoutly resisted sharing unclassified maps readily accessed on Google. Worse still, all records of troops in contact—indeed, practically all written communications during the Afghanistan war—were transmitted via a classified network called SIPRNet. All data were automatically stamped Secret. While the Pentagon provides generals and former secretaries of defense access to the records and expedites declassification, this courtesy is not provided to civilian historians. This means that a generation of writers will lack access to basic materials. My special thanks, then, go to 3rd Platoon and Kilo Company for taking the time each evening in the field to keep a hand-printed, unclassified diary of the day's events.

On a personal note, I extend my heartfelt thanks to my loving wife, Betsy. I know she has wondered over the years about luck and odds, yet never once has she expressed apprehension. Trip after trip, book after book, she is encouraging, understanding, and supportive.

Appendix A

ADDRESS BY LT. GEN. JOHN KELLY, USMC

(To the Semper Fi Society of St. Louis, November 13, 2010)

Nine years ago four commercial aircraft took off from Boston, Newark, and Washington, with men, women, and children—all innocent, and all soon to die. These aircraft were targeted at the World Trade Towers in New York, the Pentagon, and likely the Capitol in Washington, D.C. Three found their mark. No American alive old enough to remember will ever forget exactly where they were, exactly what they were doing, and exactly who they were with at the moment they watched the aircraft dive into the World Trade Towers on what was, until then, a beautiful morning in New York City. Within the hour 3,000 blameless human beings would be vaporized, incinerated, or crushed in the most agonizing ways imaginable.

In the darkest times Americans seek refuge in family, and in country, remembering that strong men and women have always stepped forward to protect the nation when the need was dire. Our enemy fights for an ideology based on an irrational hatred of who we are. We did not start this fight, and it will not end until the extremists understand that we as a people will never lose our faith or our courage. America's civilian and military protectors both here at home and overseas have for nearly nine years fought this enemy to a standstill and have never for a second "wondered why." They know, and are not afraid.

Their struggle is your struggle. They hold in disdain those who claim to support them but not the cause that takes their innocence, their limbs, and even their lives. As a democracy—"We the People"—and that by definition is every one of us—sent them away from home and hearth to fight our enemies. We are all responsible. I know it doesn't apply to those of us here tonight but if anyone thinks you can somehow thank them for their service, and not support the cause for which they fight—America's survival—then they are lying to themselves and rationalizing away something in their lives, but, more importantly, they are slighting our warriors and mocking their commitment to the nation.

Since this generation's "day of infamy" the American military has handed our ruthless enemy defeat after defeat. But it will go on for years, if not decades, before this curse has been eradicated. We have done this by unceasing pursuit day and night into whatever miserable lair Al Qaeda, the Taliban, and their allies might slither into to lay in wait for future opportunities to strike a blow at freedom. America's warriors have never lost faith in their mission, or doubted the correctness of their cause.

Yes, we are at war, and are winning, but you wouldn't know it because successes go unreported, and only when something does go sufficiently or is sufficiently controversial, it is highlighted by the media elite that then sets up the "know it all" chattering class to offer their endless criticism. These self-proclaimed experts always seem to know better—but have never themselves been in the arena. We are at war and like it or not, that is a fact. It is not Bush's war, and it is not Obama's war, it is our war and we can't run away from it. Even if we wanted to surrender, there is no one to surrender to.

Our enemy is savage, offers absolutely no quarter, and has a single focus and that is either kill every one of us here at home, or enslave us with a sick form of extremism that serves no God or purpose that decent men and women could ever grasp. Given the opportunity to do another 9/11, our merciless enemy would do it today, tomorrow, and every day thereafter. If, and most in the know predict that it is only a matter of time, he acquires nuclear, chemical, or biological weapons, these extremists will use these weapons of mass murder against us without a moment's hesitation.

I don't know why they hate us, and I don't care. We have a saying in the Marine Corps and that is "no better friend, no worse enemy, than a U.S. Marine." We always hope for the first, friendship, but are certainly more than ready for the second. If it's death they want, it's death they will get, and the Marines will continue showing them the way to hell if that's what will make them happy.

It is a fact that our country today is in a life and death struggle against an evil enemy, but America as a whole is certainly not at war. Today, only a tiny fraction—less than a percent—shoulder the burden of fear and sacrifice, and they shoulder it for the rest of us.

The comforting news for every American is that our men and women in uniform, and every Marine, is as good today as any in our history. While some might think we have produced yet another generation of materialistic and self-absorbed young people, those who serve today have broken the mold and stepped out as real men, and real women, who are already making their own way in life while protecting ours. They know the real strength of a platoon.

It doesn't matter if it's an IED, a suicide bomber, mortar attack, sniper, fighting in the upstairs room of a house, or all of it at once; they talk, swagger, and, most importantly, fight today in the same way America's Marines have since the Tun Tavern. They also know whose shoulders they stand on, and they will never shame any Marine living or dead.

The chattering class and all those who doubt America's intentions and resolve, endeavor to make them and their families out to be victims, but they are wrong. We who have served and are serving refuse their sympathy. Those of us who have lived in the dirt, sweat and struggle of the arena are not victims and will have none of that. Death, or fear of death, has no power over them. Their paths are paved by sacrifice, sacrifices they gladly make . . . for you. They prove themselves everyday on the field of battle . . . for you. They fight in every corner of the globe . . . for you. They live to fight . . . for you, and they never rest because there is always another battle to be won in the defense of America.

We Marines believe that God gave America the greatest gift he could bestow to man while he lived on this earth—freedom. We also believe he gave us another gift nearly as precious—our soldiers, sailors, airmen, Coast Guardsmen, and Marines—to safeguard that gift and guarantee no force on this earth can ever steal it away. Rest assured our America, this experiment in democracy started over two centuries ago, will forever remain the "land of the free and home of the brave" so long as we never run out of tough young Americans who are willing to look beyond their own self-interest and comfortable lives, and go into the darkest and most dangerous places on earth to hunt down, and kill, those who would do us harm. God Bless America, and . . .

SEMPER FIDELIS!

Lt. Gen. John Kelly

Appendix B

3RD PLATOON AND KILO COMPANY
3/5 EXCERPTS FROM DAILY LOGBOOKS

OCTOBER 2010

14 SH Catherwood KIA, 2 amputees, 1 other wia

15 SH-3 [Sledge Hammer 3rd Platoon] clearing bldgs. Continuous firefight. Lt. West, Boelk Ubrando, IED SAF

16 Patrols night (14-20 Marines) with no contact.

16 Afghan digs hole in road; sniper misses him

18 3-1 patrol in contact in cornfield; 3-3 hit with mg [machine gun]; 2 en [enemy] kia; 2 civ kia; one civ wia

19 3-1 blows up an IED; trip wire ied wounds two snipers; three hours later, Q1E moderate SAF; CAS 2 GBUs; one hour later, blow IED; one hour later, blow Brit mine

20 17 q1e; gunshot in ribs

3-3 saf 62 83 q1f

3-1 takes saf [small arms fire]; kill one with icom; Sibley hit by
SAF in ribs; 3-3 out as qrf [Quick Reaction Force]; women
and kids flee; 2d round of saf; 81s ([mortars] fire; Hughie hit
at PB Fires, followed by another firefight

21 3-2 takes saf; 3-3 takes out 7-ton truck as qrf

22 3-1, 3-2 and 3-3 all on patrol; explosion for unknown
reasons

23 ied Dominguez double amputee b17 q1e + 3 concussions

24 3-1 gets radio HET ID B6 Q1A Finds 12.7 heavy rounds. SAF
I en kia

26 3-1 ptl pb fires hit by saf

27 3-3, 3-2 on ptl; find and blow an ied

28 SH-3 with 40 pax out for 3 day ptl. 3-2 ambushed in canal/
Weese evacd/ fight Q1A e pos + mosque 2 500 lbs bombs; at
night, 20 w/IR try to move on 3-2 Was this patrol a turning
point in terms of morale and aggression?

29 find wpns and ied stuff

30 still clearing Gorcie, Fearon and Hess are bitching

31 farmer steps on ied single amp 15 yr old;

NOVEMBER

3 Nov all 3 sqds in contact; mark ied with ir chem

6 1 cas kia farmer

7 cpl cook shoots man with icom; find 3 ieds

8-15 Nov too busy to keep log

10 McCulloch takes shrapnel

16 census ptl; boy shows ied, leads 3-2 across field but won't go
near tree line; usual bounding by one ft w/sbf by other to
search compounds; farmers complain re damage; shot at en

spotter; pics and info taken and put into computer; takes too long

16 std ptl sqd + 5 ANA, PC, 2 STA, 3 MG, 1 engn, 1 NE [Navy enlisted], 1 RO [straight radio operator], route to mosque ied signs; 3 on mopeds shadow ptl; cut through vines to avoid; in courtyard ana eventually uncover two shovel heads, 3 illums, 6 mortar fins, 2 icom chargers, opium tar, blue powder, wires, vials of animal medicine, AK clng gear in mosque, man in next field seen running away, no LNs in area

16-18 afghan holiday; no enemy shoot in zone

16 3-1 finds ied; p8t bldg. 6 family happy to see marines; moped man searched an let go; 2 hrs later same man with icom on moped hit; moped destroyed; meet farmer who says he shuts all doors at 1800, so never sees T; poor and asks for money; told about ied for money program; found blood in compound near where moped guy shot; farmer said it was a lamb

17 PB Fires post shoots at two men

17 3-2 confirms some compounds have elec power

18 3-3 provides basic med care to a few kids

19 At bldg 23, family came out. Took pictures of man, of house, his kids and elderly woman. Claimed to be his mother who[se] husband had been killed several months ago. Elderly woman acted unhappy with our presence. All lns [local nationals] saying they were afraid we would kill them. Also a woman at bldg 18 with no husband and young kids said she had to move there because her house had been bombed 10 days ago and the kid's father had been killed. She was their grandmother.

19 shoot at icom; farmers bring body to patrol base

19 3-1 himars ville P8S bldg15, 16 talks to farmer who said he commuted to work from desert; showed damage; took his pic and gave him chit on rite in rain paper; another wanted $ for

4 dead goats and 2 cows; dogs had eaten. Asked for pics of bones; took census of two families afraid of us; thought we'd kill them; house had been bombed; kids' father killed signed chit for 14 trees blown up; find two batteries in waterproof plastic with wires (3-2)

20 0900 P8Q garcia double amp ied was at point with vallon eod finds 2d ied Delany spotted—set up u shaped ambush in buffalo grass; Hur saw mam outside bldg. 39 w icom; shot and missed; mam ran into bldg. and ten mins later came out with shovel did this twice in and out; snipers hit center mass;

20 3-1 engineer wia by ied; find a 2d ied; farmer again asks for damage money "must try to take care of him soon to avoid him getting frustrated and helping Taliban with his land next to PB Fires."

20 3-1 finds ammonium nitrate cache and receives accurate saf 200 m

21 3-2 w conducts census under harassing fire

21 3-1 withholds fire to avoid hitting kids (per usual, not reported to company level because no TIC)

22 3-2 Garcia calls 6omm vs bldg. 11 himars ville, clear with m67 frags, begin tse bldg. 19 firefight Delany throws frags banshee in bldg. 3 takes fire 10 ieds destroyed during ptl

22 3-1 kills two w aks, chest rigs, radio antenna in himars fight all day

23 3-1 again engaged

24 ist night ptl 3-3 out at 0400 and back at 0900

24 3-3 Sgt Byram? [Sgt. Deykeroff] ied tripped by engr from 1-1 in P8T 10 lbs kia

2d ied hit Gonzales and gunny Carlisle and sgt peto Delany and Wagner fire LAWs at treeline evac under fire

25 THANKSGIVING BATTLE 1100 qrf to help 2d plt at transformer en fire—old breed 2-1—push east thru P8S and P8R;

2-1 pinned in Q5G; 3-2 bounding south in Q5H ambushed by 3 shooters (1mg, 2ak); Espinoza shot; myers called gun run; 3 en kia; joined plt in bld 34 Q5H moved east with cas and kia [Lt. Donnelly] gsw in head; swept Belleau Wood while 2d plt & ANA provided base of fire; ungodly amount of excalibers plus Shootout one Huey stayed in overhead while (120s?); LN evac w/gsw

26 3-2 left to find Sgt Petos rifle M203 barrel, engaged enemy spotters and returned

27 3-1two enemy shadow ptl; one en kia; hvy fire; tic; 60s; 4 gbus hit bldgs

27 3-2 fight

29 shoot at en with ak and binos

30 OB3 eod double amp ied; find 4 ied; PB Ezaway?

DECEMBER

2 Abbate killed; 60mm and 2 gbus; sector P8Q

2 Abdul Ahad captured; fired RPG at platoon

3 (Co. log) Old Breed 3-1 under fire; calls 120s; sees icom spotter and takes shot; finds ppied

6 (Co. log) 3-2 at 787 540 takes mg, rpg, calls hellfire; two hour fight

8 3-3 in Q1D pid TB call 60s; saw MAM on cycle w icom; shot cycle; man alive, no icom, let him go

9 3-2 vs one ak; dicker in trees; sniper killed

9 3-3 in Q1D at 0900; gets LN to show compound where Tb occupy 0500 to 0900 daily; clear ten bldgs.; get hit by mg; sh 1 in contact to north and some stray 40mm; constant bounding and sbf with no joy; rtb 1600

9 3-2 dfl 1030 to P8Q; crosses huge canal running east-west; questions 2 on cycle; Banshee 3 drops spotter; hit by 7 in

treeline; mg suppt and try to flank; Williamson uses at 4 at compound; en carrying off wounded; vargas (don't have this guy) uses 40mm; used hellfire on bldg. 52

10 3-2 finds ied; Delaney and wagner and Harmon blow it up

10 3-2 "sensitive situation in Jackson" ??? ordered to rtb

10 3-3 on 3-2 flank detain a guy with money and cell phone

11 3-3 in Q1D find two ieds; kill two running away in ditch; bldg. 42 Q1A find icom parts and atm tube and rounds in the corn

13 3-2 sniper shoots ied emplacer

14 LN leg taken off by ied

14 3-3 ordered to rtb due to issue with local officials

16 Sgt Esquibel 3-1 was the squad leader tasked to cross route carrot into southern green zone. 3-3 Sgt McCulloch and myself had a support by fire established and the maneuver element was clearing structures to west. 3-1 was initiating an Apobs to clear a suspected enemy mine-field on route carrot, when the enemy initiated an ambush from multiple directions catching 3-1 and the remainder of 3-3 in a massive hailstorm of bullets. Sgt mac, yazzie, and myself utilized the buildings to run 500 meters towards to flank the enemy in minutes. I used 60mm mortars to suppress enemy positions while we subsequently silenced and cleared them.

Cpl Xiong leads 60mm thru ied-cleared path to bring fire on enemy, treeline Carrot? 3-1 Palmer and Hess terrific ssgt cartier with us; Palma took Vallens from nervous engr and led us

18t platoon moves overnight to pb America, estab at 1100

22 depart America to Q9L at PhaseLine India drop excel and f18 gun runs on spotters; in treeline found 2 kia, one ak with 30mm ubgl and battery pack for ied; searched corn outside mosque; found rpg, 4 rockets, ied ak rounds; burned corn and set off another ied. Rtb 1700

23 3-1 engr loses his Vallen in canal

23 3-3 ptl from America; Yazzie get bad feeling, digs and finds lamp wire leading to 30 lbs explosives and 1016 ? jug [pressure cooker wrapped in plastic]

26 3-3 from America crosses rope bridge, meets nice family, enters bldg. 103 104, 109 finds one pp in front of firing hole in window and then another on back wall; blow one and leave other for eod. EOD brought to scene to destroy remaining IEDs

26 3-1 dfl America to Jackson

27 3-1 dfl America to blow ieds found by 3-3; found two more

28 3-2 dfl Jackson; Delaney and Wagner find three ieds and one command wire ied in gravel along Helmand river

28 3-3 dfl America; yaz finds and blows 3 pp ieds

29 at pb fires, en with scoped rifle duels watch standers

29 3-3 in p9L sector with ana; bldg. 41 Mcc and yaz find one ied; ana find a bag of pps; blew the bag in place

29 3-1 dfl America 29 pax, dog and donkey, spotter on west bank of river

30 3-1 blows five ieds found by other sqds

30 3-1 night ptl w Garcia; saw two flashlights; palma falls into icy water to chest; no complaints thru night; covered in ice in morning; still leads ptl back

31 3-2 cpl hur killed ied emplacer bldg. 35 P9L

JANUARY 2011

1 3-1 routine dfl America

2 3-2 hit ied Walker or Harmon? It was a sniper attachment from India, single amp at ankle, can't remember his name.

2 3-1 last ptl from america

2 3-1 last ptl from America

2 3-2 pp ied found; lcpl meirini mangled foot; danger ranger evacd him; ?? not reported as wia on plt list

2 3-1 found 3 ieds daisy chain; Palma clears rooftop to drop in; search long line of motorcyles at foot bridge

3 3-3 calls 60s twice in p8q; finds pkm shells in bldg.

4 3-3 24 hr stakeout p8q with nothing

5 3-3 find shooting room only 800m from pb fires

5 3-2 wagner and harmon find ied; Williamson and delany find another; 2 spotters killed; under fire, use smaws; kill another spotter

6 3-1 banshee kills cyclist with icom; Hess and Palma hit ied; palma limping lft foot; refuse medevac

6 3-3 zero

7 3-2 find toe popper; palma crossing roofs; p54g

8 3-2 finds ppied

8 3-3 get co info re en casevac to west in P8T—hit by PKM crossing river—Laaw used vs bldg. 34 p8q; brass and blood; more en firing; 60mm used; pinned; jfo to rotatrs 5 gun runs in tree line; hellfire vs bldg. 32 q5h; in rubble one en kiqa and 3 civ wia; again pinned; moved fwd; 60s vs bldg. 21 q5h; low on ammo; egress under fire; rtb

8 3-1 no. thru Taliban town near old pb bulldog; Harmon in lead; saw en; laird used at4; 3-3 moved up but dangerous geometries of fire; oriented shootout for gunrun; rpk fires continued; rtb

8 post 5 at pb fires engages en shooter

9 3-3 engaged in p8q; used 60s

9 3-1 banshee takes out spotter at 820m; en single shots; clear two compounds so cag and bbc can talk to lns

10 3-2 saw mam putting ied in canal; delany saw lamp wire, threw flashbang into hooch, capture mam; lantznester stepped on ied and ok

10 3-1 found laptop hidden at previous arms cache; in weeds

found two wht vans shot up. Cobras saw mams following us all the time.

11 at 1118 3-1 dfl w/ cariter and 23 pax because 3-3 in contact; find one ied; rtb

11 3-3 crossed bridge sw of bldg. 40 p8q ; at bldg. 112 blew ied; pushed w and blew another; in contact; broke contact, reduced two more ieds; rtb p6411 at 1507 3-1 20 pax and bbc qrf to 3-3; Palma on rooftops despite turned ankle from ied on 6th

12 3-1 1206 dfl 19 pax and bbc; soto and cook shoot spotter at 600m; bolo brown Toyota no lic plate tries to stalk us; can't get shot; pinned en mg between us and 3-3; got to bldg. 40; great en pos; cut down trees. Rubble and fire indicated en just left.

Cpl cook kills another at 440m with mk 12; two mams carry him off

12 3-3 in contact; also take pics of wanted bolo

13 3-2 dfl 1359 trails into p8q, where 3-3 in contact; get both sqds on line; remain with Garcia overnight at hideout

13 3-1 dfl 1400 w/23, 15 min after 3-3 and 3-2; heard 3-3 in contact; en mg 200 m front

15 3-2 ft appch from rear ruined chance of getting into 3-1's gun fight but Sullivan grabbed a guy with a battery pack attached to his cycle

15 3-1 credits everyone p8q in fight mams in blk using families as shields—palma in fight hvy en in 7 pos; ana saw second en gang moving up; xiong led ft vs en mg; alvarex engaged; 60s shoot; got a coupe; Garcia adjusting fire

16 3-2 banshee shot at spotter at 400m

16 3-1 dfl 1020cook killed spotter at 375m' families worried we won't stay; at en kill, footprints of second guy; cash, names of talibs, petition to let prisoners go, bank acct number

17 3-3 nothing

18 3-3 p8q hit by hvy mg; called in rotors; found pkm brass

18 3-2 p8q dfl 0830 to destroy boats; find one ied, set off 2d; Marcum and sgt browning shaken up; delany pulled harmon back with broken leg

8 3-1 1015 23 pax and dog; palma at pt hacks thru vines; gonzalez with 117 calls in f18 Maker 32 as three t maneuver; yaz finds ied; use wolf hound icom triangulationto locate them 700 m to south; t saying bag is full where do you want to go? Meaing have ieds where go to lay them and avoid 3-1 ; casevac rodrigquez rolled ankle broken??/ cpl had with mk 12 kills one ; icom cut saying: put in ied; you are safe

21 3-1 w 35 goes to Taliban Town across river; nothing; affluent family cooperative; destroy two boats and cables across river; CAG with us

22 3-2 dfl 0730 census atmos good when 1-3 hit two ieds

22 3-3 hit ppied; routine casualty kw5865 broken ankle

23 3-3 in Q1B find a man who teaches secretly out of his house; find ied

23 3-1 w 24 in Q1B; guy said t stayed in bldg. 91 for 8 days;

26 3-3 in P8Q finds two ieds with yaz

27 3-1 in Q1C w sgt dwyer cag who speaks Pashto; blow wall near pb fires for exfil

29 3-3 dfl fob Jackson to pb America??

29 3-3 finds two rifles ist plt lost in river??

31 3-2 Q1C VCP many avoid us easily on cycles; find one ied; atmos good; farmers preparing to plant poppy

FEBRUARY

1 3-2 finds two ieds

1 3-3 in P8Q finds p pied two and blows both

4 3-3 with eod blows 70 feet of trees

4 3-2 in riverbed; blimp spots guy w ak; found cache of ied material; blew two ieds

7 3-3 find cache 6pp, 300 lbs explosives 200 feet wire; soldering iron pr 775 544

8 3-2 finds 82mm mortar shell

11 pb fires takes fire from west

17 3-1 finds 3 ppieds

21 3-1 finds eight pounds explosive in pipe charge

24 3-3 in fight with en

27 3-3 in Q1D finds 4 ieds

MARCH

1 3-3 crosses canal between P8T and P8Q; accurate PKM and Ak fire; rtb

2 3-3 P8Q found an 82mm mortar in a false wall

2 ob 3 wounds one en

4 3-1 shoots at one spotter with icom

5 3-2 same location; hit from Q5H; destroyed one ied; Wagner did good work with law; found two ppied

6 3-2 chased a guy in Q5G; under fire, 3-1 moved to support; hvy contact at bldg. 73 Q5H; called mortars and smoke; exfil; hit guy on cycle with wpn

7 3-3 under light saf in Q5G on line with Transformer; found one ied

8 3-2 bldg 7 P8Q cache found ak pkm, at4, 14 mortar rds; cpl bradach ied broke his foot

8 secdef at 3/5

13 3-3 #82 p8q pkm 200m north

16 3-3 to #26 p8q but weather turned air red so rtb with no contact

19 Esquibel hits IED and is evacuated

20 Doc Ramos and Yazzie evac'd

Patrol Log ends

Appendix C

NAMES IN APPRECIATION

Thank you for your comments and for your service . . .

Staff Sgt. Siege Amey
Gen. James Amos
Col. Kevin Anderson
Capt. Peter Ankney
Gunny Lorenzo Arballo
Staff Sgt. James Archbell
Sgt. Joel Bailey
Jim Banion
Mushtaq Baqikhel ("Max")
Capt. Richard Barclay

Capt. Chuck Beardsley

Lt. Col. David Bradney

Sgt. John D. Browning

Maj. Kirk Bush

Sgt. Josh Byram

Gunny Chris Carlisle

Maj. Mark Carlton

Staff Sgt. Cartier Coleman

LCol. Juan Covarrubias

Capt. Clay Davis

Lt. Col. Sean Day

Capt. Todd Eysenbach

Capt. Scott Foster

Lt. Col. Richard Fuerst

Maj. William Ghilarducci

Lt. Nick Gidden

Sgt. Nickolas J. Glidden

Lt. Col. Steve Grass

Capt. Hamid, ANA

Faisal Haq

Sean Heinz

Maj Hekmatulah

Sgt. Jordan Hintz

Lt. Kurt Hoening

Lt. Col. Jeff Hogan

Capt. Nicolai Johnson

LCpl. Jaspar Jones

Lt. Karl Kadon

Capt. Thomas Kearns

Maj. Travis Kelley

Father William Kennedy

Capt. Jimmy Knipe

Lt. James Koch

Col. J. T. LeBonne

Col. Craig Leflore

1st Sgt. Alex Leibfried

Staff Sgt. Edward Marini

Maj. Eric McDowell

Maj. Mcleash

1st Sgt. Jorge Melendez

Maj. Gen. Richard Mills

Col. Mike Moore

Capt. Pat Murray

Sgt. Joseph Myers

Capt. Reid Nannen

Maj. Mike Nesbitt

Capt. Geoff Newton

Capt. Timothy Nogalski

Ali Nor

Maj. Chris O'Donnell

LCpl. Jorge Ortiz

Brig. Gen. Jodie Osterman

Maj. Jennifer Parker

Lt. Chuck Poulton

Capt. Joshua Rogers, air kilo

Lt. Stephen Russell

Sgt. David Sarragoza

Patty Schumacher

Col. John Shaefer

Lt. Col. Dan Shipley

Amo Shuaraz

Cpl. Jeff Sibley

Sgt. Brandon Smith

Capt. Richard Stinnett

Staff Sgt. Nicholas Tock

Lt. Gen. John Toolan

Lt. Col. Stu Upton

Terry Walker

Maj. Walker

Capt. Kyle Walton

Brig. Gen. Wasea

Maj. Vincent Welch

Lt. Cameron West

Capt. Dan Wilcox

Maj. Steve Wolf

Paul Wood

Sgt. Maj. George Young

Capt. Andrew Zetts

Appendix D

3RD PLATOON QUESTIONNAIRE

PART I: INDIVIDUAL SURVEY AT PATROL BASE FIRES OF 3RD PLATOON,

MARCH 11, 2011

(51 Marines separately filled out the form)

Two-parent family: 75%

High school graduate: 100%

Age 23 or younger: 80%

Married: 32%

Have children: 29%

I plan to:

    [1] reenlist 54%

    [2] get out 46%

      [Note: by 2014, 70% of the platoon had returned to civilian life.]

Are your tastes in music, movies, etc. the same as your civilian friends?

[1] Yes 63%

[2] No 17%

[3] Don't know 20%

Do you see American civilian males your age as being:

[1] just like you 6%

[2] different, but the difference is of no importance to me 53%

[3] softer and more spoiled 41%

If you had it to do over again, you'd

[1] not enlist 4%

[2] enlist, but not in grunts 4%

[3] I'd be right here 92%

Did Marines change you:

[1] a little bit 27%

[2] a fair amount 50%

[3] a lot 23%

Did combat change you:

[1] a little bit 27%

[2] a fair amount 30%

[3] a lot 43%

Because of combat:

[1] I am more caring of those close to me 33%

[2] I'm harder 15%

[3] I appreciate life more 52%

Belief in God:

[1] I believe in God, his rules and heaven 65%

[2] I'm so-so about God and hereafter 25%

[3] Probably a myth 10%

Why did you join the Marines?

[1] role model of a relative 12%

[2] discipline & toughness 40%

[3] straighten myself out 40%

[4] learn a trade 8%

PART II:

Enemy: I have seen

[1] 1–3 Taliban 12%

[2] 5–10 Taliban 14%

[3] Over 10 14%

[4] Over 20 60%

[Note: at the time of the survey, the average Marine had conducted over 65 patrols. Obviously, many of the same Taliban were seen on different occasions. In about one patrol in three, the average Marine saw one Taliban.]

Enemy Casualties: I have hit

[1] 1–2 Taliban 45%

[2] 3–5 28%

[3] 6–10 10%

[4] Over 10 17%

[Note: the sniper section accounted for all the kills in the "Over 10" category. In total, the Marines believed they had hit with small arms fire 221 of the enemy. It cannot be judged how many were actually hit, or how many others were hit by mortars, bombs, and helicopter gunship runs. Even if the individual estimates are cut in half, it is probable that 3rd Platoon by direct and indirect fire killed close to 200 Taliban over the course of 400 patrols.]

PTSD. In your squad, how many do you believe have or will have PTSD?

No one 25%

One 18%

Two 18%

Three or more 36%

Average guess March of 2011: 6 among the 51 Marines in 3rd Platoon have or will experience PTSD

[Note: the 2014 actual number was 3 with PTSD diagnoses.]

Afghan Soldiers vs. Taliban

[1] Taliban better fighters than Afghan soldiers 37%

[2] Both sides are about the same 43%

[3] Afghan soldiers are better 20%

View of Afghan people

[1] can't trust; they support the Taliban 36%

[2] people OK, but intimidated by Taliban 58%

[3] worth fighting for; they're aligned with us 6%

Endgame

[1] Afghan people will side with government against Taliban 20%

[2] We can train Afghan soldiers so they can defeat Taliban 25%

[3] When we leave, Afghanistan will remain a mess 55%

Appendix E

3RD PLATOON, KILO COMPANY, 3RD BATTALION, 5TH MARINE REGIMENT AT SANGIN, AFGHANISTAN

1ST SQUAD

Cpl. Porfirio Alvarez
Cpl. Chatchai Xiong
Cpl. Juan Palma
Cpl. Anthony Gonzales
Cpl. Dylan Nordell
Cpl. Edwardo Soto
Cpl. Victor Valdez
Cpl. Clayton Cook
Cpl. Darin Hess
Sgt. Dominic Esquibel
LCpl. Brandon Weese

MORTARS

Sgt. Joshua Byram

Cpl. Mike Domico

Cpl. Christian Wall

Cpl. Jim Parvin

Cpl. Zach James

Cpl. Philip Chronis

Cpl. Paul Sharon

Cpl. Leland Vaughan

Sgt. Joe Myers

LCpl. Ryan Echelbager

2D SQUAD

Sgt. Alex Deykeroff

LCpl. Timothy Wagner

LCpl. Trevor Halcomb

LCpl. Mike Williamson

LCpl. Aaron Lantznester

Cpl. Armando Espinoza

LCpl. John Payne

LCpl. Oscar Orozco

Cpl. Richard Hur

LCpl. Zachary White

ATTACHED

RTO LCpl. James Helton

HM3 Juan Hernandez

HM3 Stuart Fuke

Engineer LCpl. Colbey Yazzie

Engineer Cpl. Kameron Delany

HM3 Emmanuel Gonzalez

Staff Sgt. Nicholas Tock

Cpl. Kacey Harmon

HM3 Redmond Ramos

HM3 Stephen Librando

3RD SQUAD

Sgt. Phil McCulloch

Cpl. Jaceon Skramstad

LCpl. Kyle Doyle

LCpl. Leonard Rausch

LCpl. Adrian Barbiera

LCpl. Jeffrey Rushton

Cpl. Sam Saephan

LCpl. Brett Stieve

Sgt. Clint Thoman

LCpl. Patrick Walker

LCpl. Juan Dominguez

MACHINE GUNS AND COMMAND

LCpl. Jorge Ortiz

Cpl. Jeremy Moreno

LCpl. Robert Baskins

LCpl. Cole Christopher

LCpl. David Hickle

LCpl. Juan Covarrubius

Cpl. William Lefevers

Lt. Cameron West

Staff Sgt. Siege Amey

Lt. Vic Garcia

Staff Sgt. Matthew Cartier

LCpl. Joseph Miller

Sgt. Ryan Krochmolny

SNIPERS

Cpl. Jacob Ruiz

Cpl. Royce Hughie

Cpl. Jordan Laird

Cpl. Jeff Sibley

Sgt. Brandon Rokahr

LCpl. Willie Deel

Cpl. Brett Sullivan

Cpl. Kevin Henson

Cpl. Sloan Hicks

Sgt. John D. Browning

Cpl. Logan Stark

Sgt. Kevin Smith

Sgt. Matt Abbate

Notes

INTRODUCTION

xx   **"moral obligation"** George W. Bush, *Decision Points*. New York: Crown, 2010, p. 205.

xx   **"squeezed into extinction"** General Tommy Franks, *American Soldier*. New York: Easton, 2004, pp. 338, 377.

xx   **opium** Alissa Rubin, "Opium Cultivation Rose This Year in Afghanistan, U.N. Survey Shows," *New York Times*, November 20, 2012.

xxi   **"The central theme"** Brig. Gen. Edward Butler, quoted in Bing West, "With the Warriors," *National Review*, March 7, 2011.

xxi   **"Sangin was no safer"** Patrick Bury, *Callsign Hades*. London: Simon & Schuster, 2010, p. 281.

xxii **"ringed in"** Ibid., p. 281.

xxii **"stop referring"** Gretel C. Kovach, "Darkhorse Battalion," *San Diego Union-Tribune*, April 23, 2011.

xxii **"I have pulled"** *Christian Science Monitor*, December 6, 2006.

xxiii **"I'm pleading with you"** Robert Johnson, "How to Work a Room Like Badass 4-Star Marine General 'Mad Dog' Mattis," BusinessInsider.com, September 25, 2012.

xxiii **"We can't"** Admiral Mike Mullen, House Armed Services Committee testimony, September 10, 2008.

xxiii **"diminish"** Anne E. Kornblut, Scott Wilson, and Karen DeYoung, "Obama Pressed for Faster Surge," *Washington Post,* December 6, 2009.

xxiii **"I urge our troops"** Admiral Mike Mullen, Pentagon briefing, December 10, 2009.

xxiv **"We've got a government"** David E. Sanger, "A Test for the Meaning of Victory in Afghanistan," *New York Times,* February 13, 2010.

xxiv **"We [Marines] can't fix"** Gen. James Conway, Pentagon press conference, August 14, 2010.

xxv **"biggest mistake"** Robert M. Gates, *Duty: Memoirs of a Secretary at War.* New York: Knopf, 2014, p. 340.

xxv **"He [Conway] insisted"** Ibid.

xxv **"Marine-istan"** Rajiv Chandrasekaran, "Marines Gone Rogue," *Washington Post,* March 14, 2010.

xxvii **"It's a hard pill"** Tom Coghlan, "American Marines Pay Heavy Price in Fight for Sangin," *The Times* (London), December 6, 2010.

CHAPTER 1: SHOCK

3 **he wrote to the families** Lt. Col. Jason Morris, letter to 3/5 families, October 13, 2010.

4 **"Colonel Morris looked"** Excerpt from the YouTube video "For the 25," posted by Logan Stark, May 5, 2013.

4 **Lance Cpl. John Sparks** *The Story of the 3/5 Darkhorse Marine Battalion in Sangin, Afghanistan,* p. 18.

4 **killing four Marines** Corp. Justin Cain hailed from Manitowoc, Wisconsin, where a motorcycle club escorted his casket through town.

   In Eugene, Oregon, at the funeral of LCpl. Joseph Rodewald, hundreds wore a red jersey with his number, 33, honoring his passion for football.

   The Boy Scout troop in St. Charles County, Missouri, turned out at the Church of the Shepherd to say good-bye to LCpl. Phillip Vinnedge, who had once dressed up as the Easter Bunny to entertain children.

   Pfc. Victor Dew of Granite Bay, California, left behind a fiancée. His mother said that his desire to join the Marines was "every mother's worst fear," but she understood his determination." Victor joined the Marines," his father said, "to be on the front lines, where he felt he could make a difference."

4 **five fatalities** *Marine Corps Times,* October 18, 2010.

7 **a squad of thirteen Marines** This was Sgt. Decker's squad from 1st Platoon.

7 **second squad** Sgt. Nick Glidden from 2d Platoon.

8 **Covered by** Abbate suggested they head to Building 29 in P8T, 600 meters north of Fires.

11 **since he was three** *Rockford* (Ill.) *Register Star,* October 15, 2010.

13 **trusted his judgment** *Los Angeles Times,* November 21, 2010.

14 **Ceniceros** "Irvin admired the strength of character of the Marines," his sister said. "He wanted to be in the Marines because he was the same way." *Times Record* (Fort Smith, Ark.), October 19, 2010.

16 **eight killed** *Marine Corps Times,* October 18, 2010.

CHAPTER 2: LEADER LOST

22 **"Wow, my son's unit"** *Los Angeles Times,* November 21, 2010, and NPR, November 1, 2010.

23 **honor man** *The Oregonian,* October 18, 2010.

23 **"I have decided"** Lt. Col. Jason Morris, letter to 3/5 families, October 18, 2010.

23 **"At the time"** Tom Bowman, "Afghan Success Comes at High Price for Commander," NPR.org, October 30, 2011.

CHAPTER 3: WITH THE OLD BREED

28 **Seven out of ten civilian casualties** Associated Press, November 26, 2010.

28 **Karzai had pointed** as reported by CNN, July 27, 2010.

33 **The sentry** Lance Corporal Kane was shot. Abbate, Ruiz, Sibley, and Laird then left the outpost.

37 **the summer of 1966** Capt. Francis J. West, Jr., *Small Unit Action in Vietnam.* U.S. Marines monograph, p. 5 (also New York: Arno Press, 1981).

42 **"Despite taking"** Lt. Col. Jason Morris, letter to 3/5 families, October 25, 2010.

43 **"There is nothing out of the norm"** *Marine Corps Times,* October 20, 2010.

CHAPTER 4: LEADERS FOUND

49 **he decided** Shortly after taking over, Garcia sent Esquibel's 1st Squad to a cemetery north of Fires, searching for a path through the minefields along the edge of Route 611. The Radio Battalion intercept team at Inkerman warned Esquibel that Taliban were watching and talking excitedly over their Icoms. At the edge of a cornfield, the Marine at point, LCpl. Victor Valdez, saw two men crouching over a PKM not twenty-four meters away.

"Machine gun!"

The Marines went flat and bullets zinged in a dozen different directions. Once the Marines began plunking .203 rounds into the corn, the PKM gunners pulled back. Thinking they were under mortar shelling, the Taliban ran to the nearest compound. Garcia came forward from Inkerman with a quick reaction force. The two squads maneuvered slowly toward the compound. The intercept team radioed that inside the compound a man was calling for help over his Icom. His comrade had been hit in the chest and blown up by a .203 explosive. But by the time the compound was reached, the Taliban, both alive and dead, were gone.

49 **covering fire** In late October, compass readings from several radio intercepts pointed to an enemy position on an azimuth of 300 degrees from Fires, which pointed at Compound 2 in sector Q1E. Esquibel went out, divided his squad into two maneuver elements, and closed on the compound from two sides. They killed one shooter and in the corner of a shed found a bag full of 12.7mm rounds. The 12.7 was a heavy Russian machine gun called a Dishka, a World War II antiaircraft

weapon. The Taliban almost never made the mistake of shooting at helicopter gunships. Instead, they used the 12.7 to harass combat outposts from positions a mile away. The Marines' seizure of the cache meant a month-long round-trip to Pakistan for the Taliban to resupply. The successful patrol confirmed Esquibel's faith in his methodical approach.

CHAPTER 5: TOE-TO-TOE

62 **Costing $500,000 each** www.money.msn.com, January 23, 2014.

64 **outdoorsman** *Denver Post,* November 6, 2010.

64 **"He is with God now"** *Arizona Republic,* November 9, 2010.

66 **No American squad dared to live** There were some exceptions, like Maj. Jim Gant of the Special Forces; see Ann Scott Tyson, *American Spartan: The Promise, the Mission, and the Betrayal of Special Forces Major Jim Gant.* New York: Morrow, 2014.

66 **xenophobic tribesmen** Meanwhile, Afghan president Karzai railed against the American presence among the villagers, adding greatly to an atmosphere of distrust. The Afghan soldiers admitted that they did not know who among them would, on a whim or conviction, murder them as they slept. The high command issued a countrywide order that an armed American soldier keep watch over Afghan soldiers at all times.

68 **That night, the Marines ate Stacy** The next day, 2d Squad was patrolling east of Fires when they saw a set of wires. Uncertain which wire to cut, the squad called an engineer team from Inkerman. While waiting, Sergeant Dy and Corporal Laird casually questioned a few passing farmers. Stevie, their shrewd translator, whispered that the farmers were subtly gesturing toward three men standing off to one side. When Stevie approached them, one nervously replied with a Pakistani accent. The three were flex-cuffed. After the engineers arrived, they uncovered an intricate network of seven IEDs.

69 **Lt. Gen. John Kelly** Speech in St. Louis, November 11, 2010; see Appendix A.

70 **In London, the *Sunday Times*** "We were there for four years," said a British veteran, "and we'd already tried what they are now trying, which is obviously not working judging by the casualties." Miles Amoore, "US Humbled in Bloody Sangin," *Sunday Times* (London), December 12, 2010.

71 **Gen. James Amos** Tom Bowman report, NPR, October 31, 2011.

71 **"I thought to myself"** Gates, *Duty,* p. 561.

71 **"I don't think there's ever been"** Gretel C. Kovach, *San Diego Union-Tribune,* November 10, 2010.

73 **"Military history must never stray"** Victor Davis Hanson, *Carnage and Culture: Landmark Battles in the Rise to Western Power.* New York: Anchor, 2001, pp. 56.

73 **"I directed all units"** Gen. Stanley McChrystal, *My Share of the Task: A Memoir.* New York: Portfolio, 2013, p. 313.

73 **McChrystal even supported** Ibid., p. 312.

75 **"At bldg 23"** Platoon log, November 18, 2010.

CHAPTER 6: THANKSGIVING

85 **"I like meeting people"** See "Arden Joseph Buenagua," Darkhorse Heroes Remembered, http://darkhorse35.com/Buenagua/.

86 **called LAAWs** Delany and Wagner fired the LAAWs.

90 **Other Marines** These were Cpl. Jake Romo and Sgt. Patrique Fearon, an engineer.

91 **"I don't think he would have"** *Maryland Independent,* December 1, 2010.

91 **The Marines traded shots** Lance Corporal Schoemaker did most of the shooting.

91 **nearby compound** Cpl. Ayala was at point.

101 **Thanksgiving 2010** On November 27, 1st Squad was back to shooting. When the Marines saw two Taliban shadowing his patrol, they responded with machine gun fire, killing one enemy. In seconds, several others opened up from an irrigation ditch and a compound. Garcia called for his 60mm mortars to start dropping shells. Back at company headquarters, Beardsley called for air and brought in two F-18s. The pilots dropped four GBU-12s—Laser-Guided Bomb Units attached to 500-pound bombs. The enemy firing ceased.

The battalion continued to take losses. On November 30, four IEDs were uncovered about 300 meters south of Kilo Company headquarters at Inkerman. A fourth IED exploded, shearing off the legs of the engineer who was disarming another IED.

CHAPTER 7: GONE

107 **But they don't cope with death** "In the States, the young don't have to think about death," Father Bill Kennedy, the regimental chaplain, told me after Abbate's death. "But out here in Afghanistan, the grunts can't avoid death. They gain a rough belief in God and eternity." In the questionnaire answers 3rd Platoon provided to me, thirty of the fifty-one Marines said they "believed in God and His rules," five said they did not believe in God, and sixteen were uncertain.

CHAPTER 8: ENEMY RESPITE

110 **Eli** *Corpus Christi Caller-Times,* December 6, 2010.

110 **their son, Michael** *Akron Beacon Journal,* December 12, 2010.

113 **"God has a plan"** *Evansville* (In.) *Courier & Press,* December 30, 2010.

115 **"You've had your fun"** That same day, 1st Squad came under fire in sector P8T and called in 120mm mortar shells that packed a heavy punch. While pursuing a man with an Icom, the squad found and destroyed an IED. Next, they captured a man named Abdul Ahad, who had fired an RPG at them. Ahad was turned over to the police at the district center. Third Platoon never heard what happened to him.

115 **hailstorm of bullets** Platoon log, December 16, 2010.

115 **base of fire** Staff Sergeant Cartier and Corporal Hess led this flanking party.

116 **"Frankly, progress"** Department of Defense press release, December 10, 2010.

116 **"Earn the support"** Fred Kaplan, *The Insurgents: David Petraeus and the Plot to Change the American Way of War.* New York: Simon & Schuster, 2013, p. 326.

117   **"a fully resourced"** Gates, *Duty*, p. 342.

117   **"fantasy"** Ibid., p. 336.

120   **"There was a pledge"** Patrick Quinn, Associated Press, January 3, 2011.

120   **with the British** In 2007, the district governor confided to the British that the Alakozai, the largest tribe in northern Sangin, had decided to revolt against the Taliban that were aligned with the Ishaqzai, a rival tribe. The British gave the Alakozai ammunition, but no supporting troops. The Alakozai were crushed. Yet somehow the few British civilian officials still remaining in Sangin in 2010 as economic and political advisers had encouraged the Alakozai to try again. The Alakozai, particularly strong in the Kilo's area north of the market, insisted they could persuade the local Taliban to cease fighting if the Marines pulled back.

122   **an IED cooked off** Platoon log, December 22, 2010.

122   **"I'm honored to say"** *Corpus Christi Caller-Times*, December 22, 2010.

123   **"got a bad feeling"** Platoon log, December 23, 2010.

123   **"We are all family"** "Funeral, Procession Emotional Affairs," TheTelegraph.com, January 1, 2011.

125   **"The bottom line"** Quoted in 3/5 Facebook page, December 2010.

125   **in opposition to the Taliban** On December 27, 3rd Squad encountered the baffling contradictions that define counterinsurgency. When they began their patrol, they were picked up by the usual spotter with an Icom. They shot at him, missed, pushed on, dropped off a sniper team to ambush the spotter, missed again, picked up the team, and pushed on. After searching a few compounds, they entered an abandoned building that was well decorated, with rugs on every floor. The owner was likely to be a drug dealer or Taliban, or both. Whoever he was, no one touched any of his belongings when he was away.

    Farther on, the squad bumped into a family lugging their few possessions in a wheelbarrow. Why they had left their farm was a puzzle that Stevie, the doughty interpreter, was unable to solve or, more likely, to explain properly in his pidgin English. That it involved local animosities became clear when the family, friendly and polite, pointed toward a nearby compound, indicating it was Taliban. Perhaps it was their way of getting a bit of revenge.

    The squad crossed a nineteenth-century rope bridge and entered the empty enemy compound. Yaz spotted small holes drilled through the thick walls—murder holes for enemy snipers to use. He looked around carefully and found first one and then a second pressure plate, both connected to a plastic jug filled with thirty pounds of explosive. The squad also uncovered a hidden underground room, with a bag of heroin stashed in a corner. They blew the building, took some harassing PKM machine gun fire, and returned to base.

    A decade earlier, Gen. Chuck Krulak, then Commandant, had written an article about a "Three Block War"—Marines aid refugees in one block, tussle with insurgents in the second, and confront heavy fire in the third. In the span of a few hours, 3rd Squad had encountered all three scenarios.

    Over the next few days, 3rd Platoon patrols uncovered and destroyed fourteen IEDs and Cpl. Richard Hur of 2d Squad killed a man digging in an IED. Stoic and unexcitable, Hur drove Sergeant Dy crazy because of his mumbling into the radio, thus earning the nickname "Kermit the Frog."

    During a night ambush on December 29, Palma of 1st Squad fell into a freezing canal. He climbed out and assumed the watch. By morning, he was shivering violently, an icy sheen covering his cammies.

"I'm okay," he insisted.

That was typical of Palma. Bored after graduating from high school, he had joined to get away from home in Arizona. He liked Marine traditions, tough conditions, and the challenges at Fires.

"Out here, I see life snatched away," he told me after one patrol. "When I get back, I'm going to love my family, not take things for granted. I'm going back to college, but after that I want a fast-paced job. Maybe the DEA."

125 **"He didn't drink"** "Hutto Marine Tevan Nguyen Killed in Afghanistan," *Austin American-Statesman*, December 30, 2010.

CHAPTER 9: MIDWAY TO HOME

126 **"We've reassured them"** *Washington Post*, January 5, 2011.

126 **"I want you to be honest"** Jonathan Alter, *The Promise: President Obama, Year One*. New York: Simon & Schuster, 2010, p. 390.

128 **"A commander can more easily"** Carl von Clausewitz, *On War*, edited and translated by Michael Howard and Peter Paret, Book Six. Princeton, N.J.: Princeton University Press, 1976, p. 482.

129 **the 800-man battalion** No commanding general would design one single operational template to control operations across Afghanistan. Local diversities and complexities overwhelmed central decision making. Each battalion needed the freedom to evaluate and adapt to the problems in his area. Major General Mills understood that. To the south of Sangin, seven Marine battalions were spread along seventy miles of Green Zone bordering the Helmand River. Next to the meandering river, one million people belonging to fifty subtribes lived in insular clans, resulting in a kaleidoscope of loyalties and security conditions. The Marine battalion in Nawa district, for instance, rarely heard a shot fired. In Marjah, another battalion averaged one small fight a week as the Taliban were pushed out into the desert. Down in Garmsir, a third battalion had dispersed into fifty squad outposts, each manned by an equal number of American and Afghan soldiers. Had 3rd Platoon broken down into similar squad outposts, they would have been wiped out.

130 **Back to work** The grunts in Kilo Company, though, knew they had it better than their brothers in India and Hotel Companies farther to the south in the heavily populated areas where IEDs were buried in every wall and alley.

While Kilo engaged in a few fights each day in the open, the rifle companies to the south were walking through narrow alleyways, surrounded by walls and civilians. The Taliban planted IEDs on every footpath and bridge over the stinking irrigation ditches used as sewers. It would take a patrol two hours to advance a hundred meters. Glimpses of the enemy were rare, and shooting in the crowded streets was impossible.

131 **"Concentrate on destruction"** FMFM 8-2, *Counterinsurgency Operations*. U.S. Marine Corps, 1980.

131 **"We need to challenge"** Conway quoted in *Long War Journal*, January 28, 2011.

134 **Day 82** On January 2, 3rd Platoon walked back to Fires to resume patrolling. Along the way, Lance Corporal Meirink, a sniper working with 2d Squad, stepped on an IED that mangled his foot. On January 4, Delany and LCpl. Michael Wil-

liamson, twenty-two, from Arizona, killed three dickers. Williamson planned to become a sergeant major one day, explaining that then he "could change what he didn't like about the Marine Corps."

137 **"My bad"** The tension ran deeper than any platoon commander. Afghan soldiers were independent; Marines were rigid, accustomed to strict rules. Americans weren't supposed to discipline or give orders to the Afghans. An Afghan soldier could not achieve the standards of an American grunt. An askari had a third-grade education, came from a northern tribe, and received $200 a month. If he was killed, his family was left with nothing. Yet still they left the wire as long as the Marines were alongside them.

We all sense when someone dislikes or disdains us, and we respond with surliness or disobedience. Afghans are unruly. Without firm leadership, they act like a high school class with a timid substitute teacher. To be effective, an adviser has to impose firm rules on an equitable basis. That combination of empathy and consistent discipline requires maturity. The Army Special Forces teams were terrific advisers. The average age in the Special Forces was thirty-two, ten years older than 3rd Platoon.

137 **Day 89** The previous day, 3rd Squad had tripped off a two-day battle. The patrol was headed northeast toward a wide bend in the Helmand River in sector Q5H when the G-Boss telescope spotted a half dozen Taliban ferrying a few wounded in a shallow-draft boat across the river.

The squad hastened to the spot, and the first fire team to wade across took fire from Building 20, to the east. There were dozens of abandoned compounds among several hectares of bare fields and icy irrigation ditches. When McCulloch maneuvered toward #20, his squad was hit from #34, to the northeast. When the Marines returned that fire, a PKM machine gun in #17, closer to them, opened up. The squad pummeled the building, and then closed in, finding brass and blood trails amid the corn stalks.

As the Taliban pulled back, McCulloch stayed after them. He went down momentarily when a bullet creased his thigh, a searing wound equivalent to being branded. He hopped up swearing and fired a LAAW rocket. In response, the enemy returned fire from six buildings.

Outnumbered, the squad pulled back and called for Cobras. The gunships rolled in, launching Hellfire missiles against three compounds in rapid succession. Led by Cpl. Jeremy Moreno, the Marines assaulted Compound 32, finding one dead Taliban and three wounded civilians.

"I saw motorcycles in a tree line," Moreno, twenty-one, from Riverside, California, said. "They could've left anytime. They didn't back off."

138 **"I do not believe the officers"** Ulysses S. Grant, *The Complete Personal Memoirs of Ulysses S. Grant.* Ulysses Press, 2013, p. 79.

140 **"will nurture women leaders"** Gretel C. Kovach, *San Diego Union-Tribune,* March 23, 2011.

140 **"the graduate level"** Comment by General Petraeus, February 9, 2011.

140 **"attack the enemy relentlessly"** FMFM 8-2, *Counterinsurgency Operations.*

141 **In response to my survey** See Appendix D.

148 **"The families"** Tom Bowman reports, NPR, October 30 and 31, 2011.

CHAPTER 10: THE ROUTINE

156 **"spirit of the body"** Col. Ardant du Picq, *Battle Studies: Ancient and Modern Battle.* New York: Macmillan, 1921.

167 **"Got PID"** BBC video, January 20, 2011.

167 **"We watched him"** BBC video, January 25, 2011.

168 **Time and again** Cpl. Brett Sullivan stopped a man driving by on a motorcycle with a car battery strapped on the rear. Sullivan pitched the battery into a canal and turned the man over to the police, who promptly released him.

169 **Palma took fire** While LCpl. Dylan Nordell led his fire team in a long loop to flank a PKM machine gun, Alvarez's fire team reinforced Palma.

170 **"a person of no account"** Gina Cavallaro, *Marine Corps Times,* January 21, 2011.

170 **another Marine** This was Lance Corporal Marcum.

171 **the squad was listening** It was Lance Corporal Gonzalez who was listening.

CHAPTER 11: END OF TOUR

175 **On February 8** On February 3, 3rd Squad had uncovered in Q1C a cache containing 300 pounds of explosives, six pressure plates, 200 feet of wire, and a soldering iron. A few days later, the camera on the blimp above Kilo Company headquarters showed a man hiding an AK on the riverbank in P8T. Second Squad searched the spot and uncovered another large cache of IED materials. At a nearby crossing point, Yazzie discovered and blew two IEDs.

A few days later, 3rd Squad found a pressure plate and two IEDs up in P8Q. Second squad, patrolling in the same area, saw movement in a set of compounds long abandoned. Inside were several families of destitute squatters. They had moved in because they believed the original owners were never coming back.

Garcia took this as a moderately encouraging sign. Although the families were dirt poor and likely had nowhere else to go, they were the first civilians to migrate into P8Q. One family moved in next door to the compound where Wagner had found two IEDs. Garcia hoped the local Taliban would warn the squatters which fields and houses were mined.

176 **"We have finally gotten"** Gen. David Petraeus interview, February 9, 2011.

176 **"have lost the support"** Jim Michaels, "General: Heart of Afghanistan Insurgency Beaten," *USA Today,* February 14, 2011.

176 **71 percent** smallwarsjournal.com/documents/moshtarak1.

176 **99 percent** January 2011 ICOS survey released in June 2011.

177 **sooner or later** The next day, 3rd Squad went back to P8Q. Inside one compound they found an 82mm mortar shell hidden behind a false wall. Once a pressure plate concealed in the dirt floor was connected to the shell, the resulting blast would kill all Marines in the room. The technique came from Pakistan and had been used a year earlier with devastating results in another district.

177 **On March 5** On March 4, 1st and 2d Squads had pushed into Q5H on parallel paths, hoping to trap some Taliban between them. A running firefight broke out, with intercepts of Icom chatter suggesting the enemy was trying to trap one of the squads. Dy laughed. Knowing Stevie was translating every word, the Taliban had pulled out, hoping to avoid pursuit by faking an imaginary attack.

178 **The machine gun crew** They were aided by Lantznester with his Squad Automatic Weapon.

178 **Dy decided** Corporal Halcomb was also firing his SAW.

178 **As the enemy pulled back** The Marines stepped out in Ranger file behind the engineer, Corporal Bradach, who swept a lane to the next tree line.

180 **every Taliban gang** On one out of every three patrols, the average Marine saw at least one Taliban. Obviously, many of the same Taliban were seen on different occasions. In total, the Marines believed they had hit 221 of the enemy with small arms. It cannot be judged how many others were hit by mortars, bombs, and rockets. Even allowing for exaggeration and double counting, by direct and indirect fire 3rd Platoon probably killed more than 200 Taliban over the course of 400 patrols.

180 **psychological toll** You become much more hesitant and cautious when you know the other side is diligently patrolling in a random fashion. Let me give an example.

In 2009, I had embedded with a British adviser team farther to the south. A Marine battalion moved into the area and, as in Sangin, patrolled extensively. The translator with the British team said the Taliban were radioing back and forth, asking where all those Americans had come from. After several days, I said good-bye to the Brits and hopped in a Ford Ranger with three Afghan soldiers to return to base.

But when we reached a stretch of open road, the driver abruptly stopped and the soldiers peered around, whispering. I sat silently, cursing my stupidity for not having a weapon. Why had I trusted renegade Afghan soldiers? What a dumb, brainless way to die.

Ignoring me, however, the askaris dashed into the field and within seconds were back inside the truck, clutching a half dozen watermelons. Off we sped. The Marines were paying the farmers a dollar per melon, a princely sum. They would come down hard on any Afghan soldier for stealing. The chances of getting caught in the vast fields of the Green Zone seemed low to me, but not to the thieves.

The melon heist illustrated the pressure the Taliban were feeling as 3rd Platoon rolled forward like a steamroller.

180 **"Since October"** Remarks by Secretary of Defense Robert Gates, Sangin, March 8, 2011, as reported in *Leatherneck.*

180 **"The president doesn't trust"** Gates, *Duty,* p. 557.

180 **"I was torn"** Ibid., p. 359.

181 **"dramatically weaken"** Ibid., p. 572.

181 **"rooting the Taliban"** Ibid., p. 571.

181 **"a tighter focus"** Ibid., p. 570.

181 **"the troops had become"** General H. Norman Schwarzkopf, *It Doesn't Take a Hero: The Autobiography.* New York: Bantam, 1992, p. 188.

181 **203 casualties** David W. Taylor, *Our War: The History and Sacrifices of an Infantry Battalion in the Vietnam War 1968–1971.* Medina, Ohio: War Journal Publishing, 2011, p. 634. (Parenthetically, this book is superb in describing the daily combat south of the DMZ.)

182 **Forty-five percent** Moni Basu, "Survey: Veterans Say Afghanistan, Iraq Wars Not Worth It," CNN.com, October 5, 2011.

184 **hashish** Vivienne Walt, "Afghanistan's New Bumper Drug Crop: Cannabis," *Time,* April 1, 2010.

186 **feeling very much alone** Cpls. Richard Hur and Oscar Orozco were the first to see they were missing and run back to provide supporting fire.

CHAPTER 12: THE ENDLESS GRUNT

191 **"I put out a memo"** Gen. David Petraeus interview, June 3, 2011.

192 **"The more time you spend"** Gates, *Duty*, p. 563.

195 **"As I strolled"** Eugene Sledge, quoted in *"The War*: Face of Battle: Aftermath,"* http://www.pbs.org/thewar/at_war_battle_aftermath.htm.

195 **"Lady"** E. B. Sledge, *China Marine: An Infantryman's Life After World War.* Oxford, U.K.: Oxford University Press, 2002, p. 135.

196 **"Some were very angry"** NPR interview, October 30, 2011.

196 **Old Breed** 3/5 was proud of its brotherhood. For example, in Iraq in 2005, Cpl. Larry Hutchins, a squad leader in Kilo 3/5, killed an Iraqi civilian in mistaken retaliation for the death of a Marine. In 2013, Hutchins sent me this letter from the brig.

> Someone once told me that *"where the Institution will sacrifice one of its own to save itself, the Brotherhood will sacrifice itself to save one of its own."* I never really understood what this meant.
>
> Seven years ago when I was arrested for the murder of an Iraqi, I felt abandoned by the Marine Corps. I'll never forget arriving in the middle of the night, pulling up to the prison and seeing parallel lights running in straight lines for what seemed to be miles. It was the gates of hell in Dante's Inferno: "Abandon all hope ye who enter here." I had never felt more alone in my life.
>
> Here I sit today, understanding the differences between the Institution and the Brotherhood. Men from all over our country have written to me, telling of their battles in WWII, Korea and Viet Nam. One man set up an allotment for my wife. Another has become like family, seeking out congressmen and coming to the brig every week. I prayed asking God send me help, not knowing he had sent me angels.
>
> My heart is with my wife and children. They are my home. Every home needs four strong walls. These men are the walls of my home.
>
> I am a proud member of the "Old Corps" Brotherhood. It is because of the Brotherhood that I have regained my pride in being a Marine. Because of the Brotherhood, I fought in Iraq, and would fight again. As I sit writing this in prison, I have come to believe there are those of us who are Semper Fi.

Hutchins's letter is testament to a strict institution that imposed hard punishment for wrongdoing, and yet remained a brotherhood that did not sever its bonds. The Marine Corps is so small that a first sergeant can call his contacts to get an informal evaluation of every Marine in his unit. When the enemy is rushing the wire, a commanding officer can call on Marines decades in their graves to motivate the living. No one scoffs when a captain like Johnson stands in the muddy waters at Patrol Base Fires, invoking the memory of a long-dead corporal named Sledge.

CHAPTER 13: WHO WILL FIGHT FOR US?

202 **"What does Sangin mean?"** *Marine Corps Times,* May 14, 2014.

203 **"Violence has subsided"** *Marine Corps Times,* April 26, 2012.

203 **"Sangin is like"** Azam Ahmed, "Afghan Army Struggles in District Under Siege," *New York Times,* September 11, 2013.

204 **"It's difficult"** Ibid.

204 **highest percentage of drug addicts** Tahir Qadiry, "Afghanistan, the Drug Addiction Capital," BBC News, April 10, 2013.

205 **A majority in 3rd Platoon** See Appendix D.

205 **handed several outposts in Sangin over** Afghan News Agency, December 16, 2013, and *Marine Corps Times,* December 17, 2013.

205 **"Local residents and officials"** Azam Ahmed and Taimoor Shah, "Local Turf-Sharing Accord with the Taliban Raises Alarm in Afghanistan," *New York Times,* December 18, 2013.

206 **"The war doesn't stop"** *Fresno Bee,* January 18, 2014.

206 **"Write this down"** Peter Baker, *Days of Fire: Bush and Cheney in the White House.* New York: Doubleday, 2013, p. 219.

206 **one trillion dollars** Linda J. Bilmes, "The Financial Legacy of Iraq and Afghanistan: How Wartime Spending Decisions Will Constrain Future National Security Budgets." Harvard Kennedy School Faculty Research Working Paper Series RWP13-006, March 2013.

206 **"Soldiers and Marines"** Foreword, *FM 3-24, Counterinsurgency.* Department of the Army, December 2006.

207 **"Afghanistan is the war"** *New York Times,* July 15, 2008.

207 **"What was interesting"** Anne E. Kornblut, Scott Wilson, and Karen DeYoung, "During Marathon Review of Afghanistan Strategy, Obama Held Out for Faster Troop Surge," *Washington Post,* December 6, 2009.

207 **"a fully resourced counterinsurgency strategy"** Gates, *Duty,* pp. 342 and 367. It is worth noting that Gates, McChrystal, and Petraeus all agreed that the strategy was based on the "oil spot" or "ink blot" technique used in the Malayan War (1948–1960). In Malaya, then a British colony, the oil spot consisted of placing villagers inside stockades guarded by Malayan soldiers commanded by British officers. The oil spot in Malaya was a means of controlling the villagers, regardless of what they wanted.

Unlike in Malaya, the American oil spot in Afghanistan would not control the villagers; instead, it would win their support. After "clearing" (killing) sufficient Taliban, the Americans would move on to another district, spreading the oil spot, while Afghan government officials and soldiers moved in behind them.

In Vietnam, the Marines had used the oil spot in the villages along the coast. By 1970, Marine squads were living in 117 villages. Each shared sleeping quarters and patrols with the village militia. The Marines moved on, usually after a year rather than a few months. It took that long to provide the militia with the training, combat experience, and self-confidence to stand up to the guerrillas still remaining in the area. The oil spot succeeded against the local guerrillas, but eventually the weight of the North Vietnamese army crushed South Vietnam.

In Afghanistan, the oil spot strategy was an arithmetic impossibility. Sixty coalition battalions could not be scattered across 300,000 square kilometers (an area equivalent to the distance between Boston and Atlanta) to protect eight million tribal Pashtuns living in 5,000 villages, while the president of Afghanistan whipped up popular opinion against the coalition and the Taliban enjoyed a 2,600-kilometer-long sanctuary called Pakistan.

208 **credible proposals** Lt. Cols. William Jurney and Dale Alford, Majs. John Nagl and Jim Gant, Capt. Matt Golsteyn, and Col. Randy Newman, to name only a few, all advocated creating conventional and Special Forces task forces to work intensively with the Afghan forces, at a fraction of the size and cost of our standard force structure.

208 **lessons from Vietnam** On both sides—the North Vietnamese Army with its guerrilla Viet Cong groups and the United States with Special Forces and Combined Action Platoons—the concept of placing experienced leadership among less capable forces was frequently applied.

208 **"We are in this thing"** Pentagon press briefing, December 10, 2009.

208 **kill the enemy and train** Gates, *Duty,* p. 572.

208 **Petraeus** After 3rd Platoon and General Petraeus had both left, Marine Gen. John Allen took command in mid-2011. "We will prevail," he said. "The insurgents have been ejected from the population by counterinsurgency operations.... We will continue the counterinsurgency campaign as long as we can, or until we might get a change in mission." General Allen video talk posted at wn.com on May 20, 2012, videotaped August 11, 2011.

209 **"our country"** Lt. Gen John Kelly, speech in St. Louis, November 11, 2010; see Appendix A.

210 **"Troops risking their lives"** Gates, *Duty,* p. 475.

210 **"resolve that terrorists"** President Barack Obama, State of the Union address, January 28, 2014.

211 **"This is how"** President Obama, address at West Point, May 28, 2014.

211 **"be viewed as a strategic defeat"** Gates, *Duty,* p. 567. In the fall of 2013, the vice chairman of the Joint Chiefs of Staff addressed the topic before the Association of the U.S. Army. "I simply don't know," Adm. James Winnefeld said, "where the security interests of our nation are threatened enough to cause us to lead a future major, extended [counterinsurgency] campaign." Counterinsurgency as nation building ended with a thud.

214 **"To fight a war"** Quoted in Tom Donnelly, "Currents of Cooperation, Currents of Conflict," AEI Center for Defense Studies website, May 24, 2010.

214 **"A set of ties"** Aaron B. O'Connell, *Underdogs: The Making of the Modern Marine Corps.* Cambridge, Mass.: Harvard University Press, 2012, p. 41.

218 **"We become"** Aristotle, *Nichomachean Ethics,* classics.mit.edu/Aristotle/nicomachaen.2.ii.html.

Index

About the Author

BING WEST, a Marine combat veteran, served as an assistant secretary of defense in the Reagan administration. He has been on hundreds of patrols in Vietnam, Iraq, and Afghanistan. A nationally acclaimed war correspondent, he is the author of *The Village; No True Glory: A Frontline Account of the Battle for Fallujah; The Strongest Tribe: War, Politics, and the Endgame in Iraq;* and *The Wrong War: Grit, Strategy, and the Way Out of Afghanistan.* Most recently, he was the co-author of Medal of Honor recipient Dakota Meyer's memoir, *Into the Fire.* A member of the Council on Foreign Relations and the Infantry Order of St. Crispin, West is the recipient of the Department of Defense Medal for Distinguished Public Service, the Colby Award for Military Writers, the Andrew J. Goodpaster Prize for military scholarship, the Marine Corps Heritage Foundation award (twice), Tunisia's Médaille de la Liberté, the Marine Corps Combat Correspondents Association Award, the Father Clyde Leonard Award, the Free Press Award, and the Veterans of Foreign Wars News Media Award. He lives with his wife, Betsy, in Newport, Rhode Island.

www.westwrite.com

About the Type

This book was set in Minion, a 1990 Adobe Originals typeface by Robert Slimbach (b. 1956). Minion is inspired by classical, old-style typefaces of the late Renaissance, a period of elegant, beautiful, and highly readable type designs. Created primarily for text setting, Minion combines the aesthetic and functional qualities that make text type highly readable with the versatility of digital technology.